# LIFE *from the* LIVING WORD

# COMMENDATIONS

There are three things to love about this book. The author cares about Christ - he keeps in mind the goal that we know Christ better and give glory to him. The author cares about the *whole* Bible - there are examples and explanations from every corner of the Old and New Testaments. The author cares about people - he's taken great care to make his explanations as accessible as possible to people of all backgrounds and cultures. I pray God will use it to open the eyes of many to the wonderful things in his law (Psalm 119:18).

**Andrew Sach**
*Tutor on the Cornhill Training Course and author of the Dig Deeper books*

In a world of great deception like ours, where the authority of Scripture is minimised, and Scripture often misinterpreted and misapplied, here is a book which makes a compelling invitation to proper Scripture interpretation. Speaking through various illustrations and case studies to bring clarity, "Life from the Living Word" empowers readers to study the Bible for themselves with great conviction and courage. The book helps ordinary Christians especially with little or no theological background to appreciate the treasures of God's Word in ways that are biblical, simple and relevant. Here is a treasure chest and a tool kit for every believer who longs to faithfully interpret Scripture.

**Rodgers Atwebembeire**
*Eastern Africa Regional Director, Africa Centre for Apologetics Research*

The writer's enthusiasm bubbles through page after page of this very readable handbook. The style is simple to understand and accessible to beginners. While there is always room for debate about details of interpretation, we are offered a clear and accessible method, conveyed with an infectious zeal. I hope this helpful book will get many started on working hard at understanding the Bible.

**Christopher Ash**
*Writer-in-Residence, Tyndale House, Cambridge*

If understanding the Bible is like working a garden to yield an abundance of fruit and flowers, here is a wonderful handbook for any gardener. Not only does "Life from the Living Word" provide some useful tools, but it carefully teaches a method to use those tools. With plenty of examples and encouragement along the way, here is a fresh and very welcome guide for anyone longing to meet with God in the pages of his Word.

**Syldio Determine Dusabumuremyi**
*Director of Studies, Word Increase Ministry, Rwanda*

As a homegroup leader, I want to help others see what the Bible says for themselves. This book offers practical, clear and true guidance in doing just that. Most importantly, Stuart helps us see the Bible's greatest treasure on every page: Christ. It is rare to find a book that can effectively train you to read the Bible better. It is even rarer to find one that consistently shows you Christ. This is that book.

**Laurent Repond**
*Homegroup and Youth Group Leader*

This should be on the bookshelf and in the hands of everyone who wants to understand the Bible and explain it clearly to others. It's an invaluable resource for teachers and students of God's Word.

**Anne Orange**
*Teacher and Women's Ministry Leader*

When I got an opportunity to read this book, my first feel as someone whose second language is English, was concern that this book might be too hard for me, but there was no need to worry! I found it so easy to understand and personally I loved the fact that it refers you to the Bible making it relevant and fun to read. Thank you for getting yourself a book that will change your life.

**Fortunate Aharimpisya.**
*Shop Keeper, Entebbe Uganda*

Read this book! It has given me a new perspective and confidence as I read the Bible. Stuart Creed provides tools that equip you to read, use and share how all the Bible points to Jesus. I'm sharing it with my mates.

**William Buchanan**
*Undergraduate Student, University of Durham*

You have here an encouraging, refreshing, accessible, informative and practical book that will help you grow in the amazing gift of understanding the very word of God revealed in Scripture. Thank you Stuart.

**Nat Schluter**
*Principal at Johannesburg Bible College, South Africa*

To Julia…

# LIFE *from the* LIVING WORD

## A GUIDE TO HELP UNDERSTAND THE BIBLE

## Stuart Creed

**Foreword by Jonathan Lamb**
**With illustrations by Michael Hobbs**

First published in Great Britain by
Living Word Literature
an imprint of Inspiration - Assurance Publications
PO Box 212 Saffron Walden CB10 2UU UK
Website: www.livingwordliterature.org


**ISBN 978-1-913741-12-9**

Printed in Great Britain by Imprint Digital, Exeter
and worldwide by Ingram-Spark

# CONTENTS

# ACKNOWLEDGEMENTS

I first had the privilege of meeting Mrs Wise at university in the person of Jim Packer as a young Christian in 1991. (If that sentence appears strange, please read on. Hopefully some sense will follow!)

Mrs Wise then appeared briefly on a number of other occasions, but I didn't get to know her well until 1994 when studying at the Cornhill Training Course in London under David Jackman and Dick Lucas. Since then, Mrs Wise has been visible in many wonderful men and women whom I have had the pleasure to meet. Several of these people have been instrumental in the writing of this book. All of whom are passionate for God's Word to speak as his living Word.

In the writing of "Life from the Living Word" I am immensely thankful to Jonathan Lamb for his contribution and kind words in the foreword. I am also greatly indebted to Fortunate Aharimpisya, Rodgers Atwebembeire, Geoff and Carolyn Bridges, Syldio Determine Dusabumuremyi, Andy and Kate Gilmore, Florence Menzies, David Moore, Pam Morrell, Anne Orange, Laurent Repond and Derrick Rugumba for their insightful comments and feedback on the manuscript. In all these people, Mrs Wise has been wonderfully evident with their godly advice. But much credit must also go to the many Rachels and Joes whom I have had the joy of teaching over the years - all have helped me with their questions and insights.

Justyn Hall has my sincere thanks for his inspired cover design, and I am particularly grateful to Michael Hobbs for his brilliant sketches which I am sure you will enjoy. My greatest thanks, however, belong to my dear wife Julia. Not only has she been a constant source of encouragement, wisdom, patience and love, but her meticulous attention to clarity will have saved many from confusion in the pages which follow.

I pray that as you read the book, you too will meet Mrs Wise, or rather the person that she represents, the Lord Jesus Christ our great teacher, to whom be all glory, both now and forever.

# FOREWORD

Some years ago a man called J B Phillips was working on a paraphrase of the New Testament, and he explained that it was like working on the mains electricity of a house, but doing so with the electricity still switched on! It was an "electric" experience. The book was "live", it was powerful and energising.

Martin Luther said something similar: "The Bible is alive - it has hands and grabs hold of me, it has feet and runs after me." And of course, the Bible itself is full of dynamic descriptions of the Word of God. Jeremiah said the Word was like fire in his bones, or like a hammer that breaks a rock in pieces. Paul described it as the sword of the Spirit. Jesus said that the Word was the seed which produced a wonderful harvest.

Then we must add the lovely story in Luke 24, when two disciples were walking home to Emmaus after Jesus' crucifixion in Jerusalem and were joined by the risen Jesus. Luke explains that the disciples didn't recognise him, and Jesus deliberately chose not to reveal himself, other than through the Old Testament Scriptures. "He explained to them what was said in all the Scriptures concerning himself." In other words, it was through Scripture that they encountered the living Christ.

The reason why we seek to understand the Bible and explain it to others is because we believe God's Word has the same dynamic impact today. It transforms lives, because it draws us into a living relationship with the author, with God himself.

I can say with certainty that it is this fundamental conviction that has motivated Stuart Creed to write this book. Throughout the following pages we will come to understand the truth that all Scripture is God-breathed, and therefore it is authoritative and powerful. This is the most important reason for giving our time and energy to understanding and explaining the Scriptures: it is a matter of life and death.

Alongside this fundamental reality, the following pages take seriously a second significant truth: that the Bible is written by human authors. We often refer to the Bible's dual-authorship - the many human authors who wrote under the inspiration of the one divine author. In turn, this demands both a humble submission to the Lord of the Word, and a careful study of what the human authors themselves recorded so skillfully.

That's why Stuart's book is particularly valuable. Founded on the conviction of the life-giving power of Scripture, it is an accessible handbook that opens up the key ways in which we can understand what the human authors were saying. By understanding their cultural context, their place in history, their writing style and their deployment of images and ideas, we come to understand their message, and why that is so significant for our own culture and our own day.

Let me give a few hints for reading this helpful resource. First, the author repeatedly urges us to read the Scriptures themselves - to read, and to read, and to read! This is the first and most important discipline that will help us understand and apply the Bible. No short-cuts! Might I encourage every reader to look up the Bible references and work on the passages which are suggested in each chapter. One of the helpful features of the book is the many examples used in every section, as well as well-chosen exercises to work on, ranging across both Old and New Testaments. Please do work on these passages, since they are windows which allow us to understand what the Bible authors were saying, and provide a model for our careful reading of different parts of the Bible.

Second, the book is built around the three important disciplines of "observing, understanding and applying". This is the simple but demanding journey we must take with every Bible passage, and the book will help us with each step, using some key questions and memory aids. As I worked through the book, I realised that this is probably not a book to read in one session (though that would be worthwhile), but a book to have alongside your Bible as you work on different sections week by week, practising the exercises which the author so helpfully provides. The book is best read slowly because it is packed with many valuable study ideas. Many of them can be found in other books, but rarely in such a concise and comprehensive format - it is like having a small library in your hands, a one-stop shop for some of the most important ways to understand and apply Scripture.

And third, it is a book which provides much encouragement along the way, so that we will not feel overwhelmed or disheartened, but will begin to see the illuminating and life-changing truth embedded in every corner of the Bible. So if we would like to understand both the grand sweep of the story-line of the Bible alongside the rich details and insights of its individual sentences, and if we long to experience its life-giving power and want to be equipped to explain its truth to others, then here is an engaging resource to help us.

Like J B Phillips working on the New Testament, or like the early disciples from Emmaus, I am sure that, as we read the Scriptures using the guidance of this book, there will be moments when we too will encounter the Lord Jesus and will also exclaim: "Were not our hearts burning within us while he talked with us on the road and opened the Scriptures to us?" (Luke 24:32).

**Jonathan Lamb**
Minister-at-Large, Keswick Ministries

"A loving trust in the Author of the Bible
is the best preparation for a wise study of the Bible."
**Henry Clay Trumbull**

# INTRODUCTION

---

*Jesus said: "If you abide in my word, you are truly my disciples and you will know the truth, and the truth will set you free."*
**John 8:31-32 ESV**

---

"Coughing, your throat burns as you breathe the foul smelling, acidic air. You are lost. It is a lifeless, cold world where everything is hard, grey and dull. You walk on. You have no choice.

Suddenly there is a flash of colour from a plant nearby. But no sooner have you noticed it than the colour has gone. The plant, like all the others, is plastic.

Thirsty, you spot a stream. You drink and for a moment it tastes so sweet, but then the feeling of sickness starts, and the pains come in your stomach. It's like this every time. You need to drink, but this deceptive water is all there is. It's the same with the food. The first bite tastes good, but then the nausea and the realisation that what you have just eaten is so bad and stale.

But what is that in the distance, beyond the grey plastic trees? Straining your eyes, you can just make out what looks like a house. Excited, you rush over to discover the house is truly impressive, bright and dazzling with colour which lasts.

Looking up you notice some giant words written over the front door. They read:

'All welcome into the Word of God'.

You try the door, but it is closed and locked.

Standing there thinking about what to do, the door swings open all by itself. Amazed you step inside.

The first thing you take in is the air - fresh, clean, pure air, filling your lungs. It's warm too, wonderfully warm. But as you breathe, you notice something else - the smell on your clothes, the foul stench which seems so out of place here. You throw off your stinking coat and step further inside.

A delightful red flower welcomes you in the first room with a wonderful perfume. Its petals are soft and real, as are its leaves. Looking around, everything in the house is light and in colour, and there on a table of real wood laid out before you, is food and water. You drink and eat. The water seems to live it is so fresh, the food perfect and satisfying. No sickness, no stomach pains.

You walk on. The next room is even larger and more colourful than the one before. A comfortable chair catches your eye. You take a seat to rest and enjoy the warmth and fresh air. But as you relax you begin to feel a cold breeze.

Turning around there is an open door leading back to the outside world. Then beyond the door - a sign: 'All in the house are trapped, slaves

18

to the thinking and rules of the house. Escape! True freedom lies outside.' There is a flash of colour on the sign and the trees behind. But you only need a moment to think 'I could leave, but why would I want to?'

Smiling, you turn around and note another door and another sign. It simply reads, 'This way to explore further.' Cautiously, you turn the handle underneath. But far from being easy, this door requires great effort to open. Eventually it moves to reveal a room even larger and brighter with yet more colour. You step inside with a strange knowing sense that in this house there are many, many rooms beyond, and that getting to them won't be easy, but that each room will be better than the one before."

Jesus said "If you abide in my word, you are truly my disciples and you will know the truth, and the truth will set you free." (John 8:31-32 ESV).

It's an amazing promise. To "abide" is to live somewhere. To abide in the Word of Jesus is like living in the house. Outside is what Jesus calls "slavery to sin" (John 8:34) - a cruel slavery to the thinking, values and desires of sin. Inside the house there is truth and freedom. There are more and more rooms the further in the Word we go. Each room gives us a greater experience and confidence of that truth and freedom. Each room provides a greater joy in Jesus.

"For the Word of God is living and active," continued the preacher quoting Hebrews 4:12, "not dead and inactive!" Picking up a Bible he continued, "This book is God's Word to us - God's living Word to enjoy, to live in, to explore, to understand."

Joe and Rachel were listening, and they couldn't help but agree. They had taken in the illustration of the house and could relate to that joy of entering themselves some time back. They were thankful, for they had once lived in the world outside and God had opened the door in their lives to the clean, fresh air - they had tasted joy from the Word of God. Now they were excited about exploring further; yet as the preacher continued passionately to explain the benefits of growing in understanding the Word of God, a question filled each of their minds: "But how do I do that? How do I open those further doors inside the house?"

Joe and Rachel were regular readers of the Bible and had done their best to contribute wisely in the fellowship group they attended, but being honest they struggled. The Bible was hard. Some bits were not too difficult. Joe particularly loved the Gospels. Other parts were fun to read. Rachel's favourite was the stories in the Old Testament, but it was a complete mystery as to how they actually applied today. They seemed like a closed door. Then there were the really obscure books: Leviticus, the Prophets and Revelation! Those were distant rooms. The Bible was far from easy.

## Understanding the Bible

Has that been your experience? You have tried to study the Bible, but without much progress? You want to know more, but feel that in your understanding you are still in the first few rooms?

Perhaps now you've settled on reading a few verses each day. You get help from some notes and try to find a "thought for the day." You look for promises and commands, but anything difficult is a struggle and you pass it over. Perhaps, like Joe and Rachel, you sense this is not as it should be and you want more. Indeed, deep down you know that God wants to give you more. If so, this book is written for you.

Perhaps your situation is different. You have been a Christian for some time now and you have some responsibility to teach: the children's group at church, the mid-week Bible study group or your own children. You enjoy this, but (being honest) you lack confidence. Repeating a good point you've picked up from a book or heard in a talk is OK, but you lack conviction with your own insights, particularly with how to apply them. You'd love to have more certainty that what you teach is faithful. Again, this book is for you.

Finally, I hope you'll find this book helpful if you are more like the preacher in the story. You know the importance of the Word of God and are looking for a method to teach others how to feed themselves. This book will present a way to help unearth the treasures of God's truth for group Bible study or individual learning.

## A method to help

So how do we explore the house? How do we discover the riches of God's Word, knowing and delighting in the Lord Jesus, which will set us free from slavery to sin, with its thinking and lifestyle?

The aim of this book is to provide a simple and easy-to-remember method for engaging with any Bible passage. The method won't unlock all the doors, but it's my prayer that, whatever the level of your current Bible understanding, it will help you move on.[1]

The method is written for those who particularly like a step-by-step approach, simply asking one question at a time. But if that is not your style, don't be put off. Please simply take away anything that is helpful for your own method of study.

My advice, especially if you are new to Bible understanding, would be to take the book slowly, perhaps reflecting with a friend. It will be most helpful to work through alongside regular Bible reading. That way its contents can be put into regular practice. To get you started, I have included some short exercises in every chapter. Learning takes time. Each exercise will explore one of those rooms, seeing the colour and goodness of the Word of God. I have also included some "Additional Tips" and some "Dangers to Avoid" which you will find in boxes for supplementary reading. These are not core to the method, but I hope helpful for further insight and keeping away from common errors.

## The journey

Imagine with me two great lands separated by a rough sea. In some places the two lands come close to each other, but in other places the distance between them is considerable. In "Bible Land" there are old towns and villages like Jerusalem, Ephesus and Bethlehem, and in all these places the Bible is being read. People listen attentively, for in each place a new book of the Bible is being read for the very first time. In one village it is Genesis describing the events of their past. In a town square

---

1. No method can be used as a formula that when followed guarantees finding the correct interpretation or exhaustive meaning of a text. The aim of this method is rather to offer some guidelines, some angles from which the text can be viewed so that readers may better understand the Biblical text.

it is Numbers, not heard before, instructing the people. In yet another town, the Psalms are being read and then sung. In Ephesus, Paul's letter to the Ephesians is having its first hearing and in another area a new book called Revelation is being passed on from place to place.

In "Today's World", that other great land mass on the far side of the sea, exactly the same Bible is being read and listened to. Here there are towns and villages too, but things are very different. These people live in a different time zone. Everything from the way people are dressed to the type of houses the people live in is different. Nothing looks the same as in Bible Land. In some places, things look somewhat similar, but nearly everywhere the language is different - as is the culture, the politics and general lifestyle. Nevertheless, what they read is the very same Bible.

In both lands the same thing is happening, people are reading exactly the same Bible, but in very different contexts.

Living today as you and I do in Today's World, there is a great divide, a vast sea between us and Bible Land. We are separated by time and culture and history, and in the case of the Old Testament parts of Bible, by covenant as well - that is, the way in which we relate to God is also different.

To understand the Bible today, we need to cross this great divide, the sea between the lands. We need to go on a journey. The journey starts in Bible Land and then we must travel home. As we will see, the difficulty of that journey varies depending on where we are coming from in Bible Land and where we live in Today's World, but every time we will need to make that journey.

If we read the Bible forgetting this journey, it will lead to confusion and error. Take Malachi 3:10 for example: "Bring the whole tithe into the storehouse, that there may be food in my house. 'Test me in this' says the LORD Almighty, 'and see if I will not throw open the floodgates of heaven and pour out so much blessing that there will not be enough room to store it."

This verse is often used to encourage people to give, with its promise to bring much greater blessing than what is donated. But to apply the verse in this way, directly to us, is to fail to make the journey from Bible Land.

If the Bible was meant to be applied to us directly like this, we would need to take the same approach elsewhere. Consider Leviticus 11:7-8: "And the pig… is unclean for you. You must not eat their meat…", or Leviticus 19:19: "Do not wear clothing woven of two kinds of material." We would need to stop eating pork and change what we wear. That's not too big a change (though some may disagree), but what about Numbers 31:17: "Now kill all the boys.  And kill every woman who has slept with a man"; or Deuteronomy 7:26: "Do not bring a detestable thing into your house, or you like it will be set apart for destruction."

Applying those verses directly and countless others would be more problematic.

The result is that difficult verses like these are often ignored. But they should not be ignored. They too are the Word of God and have relevance for us. They are in the house, but, to understand them correctly, indeed to understand any of the Word of God correctly, we must always start in Bible Land.

Whether it is Genesis or Galatians, Exodus, Ezra or Ephesians, we need to start with the question: "What did the text say to the original hearers?"

If we are studying Ephesians, we have to travel back in time and start in Ephesus, in the 1st century. We need to cross over the great sea dividing us from them. We have to imagine ourselves as 1st-century believers in Ephesus, hearing Paul's letter for the very first time. Only then, having understood "What did the text say to the original hearers?" can we begin our journey back home to Today's World and work out what the text means for us. But to get home we will need to cross that big divide which separates them in their context from us in ours. We will need to find a bridge.

What follows in this book is how to make that journey. We will look at how to listen, becoming an imaginary hearer in Bible Land. We will explore how to work out what the text meant to those living there. We will examine how to find a bridge over the sea and work out what the text means to us and how to apply it. In short, we will look at a method for how to bring the wonderful message of the Bible home to us in all its glory and relevance.

In chapter 2 we will start that method. But, before we begin, there are some vital truths to grasp with both hands. Without these any method is destined to failure.

## END OF CHAPTER EXERCISE

**Slowly read through Psalm 19:7-11.**

There are many blessings described that come from the Word of God in these verses. Write down each blessing. Then spend some time in prayer asking God to give you a greater understanding and delight in his word.

# CHAPTER 1

## STARTING OUT: VITAL TRUTHS TO GRASP

---

*"These are the ones I look on with favour: those who are humble and contrite in spirit, and who tremble at my word."*
### Isaiah 66:2

"A man may read the figures on the [sun]dial, but he cannot tell how the day goes unless the sun is shining on it; so we may read the Bible over, but we cannot learn to purpose [it won't lead to any purposeful learning] till the spirit of God shine upon it and into our hearts."
### Thomas Watson

---

Joe was confused. It wasn't that the Bible talk this week had been particularly difficult to understand. What's more it had been well illustrated and applied, but despite all those things, as Joe put it with brutal honesty to his wife, "it was just very, ordinary".

"Not like last week at all!" exclaimed Rachel. "His talk last Sunday was incredible, so convicting and powerful." Joe had to agree, the previous week's message had been on his mind all week. Why had that talk affected him so much?

Have you ever had that experience? Same place, same speaker, same faithfulness to the text, yet very different impact. Perhaps instead it's been with your personal Bible reading or a group study? Sometimes it's been very ordinary and yet on other occasions the words have virtually leapt off the page with such force, relevance and conviction.

As we have seen, the Bible is not an ordinary book: it is "living and active," but it can be received very differently. The apostle Paul recognised this. Reflecting on his time spent in Thessalonica in Greece he wrote:

"For we know, brothers and sisters loved by God, that he has chosen you, because our gospel came to you not simply with words, but also with power, with the Holy Spirit and with deep conviction." (1 Thessalonians 1:4-5).

These verses tell us something important. God's Word can be received in two contrasting ways.

First, we are told the teaching of the Bible can be received "simply with words". We may understand the words, we may even find them interesting or enjoyable, but that is all. There is no received impact leading to change in our lives.

But it can be very different, such as with the Thessalonians. They received the gospel "with power, with the Holy Spirit and with deep conviction." Hearing the Bible, for them, led to change. Paul continues:

"You became imitators of us and of the Lord; in spite of severe suffering, you welcomed the message with joy given by the Holy Spirit." (1 Thessalonians 1:6).

Stop for a moment and read those words again. Their content must not be missed. What happened to the Thessalonians?

Paul tells us they become imitators, they began to look like Paul and his friends, and more importantly they began to look like the Lord Jesus Christ himself. Now that is remarkable.

What's more when God's Word was preached, they welcomed the message with joy. Joy came to them, given by the Holy Spirit.

And this joy was not ordinary. It was no quick, happy moment. This was joy "in spite of severe suffering". These people had no earthly reason to be joyful, they had lots of problems in their lives, they had "severe suffering," but despite this, the Holy Spirit through the preaching of God's living Word brought them joy.

How amazing would it be if every time we read the Bible, studied the Bible or listened to the Bible, something of these two things happened: our lives changed to look more like Jesus, and we had real deep-down joy?

Is that possible? Yes, absolutely. The key, as the verses tell us, is the work of God in the person of the Holy Spirit.

So how then should we read or study the Bible in a way that is pleasing to the Holy Spirit? That is what this chapter is all about.

Since the Holy Spirit is Almighty God, he does as he pleases. There is no magic formula to twist his arm, and we must never forget that. Yet by God's grace, we have been given some important instructions for how to "keep in step with the Spirit" (Galatians 5:25) - and so every time we approach the Bible, rather than rushing ahead, we'd do well to stop and reflect and examine ourselves. Are we seeking what the Holy Spirit desires?

## Keeping in step with the Spirit

The Bible is incredible. Written over a period of 1,500 years, it contains 66 books composed by around 40 human authors. It is God's great gift to us. But the way we approach the Bible is crucial. Wonderfully, the starting place is not our ability, our education or our understanding, but having the right attitude. Crucial for having the right attitude are three truths for us to recognise.

## 1) Recognise the Bible is the Word of God.

The Bible was inspired by the Holy Spirit. Indeed "All Scripture is God breathed" (2 Timothy 3:16) so, if we are to keep in step with the Spirit, we need to recognise that the entire Bible is the Word of God.

This means that we are not at liberty to pick and choose. If something we read doesn't appear to make sense, or is something with which we don't agree, there is no fault with the Bible: the fault lies with us. The Bible is reliable, not us. To say such things about the Bible is to say there is something wrong with what God has said. That is to say there is a fault with God, which can never be the right starting place.

We should instead start by recognising that, because the Bible is God's Word, it can be trusted. Every doctrine, every chapter, every word can be fully trusted. God does not make mistakes. He knows what is best and he reveals the truth.

Indeed, we are instructed: "Do not merely listen to the word and so deceive yourselves, do what it says." (James 1:22). In other words, trust it and put it into action. Jesus likens this to building our house on the rock, not sand (Matthew 7:24-27). That attitude, wanting to put whatever is revealed to us into practice, is the right starting place.

## 2) Recognise that the Bible is all about Jesus.

After his resurrection, Jesus appears to two disciples walking on the road to Emmaus. A conversation starts, but Jesus is not recognised by them. Let's take up that conversation in Luke 24:25-26:

"He [Jesus] said to them, 'How foolish you are and how slow to believe all that the prophets have spoken! Did not the Messiah have to suffer these things and then enter his glory?' And beginning with Moses and the Prophets, he explained to them what was said in all the Scriptures concerning himself."

This teaching is so important it is repeated a few verses later:

"He [Jesus] said to them. 'This is what I told you whilst I was still with you: Everything must be fulfilled that is written about me in the Law of Moses, the Prophets and the Psalms[1].'" (Luke 24:44).

Put simply, Jesus is teaching that the whole Bible is about himself. Like his portrait or his photograph, the Bible's purpose from beginning to end is to reveal Jesus in all his splendour and bring him praise, honour and obedience.

Recognising this has a remarkable effect on these two disciples. Later in v31 their eyes were opened and they realise that it had been Jesus speaking to them. They then reflect on what had happened:

"They asked each other: 'Were not our hearts burning within us while he talked with us on the road and opened the Scriptures to us.'"

Now I find that extraordinary. We are not told that their hearts burned when they finally become aware that the man who had been teaching them was the risen Jesus. But we are told their hearts burned as the Scriptures were explained! This Bible study was not "simply with words": this was receiving the message "with power, with deep conviction and the Holy Spirit." Their hearts burned when they recognised Jesus in the Bible.

---

1. "The Law of Moses, the Prophets and the Psalms" is simply shorthand for saying all of Old Testament Scripture.

This has important implications. First, as we approach the Bible we must above all things expect to be taught about Jesus. The Bible is more about Jesus, than it is about us. Christians shouldn't therefore come to the Bible primarily for themselves, but to worship and humble themselves before Jesus.

Secondly, we should read the whole Bible. If the whole Bible is about Jesus and we ignore certain parts of the Bible, it is like blacking out a portion of his photograph, limiting our picture of Jesus.

Now some parts of the Bible, like with a photograph, are more important. Key passages in the New Testament for example are like Jesus' eyes and mouth. To miss those would be catastrophic for seeing Jesus as he truly is, but the entire photograph is valuable in revealing something of him, even if it is simply providing the background.

We should read the whole Bible. To ignore parts of the picture is to reduce our vision of Jesus. But there is another danger, which is even more important to avoid.

Imagine a picture being taken on your wedding day. It is a photograph of your wonderful bride or bridegroom. Your beloved is looking at their very best, looking fabulous in fact, picture perfect for a photo that will be sent to all your friends and family.

The photographer is, however, far from looking good. He has clearly made no effort at all for the special day. But he has the camera pointing the right way round and appears to know what he is doing. He takes his shots and you look forward eagerly to see how the pictures will turn out.

But when that exciting moment comes, the pictures are nothing like accurate. Instead your partner has been horribly distorted with images more like those from a fairground mirror. One of your partner's eyes is enormous, their face is stretched and their mouth is tiny. What is more, on closer examination, you realise that large parts of what should be your beautiful bride or bridegroom are not them at all, but the photographer, the ugly photographer. Your photos are ruined!

The Bible portrays a perfect portrait of Jesus in all his glory, yet so often the picture we see, or the picture presented to us, is ruined. Jesus is disfigured, parts are left out, features are exaggerated or minimised and, worse still, parts of us, like the ugly photographer can be imposed onto the picture as we assert our understanding onto the Bible.

If the idea of our wedding photographs misrepresenting our bride or bridegroom is horrifying, should we be surprised if the Holy Spirit, the perfect photographer, doesn't honour our distortions of his flawless picture of Jesus?

So in coming to the Bible we must always make every effort to listen with humility.

This is God's Word, God's truth to be trusted and obeyed and it is his perfect picture of Jesus. All of it is important and all of it is perfectly balanced. We shouldn't give emphasis where the Bible doesn't emphasise. If the Bible does highlight a point, we shouldn't play it down, and we should never impose ourselves, our ideas, onto the text - onto the beautiful picture of Jesus.

So the Bible's main focus is Jesus, not us. But there is another crucial lesson about how we approach the Bible which those two disciples on the road to Emmaus can teach us.

### 3) Realise our need for God.

You'll recall that the hearts of these two disciples burned within them as Jesus explained the Bible, but that it was only later in v31 that we are told, "Then their eyes were opened and they recognised him." So, they understood Jesus at one level when the Bible was explained, but something else was needed for their eyes to open. It is a point so important it is also repeated in v45: "Then he opened their minds so that they could understand the Scriptures."

A miracle was needed. Their minds had to be opened so that they could understand the Scriptures. And that is still true for us today. Without a work of God we simply cannot grasp the revelation of Jesus, the picture remains obscured. We are naturally blind (2 Corinthians 4:4), deaf (John 8:47), hard hearted (Ephesians 4:18), dead in our sins (Ephesians 2:1-2) and unable to discern spiritual truths (1 Corinthians 2:14). Only with God's work in our lives can we receive the Bible "not simply with words, but with power, with the Holy Spirit and with deep conviction."

And there is something vital for us to realise about this for the purpose of Bible understanding. This dependence on God for us to see the truth, doesn't just apply to that very first time when we become Christians. This spiritual blindness, deafness and hardness can continue into our Christian lives.

Listen to the words of Jesus to the church at Laodicea (Revelation 3:17):

"You say. 'I am rich; I have acquired wealth and do not need a thing.' But you do not realise that you are wretched, pitiful, poor, blind and naked."

These words are written to a church, to Christians not unbelievers, and yet Jesus says they are completely unaware of their true spiritual condition.[2]

They "do not realise" how they actually are. They felt spiritually

---

2. The context of the rest of this letter to Laodicea (Rev 3:14-22) is all about the spiritual condition of the church, not its material state and is described using a range of metaphors. Their deeds being like water temperatures, their relationship with Jesus being like him drinking foul water etc. As such the "riches and wealth" of v17 are also metaphors for their spiritual condition. There is no escape in thinking these verses apply only to materially rich Christians. If that were the case, they must also have been literally running around the streets poor, blind and naked!

wealthy and secure, they boasted "I...do not need a thing," yet the truth was the opposite; spiritually they were "wretched, pitiful, poor, blind and naked."

Stop for a moment and reflect on this. How do you feel spiritually right now? Are you comfortable with your understanding and your relationship with Jesus? So were they. It is possible to feel OK and not realise our true situation. Might that apply to you?

Christians can pray and go to church, live lives that appear morally acceptable and listen to good Bible teaching, as I am sure they did, but in the eyes of Jesus, they remain "wretched, pitiful, poor, blind and naked."

How is that so?

The key is to ask why do we do those things - Why do we pray and attend church and listen to the Bible?

Is it because as Christians that is what we are meant to do? We feel that it is right and good. Others encourage us, perhaps we also enjoy it, but that is all. If so, we are just like the Christians at Laodicea, for there is no real sense of need.

This lack of need was the mark of their blindness, they boasted, "I...do not need a thing," they felt spiritually fine, they felt no burden, no inability, no real need for God, and they were blind.

If that is us as we approach the Bible, if we come over-confident in ourselves, we should go no further. We need to stop and hear Jesus' words to the church at Laodicea: v19: "Those whom I love I rebuke and discipline. So be earnest and repent."

There is no question here of a Christian losing their salvation. Jesus loves us, but if we acknowledge no sense of absolute need, that love calls us to repent.

"Here I am! I stand at the door and knock. If anyone hears my voice and opens the door, I will come in and eat with that person, and they will eat with me." (v20).

It's a loving invitation. His promise is a wonderful restored relationship of eating with him, but if we will not acknowledge our need, he calls on us to repent. Overconfidence in our Christian lives, independence from

Jesus is dangerous and we must open the door at which he knocks.

Notice in this verse that the knock of Jesus corresponds to his voice, and we can do two things. We can ignore the knocking of his voice because we see no need for Jesus or we can respond by opening the door. To open the door is to admit our need for him, it is to see ourselves as "wretched, pitiful, poor, blind and naked"- it is to depend on Jesus.

This dependence is the starting place for all good Bible study. It is to "keep in step with the Spirit" who opens our minds to the Scriptures so that we can see Jesus of whom the entire Bible speaks.

Practically this means prayer. Prayer, not just as something that we say out of habit before Bible study, but heartfelt, humble prayer knowing our need as we come to the Bible. Unless God acts and opens our minds and warms our hearts, it'll only be an exercise - "simply words".

## Seeking the glory of God.

Genuine dependent prayer is vital. But it's important to realise that the purpose of prayer is not primarily to ask God for what we need.

Undeniably, such asking is an essential component of prayer. The Lord's Prayer itself contains many requests for ourselves, but it starts with "hallowed be your name," because the principal focus of all Biblical prayer is the glory of God.

The Holy Spirit himself supremely desires the glory of Jesus (John 16:14). That is why he caused the Bible to be written. So if we are to "keep in step with the Spirit" as we read the Bible we must have hearts that long, above everything else, that Jesus be glorified.

As we ask for eyes to see, we should search our hearts and ask why do I want good Bible understanding? Is this first and foremost for me or for Jesus?

Am I doing this to feel good about my understanding? Is it so that others will look up to me with my knowledge? Or is it so that I can obey Jesus so that he is honoured and worshipped? We are never to take away the glory that belongs to God and put it on ourselves.

The start of good Bible study is having the correct attitude. Dependence on God is that attitude. Recognising our need, feeling our moral failure and inability we can come to God's living Word and be changed. But we do need to come to that living Word dependent on God.

Who of us if we were physically sick and dying, but had a medicine to cure us, would read the instructions on the medicine bottle, but then decide on our own dose and our own way to take the medicine? Our approach to the Bible is infinitely more important. Our attitude matters.

"As the Holy Spirit says: 'Today if you hear his voice, do not harden your hearts'" (Hebrews 3:7-8) and "see to it that you do not refuse him who speaks" (Hebrews 12:25) and "We must pay more careful attention therefore to what we have heard, so that we do not drift away." (Hebrews 2:1).

These words were all spoken to believers and they still apply today. Coming to the living Word of God is no small thing. Approach with the wrong attitude and God's anger is provoked. (Hebrews 3:10, 12:25).

On the other hand, if we come humbly, recognising our need and willing to obey whatever we find, however tough the demands may be; if we come longing to see Jesus and longing to bring him glory then there is a great promise:

"Anyone who chooses to do the will of God will find out whether my teaching comes from God or whether I speak on my own." (John 7:17).

Now that promise is remarkable.

It says the exact opposite of what we might expect. The Bible doesn't teach that increasing study and academic understanding leads to assurance. Instead it teaches that a willing, loving obedience leads to assurance. The order is not "understanding," then "willingness," then "obedience," but "willingness" first, then "understanding" then "obedience".

Proverbs 2:3-5 puts it like this:

"…if you call out for insight and cry aloud for understanding, and if you look for it as for silver and search for it as for hidden treasure, then you will understand the fear of the LORD and find the knowledge of God."

The "knowledge of God" is not knowing about God, but knowing him in a personal and loving relationship. That is eternal life (John 17:3), that is to have the full measure of joy within us (John 17:13), that is the hidden treasure of the Bible. Let's get exploring!

## END OF CHAPTER EXERCISE

What would you say to Rachel and Joe in their confusion if you were to meet them?

**Read John 5:39-40.**

What big mistake does Jesus say the Pharisees have made in their understanding? What does he say instead they need to realise?

Spend some time in prayer asking God to help you not make the same mistake.

# STAGE 1: OBSERVE

"We must read our Bibles like men
digging for hidden treasure."

**J. C. Ryle**

# CHAPTER 2

## MEMORABLE, REPEATED AND SURPRISING

---

*"Open my eyes that I may see wonderful things in your law."*
***Psalm 119:18***

"The more of God's Word you know and love,
the more of God's Spirit you will experience."
**John Piper**

---

"This is great!" exclaimed Joe. "The whole Bible is about Jesus and knowing him is easy. All we have to do is read the Bible and wait for the Holy Spirit to work. He will make something we read come alive, jump out of the text and speak to us."

"So much easier than all that academic study," replied Rachel. "I get it now. We can't gain spiritual understanding on our own, but if we simply pray and recognise our need, God will help us."

What do you think about Rachel and Joe's conclusion?

Their humility is certainly to be commended. As we saw in the last chapter a crucial starting place for Bible study is that we depend on God. Without the Holy Spirit we are blind to the truth about Jesus, but it's important to understand how the Holy Spirit works.

Imagine a mother teaching her two-year-old boy to swim. Left on his own the little boy will simply drown in the water, so his parent supports him. But along with keeping her little one from sinking, the mother moves the little boy through the water. She does this so that he will experience the joy of movement. In response her toddler begins to kick and move his arms, exactly what his mother wants, so she responds by moving him still faster through the water. The aim is for him to learn to swim. So when he stops kicking, she stops moving him through the water for he needs to learn that kicking and moving his arms is important.

The Holy Spirit works in much the same way as the mother. Our efforts like that of the toddler are useless on their own, but the Holy Spirit loves to give us Bible understanding as we depend on him and put in effort. Sometimes he might move us in response to very little effort, sometimes only after great effort, but as our loving teacher he knows what is best. Our role is to put in the hard work, knowing that whatever movement occurs, it is always down to him.

In this chapter we will begin to learn a method by which we can put in that effort to understand, whilst never forgetting our reliance on God. It is a method that can be used for any passage in Scripture and with a bit of practice can easily be learned.

The method is a simple three-stage process: "Observe," "Understand" and "Apply".[1] We will start in this chapter with "Observe," but before we start we need a Bible and there are so many to choose from.

## Which Bible should I use?

The Bible was originally written in Hebrew, Aramaic and Greek - three different languages. Today the whole Bible has been translated into more than 680 languages and for some, such as English, there are many different translations. But with so many versions to choose from, it can all be very confusing. So which Bible is best?

Different Bible translations can be thought of on a spectrum. At one end are the "word for word" translations. These are very accurate to the original languages, sticking closely to the actual words used, but they don't tend to be so easy to comprehend. They make excellent study Bibles, but are less good for general reading. In the middle are the "thought for thought" translations. Instead of translating word by word, these focus on translating the ideas one at a time as accurately as they can, but the consequence is that they lose some of the accuracy of the

1. The method doesn't look in detail at the different Bible writing styles or "genres". This is because, as a basic method, it aims to be simple and useful for any passage of Scripture. The question of biblical genre will instead be taken up in a sequel to "Life from the Living Word" where each major biblical genre will be addressed.

"word for word" versions. Finally at the other end of the spectrum are the "paraphrase" translations. These aim to make the modern language even easier to read than the "thought for thought" translations. These have their role, particularly for those who struggle with English, but sadly the result is often a considerable loss of accuracy to the original text. As such paraphrase Bibles should generally be avoided where possible, especially for study.

| Word for Word | > | Thought for Thought | > | Paraphrase |
|---|---|---|---|---|
| New American Standard Bible | English Standard Version | New International Version | Good News Bible | The Message |
| | New King James Version | Christian Standard Version | | New Living Bible |

The best Bible, therefore, depends on whether it's for study or simply for reading.[2] For study, a "word for word" translation is best to ensure accuracy, but for reading large amounts of Scripture a "thought for thought" version will usually be easier and not miss much of the message of the original text. If possible, therefore, it's good to have two different translations, one in each category. And as we shall see later, this also has benefits for study.

### Observe – Asking "What did it say to the original hearers?"

Rachel and Joe were now stuck. They had prayed, truly dependent on God for understanding. They had a good Bible translation and had read the study passage, but there had been no special moment of revelation. Being honest, they remained very uncertain about what the passage was saying. It seemed so unconnected to their lives. They needed help.

But perhaps that help lay just next door for Mrs Wise their neighbour

---

2. If personal finance only allows for one Bible, my own recommendations are the Christian Standard Version / English Standard Version. Both combine excellent accuracy & readability.

was a mature Christian of many years and full of wisdom. Her cakes were also the best in the area.

"I'd be delighted to give any assistance I can," the old lady explained pouring them each a cup of tea.

"Understanding the Bible can certainly be difficult," she continued. "Even after 80 years I still have so many questions, but you know, at one level it's really very easy." She paused for thought and then exclaimed: "I don't wish to draw attention to myself, but all you have to do is remember my name. Remember Mrs Wise!"

Rachel and Joe were now more confused than ever, but their kind neighbour continued. "Good Bible study starts with what we observe," she explained. "Read the passage and observe carefully. In fact, read, read and read again; and as you observe carefully, be constantly remembering my name."

"Oh I'm sorry," she said seeing their puzzled faces. "Each letter in my name stands for something - a question to ask of the passage. So all you need to do is remember the letters of my name and ask the questions."

"Oh I see!" exclaimed Rachel. "So 'M' stands for something, then 'R' stands for something, then 'S' etc."

"Exactly," replied Mrs Wise, "but all along as we observe, we have to remember the aim. The aim is to come up with an idea of what the author in the Bible passage is saying. The key question is: What did it say to them, the original hearers."

Mrs Wise went on to explain how each Bible book was written by a human author who had a purpose in writing and why working out that purpose for each and every Bible passage is so important.

"Once you understand the author's purpose, you are half way there," said Mrs Wise. "The authors wrote to specific people in their particular time for all sorts of reasons," she continued. "It might be to teach something or to encourage their readers, or to correct, or to warn. So our first job is to travel back in time and imagine we are there alongside the very first readers. Then we must observe, carefully, and work out what the author's purpose was…and they leave big clues," she said excitedly. "It's like hunting for treasure!"

### MRS: The first three letters

The first three letters stand for things which overlap with each other and so can be taken together. Each is a means by which the Bible author draws our attention to what they wish to say. The method starts by simply reading the Bible passage slowly and repeatedly, "read, read and read again". And as we read, we need to observe, looking specifically for three things. At this stage it can be helpful to take notes or to print out the passage onto paper so that, once noticed, they can be highlighted.

> **ADDITIONAL TIP**
>
> To assist the process of "Read, read and read again" it may be useful to read the passage aloud, read it in a different translation or have the passage read to you. Anything that supports a fresh reading is helpful. Even reading the passage backwards may help to ensure every word is noticed. Above all though, a passage must be read in its context - more on that in chapter 5.

### M is for Memorable – What is most memorable?

One way an author can draw attention to an important point is to make it memorable. This might be by using humour or irony, a turn of phrase or an argument, but most commonly it is achieved by creating impact on our emotions or by using details to form an image in our minds.

### Emotions

Strong memories are made when we feel something deeply. Knowing this, a biblical author may target our emotions to make their point. "What does the author intend for their readers to feel?" is a good question to ask.

Let's ask that question now. Consider Paul's words in Galatians 3:1-2:

"You foolish Galatians! Who has bewitched you? Before your very eyes Jesus Christ was clearly portrayed as crucified. I would like to learn just one thing from you: Did you receive the Spirit by the works of the law, or by believing what you heard?" (Galatians 3:1-2).

Paul's words are memorable because they are shocking.

Compare that emotional impact with what Paul intends as he writes these words:

"How can we thank God enough for you in return for all the joy we have in the presence of our God because of you? Night and day we pray most earnestly that we may see you again and supply what is lacking in your faith." (1 Thessalonians 3:9).

Here the emotional impact is altogether different, but it remains memorable.

---

**DANGER TO AVOID**

In asking what is memorable, it's important to distinguish between two ideas, namely what is memorable to me and what was intended by the author to be memorable. Very often these two things will be the same, but we need to be careful for they may be different. What grips or excites us about a text may come from a particular desire within us, rather than be what the author is seeking.

---

## Details

An alternative way in which authors can make a point memorable is for them to use details to create an image in our minds.

Sometimes the use of these added details is obvious, such as when a place or an individual is purposefully named.[3] But wherever an author adds a detail, they do so to make a point. An important conviction we must have is that every word in the text matters. No Word of God is without purpose, for the Holy Spirit doesn't waffle!

A good example of an author making a text more memorable to draw attention to their purpose is when Elijah, the true prophet of God, challenges the false prophets of Baal. Which of them, God or Baal, can answer by fire to burn up a sacrifice? If you are not familiar with the

---

3. The naming of a place or person is a common way for authors (particularly in the Old Testament) to highlight their emphasis in a passage. An example would be the naming of "Ichabod" meaning "no glory" in 1 Samuel 4:21. His name, an added detail, emphasises the author's main point of the passage, the departing of God's glory from Israel after the capture of the ark by the Philistines.

story, it's in 1 Kings 18:16-46.

The challenge is set. All the people of Israel are called to meet on Mount Carmel and an altar is built. The 450 prophets of Baal go first. Our author has a clear point to make, v26-29:

"Then they called on the name of Baal from morning to noon. 'Baal answer us!' they shouted. But there was no response; no-one answered. And they danced around the altar they had made. <sup>27</sup>At noon Elijah began to taunt them. 'Shout louder!' he said. 'Surely he is a god! Perhaps he is deep in thought, or busy or travelling. Maybe he is sleeping and must be awakened.' <sup>28</sup>So they shouted louder and slashed themselves with swords and spears, as was their custom, until their blood flowed. <sup>29</sup>Midday passed and they continued their frantic prophesying until the time for the evening sacrifice. But there was no response, no one answered, no-one paid attention."

It's a memorable scene. Hundreds of prophets dancing, shouting, cutting themselves with blood flowing. Our author adds in Elijah's mockery, "Perhaps he is deep in thought or busy (the ESV has "relieving himself") or travelling. Maybe he is sleeping and must be awakened." The mockery is memorable, as is the phrase to sum up the result: "no response, no-one answered, no-one paid attention."

Our author didn't need to say all that. "They tried hard all day, but nothing happened" would have been sufficient, but by adding details, mockery and a memorable phrase, our author brings out their point. The prophets of Baal and their god are utterly powerless.

When it comes to Elijah's turn, our author again brings out what they want to say with details to paint a memorable scene. Four large water jars are filled and poured over the sacrifice, a procedure repeated three times so that the water "ran around the altar and even filled the trench" (v35). Then, when God answers with fire, it doesn't just burn the sacrifice but also "the wood, the stones and the soil, and also licked up the water in the trench" (v38). The point is made. God is powerful. He is the one who answers. The details fix God's power in our memories.

Now it is your turn to look at a text. Throughout the book I have included short "exercises" to put into practice the various aspects of the method as we cover them. Each exercise has some suggested thoughts by way of "answer" in Appendix 1. Please don't be tempted to skip these exercises. Practical learning is important and should help to deepen your confidence in Bible understanding. They are not essential for reading the book, but each exercise will only take a few minutes. Let the living word of God speak to your heart.

---

**EXERCISE**

**Read 1 Samuel 17:4-11**

What is memorable in these verses?

(HELP: What one big point is our author making with every detail in the text?)

Once you have worked through this question please turn to page 253 for some suggested answers.

---

### R is for Repeated – Is anything repeated?

The next thing in Stage 1: "Observe" as we "Read, read and read again" the text, is repetition. This is perhaps the most common way the Bible authors draw attention to a point they want to make. This is perhaps the most common way the Bible authors draw attention to a point they want to make!

The episode in 1 Kings 18 contains many examples. As soon as the fire falls from heaven we read, "When all the people saw this, they fell prostrate and cried, 'The LORD - he is God! The LORD he is God!" (v39). Our author didn't need to put in the repetition, but does so because of their purpose, to emphasise a point.

Repetition is easiest to spot with repeated words that immediately follow one another, such as in the example just given, but words are often repeated in the same paragraph. Take 1 John 1:1-3 for example:

"¹That which was from the beginning, which we have heard, which we have seen with our eyes, which we have looked at and our hands have touched - this we proclaim concerning the Word of life. [2]The life appeared; we have seen it and testify to it, and we proclaim to you the eternal life, which was with the Father and has appeared to us. [3]We proclaim to you what we have seen and heard, so that you may also have fellowship with us. And our fellowship is with the Father and with his Son, Jesus Christ."

Spend a moment looking at that text. What is repeated?

Our author uses "appeared" twice and "seen" three times. Clearly that is repetition. But, when thinking about repetition, it is important to realise that repetition isn't just about repeated words. Repetition is also about repeated ideas. Here "seen" and "appeared" are essentially the same thing, so that adds to the repetition. Then the author adds "looked at" and "with our eyes"- again to repeat the idea. In the space of just three verses the same idea comes up seven times. We are meant to notice!

Now have another look. What other words or ideas in these verses from 1 John are repeated?

I am sure you will have seen them. The word "heard" is repeated twice. Add to this the mention of touch once and the seven seeing words already noticed, and the idea of sensed (combining sight, hearing and touch) is repeated a total of ten times! Our author is making a point.[4]

So, repetition can involve words alongside each other or words in the same paragraph, or it can be of ideas in the same paragraph. But equally important repetition can be of words or ideas drawn out over several chapters or even a whole Bible book. For example, in the books of 1 and 2 Samuel the truth that God's Word never fails is repeated again and again. Just as an author will have an emphasis in a paragraph, so they will have an emphasis in a whole book. This is easily missed if we limit our Bible reading to just short passages, but a wonderful blessing when we take the time to read through several chapters or even a whole book in one go.

---

4. In addition, "life" is repeated (introducing an important theme for the whole book) along with the words "proclaim" (with "testify") and "fellowship".

Along with the repetition of words and ideas, authors can gain our attention by telling us of repeated actions by characters in the text. Abraham we are told prayed repeatedly for the people of Sodom (Genesis 18:23-33) and God sent plagues repeatedly on the people of Egypt (Exodus 7:14-12:30). Through repeated actions, the text emphasises its point.

Finally, authors sometimes use repetition, not so much to make factual points that we are meant to understand, but to communicate or create an emotion with which we are meant to engage. Take Job chapter 3 where Job expresses his deep distress:

"³May the day of my birth perish, and the night that said, 'A boy is conceived!' ⁴That day - may it turn to darkness; may God above not care about it; may no light shine upon it. ⁵May gloom and utter darkness claim it once more; may a cloud settle over it; may blackness overwhelm it. ⁶That night - may thick darkness seize it; may it not be included among the days of the year nor be entered in any of the months. ⁷May that night be barren; may no shout of joy be heard in it. ⁸May those who curse days curse that day, those who are ready to rouse Leviathan. ⁹May its morning stars become dark; may it wait for daylight in vain and not see the first rays of dawn, ¹⁰for it did not shut the doors of the womb on me to hide trouble from my eyes." (Job 3:3-10).

At a purely factual level, to communicate how Job felt after his ordeal of chapters 1 and 2, our author could simply have said, "After this, Job felt terrible." That would have done. It would communicate the truth, but of course it wouldn't communicate anything like the passage we have been given. Using repetition, Job expresses with great emotion his deep distress, so as readers we can feel something of his pain. Job knows what it is to suffer. So when he teaches us about suffering we don't have a hypocrite, we have a teacher who truly understands.

In summary, repetition can be of words, ideas or actions; the repetition can be immediate, within a paragraph or spread out over several chapters of a Bible book and it can be used to emphasise a teaching point or to create an emotion. Time again for you to look at a passage.

**EXERCISE**

**Read Mark 10:35-52**

What important question is repeated in these verses?

What is our author drawing attention to with this repetition?

Once you have thought through this, compare with the suggested thoughts on page 254.

**ADDITIONAL TIP**

Unfortunately, an author's repetition can sometimes be missed in translation from the original languages. Rather than repeating the same word the translators provide different words in their translation to make a passage more readable. This is a good example of where a word for word translation can be more helpful for Bible study purposes.[5]

Further help with knowing exactly which words are used in the original languages and so spotting repetition is available in an excellent and completely free resource called Scripture Tools for Every Person (STEP). This can be accessed or downloaded at www.stepbible.org. and enables people without any knowledge of the original languages of Hebrew, Aramaic and Greek to work out which words are used. It also provides a good understanding of their meaning. (There will be more on this in chapter 6.)

### S is for Surprising – Is anything surprising?

Surprises are one of those things you either love or you hate. Even teenagers aren't apathetic when they are shocked or amazed by something! A surprise grabs our attention, it sticks in our memory and so it makes a point. As such the biblical authors sometimes use

---

5. Even word for word translations can sometimes obscure the repetition in the original language. In Romans 3:20-31 for example, the original words for "righteousness" and "justified" are very closely related, so someone reading the Greek would count more repetitions than someone looking at an English translation. In 1 Peter, the words translated variously as "respect", "reverence" and "fear" are in fact all the same.

surprises to make their points. Again we are meant to notice: the surprise highlights what the author wants to emphasise.

By definition, surprises come when we are not expecting them. Because of this an author may deliberately say something fairly ordinary, in order to set up their surprise. Take 2 Kings 5:1 for example:

"Now Naaman was commander of the army of Aram. He was a great man in the sight of his master and highly regarded, because through him the LORD had given victory to Aram. He was a valiant soldier, but he had leprosy."

Take a look at that verse again. What are the two surprises?

A useful trick to help us spot surprises is to put ourselves into the shoes of the original hearers, in this case people in Israel living hundreds of years before Jesus. Aram (modern day Syria) was one of the enemies of Israel, so the fact that the LORD had given victory to Aram is a surprise. Wasn't he supposed to be Israel's God?

Then, the fact that this man had leprosy is another surprise. He is a "great man", "highly regarded" and a "valiant soldier", and we might expect the verse to finish "and he was popular amongst his men" or "and he was handsome in form"! But it doesn't. It finishes with "he had leprosy"- a terrible disease, something the exact opposite of greatness, high regard and valour.

Having created these surprises at the start of this section of his book, our author has highlighted two important themes to which he is drawing our attention. God is not just the God of Israel, but of the whole world, and God is all-powerful over even leprosy, the most terrible of diseases.[6]

Surprise can be "set up" by the Bible's authors, but sometimes it comes out of the blue. To spot this, careful observation of the text is important, thinking through word by word. A good question to ask is: "What might we expect the author to say?" comparing it with what they actually do say.

---

6. By the end of 2 Kings 5, not only is Naaman the Gentile healed of his leprosy, but surprisingly the Israelite Gehazi, Elisha's servant is punished with leprosy. The point is not just that God is the God of other nations too, (something that Jesus picks up in Luke 4:27) but that he cannot be taken for granted by Israel. He is not just the God who is able to cure leprosy, but also the God who can punish with leprosy.

Take as an example what Paul says in Galatians 1:15-16. What surprise is there here?

"But when God, who set me apart from my mother's womb and called me by his grace, was pleased to reveal his Son in me so that I might preach him among the Gentiles, my immediate response was not to consult any human being."

There is surprise enough in Paul not telling anyone the full content of his Damascus road experience. We would expect him to share his calling to the Gentiles with at least someone. But there is a bigger surprise here. Paul says that God set him apart from his mother's womb as someone who might preach to the Gentiles. Paul's terrible persecution of the church before he met Jesus on the Damascus road was, then, all part of God's plan, God's preparation for Paul to be his preacher to the Gentiles - for he was set apart as such, even before he was born. There is incredible comfort here: God is sovereign and uses even Paul's persecution for his purposes. But, did you spot the other surprise? This needs careful observation.

Paul says that God "was pleased to reveal his Son *in* me". That is shocking. He doesn't say that God "was pleased to reveal his Son *to* me" as we might expect. Is that how we tend to think of the revelation of Jesus? In us! But Paul has a point to make to the Galatians. In 2:20 he will go on to say, "Christ lives in me" and in 4:6 "God sent the Spirit of his Son into our hearts". The Galatians have seemingly forgotten the "new creation" (6:15), the reality of God's inward work and Christian experience and are focusing only on the external. It's a danger for us all.

## Spotting surprises

Surprises come in many ways, and we need to be careful not to miss them by becoming over-familiar with the Bible text. Imagining that we are hearing the Bible for the first time can help. When Jesus announces, "Son your sins are forgiven" to the paralysed man (Mark 2:5) it is easy for us to miss the shock, because we are so used to the idea of Jesus forgiving sins. But no person can forgive all the sins of another: only God can do that. Jesus is in effect claiming to be God!

In the well-known and much loved Psalm 46 which begins "God is our refuge and strength, an ever present help in time of trouble", there is a real surprise in the geography of verse 4. This speaks of "a river whose streams make glad the city of God." But Jerusalem has never had a river run anywhere near it. What is the author saying?[7]

Sometimes the surprise is more subtle, such as the tense of a verb. In Romans 8:37 (another favourite passage), we are told, "No, in all these things we are more than conquerors through him who loved us."

The tense of that last verb is a surprise. Wouldn't we expect Paul to say, "through him who *loves* us"? Isn't that the normal way of thinking about God's love? He loves us now.[8] But Paul wants to make a point. In 8:5 he has asked, "Who shall separate us from the love of Christ?" (present tense) and in 8:39 he will go on to say "(nothing) will be able to separate us from the love of God in Christ Jesus our Lord" (future tense).

Why can no-one and nothing separate us from the love of Jesus now and in the future? Because he loved us then, at the cross! The Christian's confidence of God's love doesn't rest on our present performance or our feelings, but on a solid, past, completed, supreme act of love then - he *loved* us. The cross, then, is the solid ground of assurance for his love now and so whatever we are up against (v36,38), we are more than conquerors! Time now for you to spot a surprise or two.

---

**EXERCISE**

**Read John 11:1-16**

What surprises are there in these verses?

What is John our author, drawing our attention to with these surprises?

Once you have thought through this, compare with the suggested thoughts on page 254.

---

7. To understand this seeming lack of geographical knowledge by the author we need look no further than Revelation 22:1-2.
8. See for example Revelation 1:5.

## Summary

In this chapter we have begun the first stage of the method: "Observe". We have considered MRS ("What is Memorable?", "What is Repeated?" and "What is Surprising?"), and we have seen that the biblical authors often use these things to draw our attention to the point that they are making. Not every passage will have something that is surprising, repeated or particularly memorable, but these are three questions that can be asked of any text and often open up insight and understanding.

In the next chapter we will consider the next thing to look for as we "Observe", but before you continue, there are two further passages to look at for your encouragement below.

## END OF CHAPTER EXERCISES

For each of these exercises, once you have read the text, aim to spend a few minutes thinking through your answers. Once you have drawn your conclusions, compare with the suggested thoughts on page 255-257.

### New Testament Exercise

**Read Matthew 4:18-22** and work through "MRS" to study the passage. What is Memorable? What is Repeated? What is Surprising? From your observations what is the author drawing our attention to?

### Old Testament Exercise

**Read 1 Samuel 16:1-13** and work through "MRS" to study the passage. What is Memorable? What is Repeated? What is Surprising? From your observations what is the author drawing our attention to?

# CHAPTER 3

## WORDS AND IMAGES

---

*"How sweet are your words to my taste.*
*Sweeter than honey to my mouth!"*
**Psalm 119:103**

"Don't say it was 'delightful' - make us say delightful
when we have read the description."
**C.S. Lewis**

---

"I'm really getting this!" exclaimed Rachel noticing yet another repetition in the passage.

"Now there is a *surprise*," replied Joe with a cheeky grin on his face.

"I see he's as charming as ever," commented Mrs Wise looking sympathetically towards Rachel.

"Yes, always one for flattery is Joe!"

"Hmm. Now that's an interesting word don't you think?" replied Mrs Wise. "Flattery! Words are such amazing and interesting things."

Rachel glanced at Joe with a smile.

"I mean where do you think the word flattery came from? After all it means making you big and important, the exact opposite of making you flat!"

Joe was now also smiling.

"Words," repeated Mrs Wise, "Words - that is the next thing to remember from my name. 'W' is for Words."

### W is for Words – Carefully think through each and every word.

In the last chapter, we began to look in more detail at the journey we must always make for good Bible understanding. We appreciated the importance of starting in "Bible Land," imagining we are there alongside the very first readers of the Bible; and we began with Stage 1: "Observe", thinking through "What did it say to them?"

Then we considered three helpful questions to ask of any passage, using "MRS" to remember these: "What is Memorable?" "What is Repeated?" and "What is Surprising?" We saw that the aim of these questions is to identify clues, to give us insight into the main points of what the author is saying. What are they drawing attention to in the way in which they write?

In this chapter, we will look at two further observation questions to collect additional clues.

### Every word matters

An important conviction for any Bible student is that every word matters. Each and every word in the Bible is given by God. As such, careful consideration of each word is important. Take Romans 8:1:

"Therefore there is now no condemnation for those who are in Christ Jesus."

There isn't a single word in this glorious sentence that is not significant. A quick read skimming over what is written may leave us with good news ("God doesn't condemn Christians"), but by reading each word slowly, and carefully in turn, we gain a much richer understanding. Let's do that now.

The "therefore" at the start of the verse links us back to what Paul has been saying previously. This is his conclusion. All the proceeding argument adds logical weight to the truth of what he now says.

And what does he say? "There is *now* no condemnation". This is a truth for now. It is not something for which we have to wait. And what is the truth? That there is "*no* condemnation"- none at all, not "decreased" condemnation or even "minimal condemnation", but none at all.

Finally, who is it for? - "for those who are in Christ Jesus." To receive this extraordinary gift of no condemnation right now, all we have to be is "in Christ Jesus." There is no "and" here: "in Christ Jesus *and* live a good moral life," or "in Christ Jesus *and* read the Bible regularly," or "in Christ Jesus *and* be happy all the time." No, to receive no condemnation now, all we need to be is "in Christ Jesus." And what an incredible phrase that is, describing not a set of beliefs or actions, but a relationship, a spiritual union with the perfect man who is God. By carefully considering every word, we gain a much richer understanding. Every word matters.

### Particular words to highlight

During the "Observe" stage of our study it's often helpful to print out the text so that certain words can be underlined or highlighted using different coloured pens.

In the last chapter, we saw how repetition is a common way in which the Bible writers draw attention to the points they wish to make. As such, repeated words should be noted. However, as we "read, read and read again", there are five other types of word to highlight. For those who like such things, these can be remembered with the word "QUACK"!

## Q - Quoted words

These are words that the author deliberately brings into the text from an outside source, usually the Old Testament. By adding a quote, the author is drawing our attention to something that is said elsewhere and we are meant to take note.

Careful observation of the exact words quoted is also important. In Luke 4:18-19 Jesus reads from the scroll of Isaiah 61:1-2:

> "The Spirit of the Lord is on me,
>> because he has anointed me
>> to proclaim good news to the poor.
> He has sent me to proclaim freedom for the prisoners
>> and recovery of sight for the blind,
>> to set the oppressed free,
>> to proclaim the year of the Lord's favour."

However, careful observation, comparing the quote with its original source, will reveal that the quote was cut short. The end of Isaiah 61:2 talks about this person also proclaiming the "day of vengeance of our God."

This cutting short is not a mistake. Either Jesus has stopped his reading at this point or Luke has cut his quote short. Either way a point is being made - the emphasis is not on judgement, but on good news.

## Finding quoted words

Helpfully, in many modern Bible translations most quoted words are identified for us. Furthermore, where they come from is often added in the footnotes. Nevertheless, we should remain alert to the fact that sometimes a reference to another Bible passage is suggested, if not directly quoted. In Numbers 22:6 for example, Balak king of Moab wants Balaam to put a curse on Israel:

> "Now come and put a curse on these people, because they are too powerful for me. Perhaps then I will be able to defeat them and drive them out of the land. For I know that whoever you bless is blessed and whoever you curse is cursed."

There is no direct quotation here, but there is a clear echo of God's words to Abraham in Genesis 12:3:

"I will bless those who bless you, and whoever curses you I will curse; and all peoples of the earth will be blessed through you."

Balak's instruction to Balaam is therefore a direct challenge to God's earlier promise to Abraham and his offspring. What is more it is to put Balaam in the place of God. Noting this reference to the earlier words in Genesis gives a far richer understanding of the passage in Numbers.

## U - Unfamiliar words (or phrases)

As we read the text, there may be words we do not recognise or understand. Such words, if they are completely unfamiliar need our attention now. A different translation may help, as may an internet search, a dictionary or a friend. Regardless, before moving on we need to make sure we have at least a basic comprehension of every word under consideration.

Perhaps instead we will understand the individual words, but there may be a phrase that puzzles us. Take Romans 12:20:

"If your enemy is hungry, feed him; if he is thirsty, give him something to drink. In doing this you will heap burning coals on his head."

In this example, all the individual words are easy enough to understand, but the phrase "heap burning coals on his head" is anything but straightforward. What is the verse saying?

Rather than trying to solve that puzzle immediately, for now, we simply observe. A good practice is to make a note, perhaps with a different coloured pen or by underlining and writing questions in the margin, e.g. "What does this mean?"

At a later stage we will need to come back to these questions (and in chapter 6 we will return to this exact question), but rather than investigating further, at this stage we simply observe.

**DANGER TO AVOID**

When faced with a puzzle such as the meaning of "heap burning coals on his head" the temptation is to go to a commentary, a book written to help us understand the Bible.

Good commentaries are a wonderful blessing and can be very useful. Nevertheless, the timing of exactly when to go to a commentary is important.

Commentaries are like conversation partners. But, just as with all conversation partners, the learning is best when we bring something to the conversation. Come too early before we have grasped the text and formed our own ideas, and we will have nothing much to offer. The danger then becomes that we simply accept what the commentary has to say. On the other hand, if we come too late, we might be so convinced of our idea that we fail to listen to others. Reading commentaries is about timing. Opening them at the end of Stage 2: "Understand" is about right.

## A - Added words

Added words are those that are added to the principal text. Without these words sentences would still make sense, but their presence provides emphasis. Typically, they are adjectives and adverbs, but they may be any word that adds emphasis to the central text. Take, for example, Luke's words at the beginning of his gospel:

"With this in mind, since I myself have carefully investigated everything from the beginning, I too decided to write an orderly account for you, most excellent Theophilus, so that you may know the certainty of the things you have been taught." (Luke 1:3-4).

What Luke says here contains many added words. His writing would still have made sense if he had written:

"With this in mind, since I have investigated, I decided to write an account; so that you may know the things you have been taught."

Instead, Luke uses added words to this central text. He says, "I myself" have "carefully" investigated "everything from the beginning" and that it is an "orderly" account and written to "most excellent Theophilus" so that he may know the "certainty" of what he has been taught.

Using added words, Luke brings a particular stress on the reliability of what he writes. Reason after reason is added to provide Theophilus with confidence. Perhaps you lack confidence in the teaching of the gospel. If so, Luke is a gospel for you. It is a carefully written orderly account so that the reader may be confident in the truth.

When considering added words, two helpful questions to ask are:

- What difference would it make if this word / phrase were not there?
- What alternative word / phrase could have been used, but wasn't?

These questions help us to grasp the significance of the specific added words used and so give insight into the author's purpose. It may be that at this stage we can't yet answer those questions. If so, writing a note in the margin: "Why this word here?" will prove helpful later.

---

**ADDITIONAL TIP**

In commentaries you may come across the comment that a particular word is "emphatic". This is because in Greek, the original language of the New Testament, there is another way in which writers can emphasise a point that doesn't exist in the same way in English. As such it is missed in our translations. It is beyond the scope of this book to explain the various ways in which this can be done in Greek, but it is essentially by altering the word order. As an example, take Hebrews 4:12: "For the word of God is living and active." Here a commentary may tell you that in the original language the word for "living" is emphatic. This means the author is adding stress to that word.[1]

---

1. Knowing that a word is emphatic may add to understanding, but there is danger in relying too much on just this observation. The emphatic position is just one way to stress a point. Where it fits with other emphasis (as covered by MRS WISE) it can add confidence to our understanding, but we need to be wary if this is the only evidence for an author's emphasis.

## C - Connecting words

Connecting words are those words which join ideas together in logical thought. They may create a contrast between ideas, or they may link together cause and effect. Examples of connecting words are provided in the box below.

| Connecting Words | | |
|---|---|---|
| Logical Progression (Cause followed by effect) | Logical Progression (Effect followed by cause) | Creates a Contrast |
| consequently | as | but |
| in order that | because | however |
| so / so that / that | for | nevertheless |
| then | since | rather |
| therefore | | yet |

At this stage, all that is needed is to observe and note any connecting words. Later, when working out the structure of the text, this will prove very helpful. If you have printed out the text, you may like to use another highlighter with a different colour.

## K - Key words

We have already seen that every word of God matters, Jesus himself said that "even the smallest letter" and "the least stroke of a pen" are important (Matthew 5:18), but there are some words that are "key" for the understanding of a passage.

Key words tend to be main verbs and nouns. They are those words which form the backbone of a sentence and, if changed, would considerably alter the meaning of what is said. They are often rich words that have different shades to their meaning.

Take for example the word "condemnation" in Romans 8:1, which we looked at earlier. This is a key word for that verse. The other words all fit around this key word, and so a detailed understanding of "condemnation" will be important.

How we understand a word in depth will be covered in chapter 6. For now, we only need to look out for key words, observe and highlight them. Which words are key? Which of these key words do we need to understand better? A comment in the margin maybe useful for later: "What exactly does this word mean?"

Usually, key words are part of the main structure of a sentence, but sometimes they can be additional detail. This is often the case when an author identifies a particular place name. The place name doesn't apparently add much to the core of what they say, but it can be key in providing us with situational context. There will be more on this in chapter 7. For now, the possibility that a place name may be important should be noted.

---

**DANGER TO AVOID**

As we read the text, it is very easy to assume that we understand the exact meaning of a word in a particular Bible passage, when actually, we have misunderstood it. The danger comes by bringing our understanding of that word in Today's World and imposing that understanding onto the word in the Bible text. But words change in their meaning according to their context. This can even be the case within the Bible, for many different authors wrote the Bible over many centuries.

Take "righteousness" for example, when applied to people. In the Psalms, it describes a morally upright (though not completely sinless) right living before God and other people. Its focus is on the actions of someone. In Romans 3:21-24 on the other hand, the righteousness of God describes a legally right standing before God which is credited to people. Here the focus is on the right legal standing of the person. If we impose this Romans understanding of righteousness onto the word in the Psalms (e.g. Psalm 18:20-24) we will make a mistake.

Time for you to have a look at a verse and think through the words:

---

**EXERCISE**

**Read 1 Corinthians 15:58**

Consider the words in this verse using QUACK. Look for "quoted", "unfamiliar", "added", "connecting" and "key" words. (Remember these don't all have to be present).

Think about the exact words, particularly the added and key words. What is challenging in the choice of words used? What encouragement is there for us here?

Once you have identified these words and answered the questions, compare your answer with the suggested thoughts on page 258.

---

## Imagination

"So you see every word is important!" exclaimed Mrs Wise. "If our minds are to understand the Bible well, we need to think carefully about every single word."

"But you know," she continued, "understanding is only half of what the mind does. There is another half, which I think is even more important."

"Really?" asked Joe, somewhat confused.

"Yes. You see a lot of what the Bible teaches is simply beyond our ability to understand in full. Take the nature of God for example. He is just so wonderful, so extraordinary, so beyond our ability to understand, that we need more than just facts and reasoning: we need…" she paused for thought, "…we need imagination!"

Joe and Rachel were now attentive to every word.

"One of my favourite prayers," she continued, "is Paul's in Ephesians 1:18-19:

'I pray that the eyes of your heart may be enlightened in order that you might know the hope to which he has called you, the riches of his glorious inheritance in his holy people and his incomparably great power for us who believe.'"

Mrs Wise's face beamed brightly.

"Our hope - the riches of his glorious inheritance and his incomparably great power for us! Now there are some things we can't get our heads around!" she exclaimed. "They are far beyond our understanding. So what is needed is that 'the eyes of our hearts may be enlightened.'"

"And that is our imagination!" exclaimed Joe.

"Exactly!" replied Mrs Wise. "Our heart is that part of us, that central part, where we desire and value and trust and so worship. So if our hearts are enlightened to the things of God, then they will desire and value him more."

"And we become more like Jesus, changed on the inside," continued Rachel.

"Yes - it's wonderful," said Mrs Wise, "but to do that the Holy Spirit works in our imagination. Facts, logic and reasoning can only get us so far. They are crucially important. We never leave them behind. We build on that understanding and never go against it, but it's our imagination based on those facts that takes us further on into a deeper appreciation, love, desire and trust. It's imagination that grips our hearts."

### I is for Images – Are any images used?

The "I" in MRS WISE is for Images. What images (if any) are there in the text being studied?

All the teachers in the Bible, not least Jesus himself, use images. Images are pictures, illustrations, similes, and metaphors to capture our imagination. They fix the eyes of our heart on things that we can't see and so easily understand. Because faith is seeing what is unseen (Hebrews 11:1), it needs imagination, and images are the windows through which faith can see.

This is particularly true when the Bible teaches things far beyond our experience such as the character of God, the realities of heaven, hell and the spiritual world. So, for such subjects, the Bible gives many images, not to confuse us, but because each image serves as a different window through which we may begin to understand realities which are so hard to see.

Let's consider an example - John's words in Revelation 1:12-16:

"I turned round to see the voice that was speaking to me. And when I turned I saw seven golden lampstands, [13]and among the lampstands was someone like a son of man, dressed in a robe reaching down to his feet and with a golden sash round his chest. [14]The hair on his head was white like wool, as white as snow, and his eyes were like blazing fire. [15]His feet were like bronze glowing in a furnace and his voice was like the sound of rushing waters. [16]In his right hand he held seven stars, and coming out of his mouth was a sharp, double-edged sword. His face was like the sun shining in all its brilliance."

These verses are full of images, metaphors - not things to be taken literally. For John a literal description won't do. Meeting Jesus made such an incredible impact. Only images can convey something of the sheer breath-taking wonder of the exalted and risen Jesus.

As readers we are meant to feel something as we read about Jesus in Revelation 1:12-16. We are not meant to ask, "I wonder what colour John meant when he described Jesus' eyes as being like blazing fire," but we are meant to have emotional engagement. His eyes are like blazing fire, all-knowing, all-discerning eyes from which we cannot escape, eyes which burn, eyes which judge. The image creates impact.[2]

Later, in Stage 2 of the method "Understand", we will consider images in more detail. We will see how, along with creating impact, they can help clarify a teaching. We will look at two important questions to ask of all images: "What impact was meant by this image?" and "How does this image clarify what is being taught?" But for now, at the "Observe" stage, our task is simply to identify the images so that we can consider them later.

## Types of Images

To identify images in the text it is useful to be aware some of the basic types of image. Once identified, there is no need to work out which particular group an image belongs to, but being aware of the different types may help us later to answer those two important questions identified above.

1. **Similes** - A simile likens two things together with an image: "As the deer pants for streams of water so my soul pants for you, My God." (Psalm 42:1). Here the picture of the deer panting for water vividly brings to our minds the author's longing for God.

2. **Metaphors** - When Paul writes, "I planted the seed, Apollos watered it, but God has been making it grow" (1 Corinthians 3:6), he is using metaphor. Paul is not speaking of literal plants. Instead, he is using something familiar - the planting, watering and growth of plants - to explain something less familiar, the teaching of the gospel and how it grows.

3. **Personification** - This is when a human attribute is given to something which is not human: "Let the rivers clap their hands, let the mountains sing together for joy;" (Psalm 98:8). In giving rivers and mountains the human ability to clap and sing, the author provides emphasis to the verse which follows, how wonderful will be the coming of the LORD.

---

2. The idea of eyes of fire being a metaphor for judgement is clear from Revelation 2:18 and its development in Revelation 2:23. This picks up Daniel 10:6 where the man in Daniel's vision has "eyes like flaming torches." His primary purpose is to reveal God's judgement (Daniel 10:21-12:13).

4. **Historical Events** - Sometimes an author will describe a particular event or recall an episode from history. Either way a vivid image is created in our minds, not just a single picture but a film, as the event unfolds. This creates impact so that we better understand and recall the truth being taught.

5. **Parables** - Like the retelling of historical events, these stories create powerful moving images in our imagination. Consequently, what they teach lodges firmly in our minds.

In summary, images are like salt in a meal, for they bring out the flavour in the text - they clarify its teaching. Yet, at the same time, they bring home a point, so that it tastes especially strong in our hearts.

Imagine constructing a fence using wooden posts and nails. To build the fence each nail must be placed into the wood with precision. But the wood is hard.

Our sinful hearts are similarly hard. Like wooden posts they don't naturally want to receive the truth. So rather than taking a box of nails and throwing them randomly in hope that some will stick into the posts, the Bible authors use images. Images hold up the nails of truth with precision so that we understand, and then knock them in with force, so that the truth lodges firmly in place.

"That picture of Jesus in Revelation is awesome!" announced Rachel. "Bit scary though."

"But what does it mean by 'the hair on his head was white like wool?'" asked Joe.

"Or that thing about his 'feet being like bronze glowing in a furnace?'" added Rachel.

Mrs Wise smiled. "Those are exactly the right questions to be asking," she replied, "but before we get to understanding we have to finish our observation and there are two more important things to look for."

"Ah, yes. The 'S' and the 'E' of Mrs Wise," replied Rachel. "What do they stand for?"

Joe looked hopefully at the remaining cakes, "Second helpings and Extras perhaps?!"

**END OF CHAPTER EXERCISES**

For each of these exercises, once you have read the text, aim to spend a few minutes thinking through your answers. Once you have drawn your conclusions, compare them with the suggested thoughts on page 259-261.

### New Testament Exercise

**Read Galatians 5:13-15**

Read through this passage highlighting words that are "quoted", "unfamiliar", "added", "connecting" and "key" (QUACK).

What image is used in these verses to add impact to what Paul is saying?

What do you think is the overall purpose of these particular verses?

### Old Testament Exercise

**Read Isaiah 11:6-9**

Spend some time thinking through the images in these verses. How do they impact your heart, what do you feel and desire?

(To help your thinking ask: What is memorable? What is repeated? What is surprising? What are the added words? What are the key words?)

What do you think is the overall purpose of these particular verses?

# CHAPTER 4

# STRUCTURE AND EMPHASIS

---

*"The unfolding of your words gives light;*
*it gives understanding to the simple."*
**Psalm 119:130**

"Don't believe everything you think. You cannot be trusted
to tell yourself the truth. Stay in The Word."
**Jerry Bridges**

---

"So if 'S' is not for 'second helpings,' what is the 'S' for Mrs Wise?"

Mrs Wise lay back further in her chair and contemplated the question.

"How's that building project of yours coming on Joe?" she inquired. "A small construction in the garden wasn't it?"

"Erm… Slowly." replied Joe, somewhat confused by the question. "It's coming on slowly."

"Make that very slowly," added Rachel. "Over two years for foundations, walls and windows. Still no roof!"

"Needs the right weather for that!" replied Joe with a smile on his face.

"And perhaps a little more attention?" added Rachel.

### S is for Structure

The structure of buildings is important. Foundations, walls, roof, windows and doors all come together (however slowly) to create the building. Each of these key parts is made up of yet smaller components - individual bricks, mortar, pieces of wood, nails, glass. Understanding structure is vital for buildings, but it is no less important for understanding the Bible. S is for Structure.

Just as a building can be separated into its component parts and each part can be yet further divided, so the Bible can also be split up. There are 66 books in the Bible. Each book has main sections, and each main section is made up of individual units, where each unit is held together by one basic idea. Each unit may then have subsections which can be further broken down into sentences and words as illustrated in the diagram below.

| Whole Bible | > | Bible Book | > | Main Section | > | Individual Unit | > | Sub-section | > | Sentences & Words |
|---|---|---|---|---|---|---|---|---|---|---|

When considering S for Structure there are two important tasks.

First, we need to identify the component parts - that is the main sections, individual units and subsections in the Bible's text.

Secondly, we need to work out how they all fit together. Sometimes this will be easy, sometimes very difficult. But with God as the author, the Bible always has structure.[1]

## Task 1: Identify the Component Parts

So how do we identify the various building blocks of a Bible passage or a Bible book?

At first glance it appears that this work has already been done for us, for the Bible is divided into chapters and verses. What is more, in many modern translations, section headings and paragraph breaks are given to help split up the text.

Unfortunately, these divisions are not an original part of the text. The chapters were added approximately 800 years ago and the verses about 500 years ago. They are of immense help for referencing, but they don't always correspond to the Bible's actual structure, indeed they can even be unhelpful. The modern section headings are much better, but again they can make the true structure of the Bible harder to see. We shouldn't necessarily rely on these divisions to be accurate.

---

**ADDITIONAL TIP**

Since the Bible's true structure can be obscured by chapters and verses, section headings and paragraph breaks; a useful exercise can be to print out the Bible passage being studied without all these distractions. This can be done from the internet, e.g. www.biblegateway.com, deleting the divisions before printing. Then, with just the text in front of you, you can underline, highlight, and write down thoughts; until you are confident the structure has been found.

---

1. Occasionally, the Bible's structure is deliberately chaotic as the skilled author writes to reflect the mood of what is written. What we should not conclude is that the Bible has no structure - if we can't see the structure, the problem lies with us, not the Bible.

The key to identifying the component parts of a text is to look for how the author has split up the text. In general, identifying where individual units start and finish is the best place to begin. These may have subsections within them, but the key for recognition is that each unit is held together by one basic idea. Once these units are identified[2], we can then look for where main sections in the book start and finish, signaled by a major shift in idea.

By way of example consider Colossians 3:18-4:1:

"[18]Wives, submit yourselves to your husbands, as is fitting in the Lord. [19]Husbands, love your wives and do not be harsh with them.

[20]Children, obey your parents in everything, for this pleases the Lord.

[21] Fathers, do not embitter your children, or they will become discouraged.

[22]Slaves, obey your earthly masters in everything; and do it, not only when their eye is on you and to curry their favour, but with sincerity of heart and reverence for the Lord. [23]Whatever you do, work at it with all your heart, as working for the Lord, not for human masters, [24]since you know that you will receive an inheritance from the Lord as a reward. It is the Lord Christ you are serving. [25]Anyone who does wrong will be repaid for their wrongs, and there is no favouritism.

4 [1]Masters, provide your slaves with what is right and fair, because you know that you also have a Master in heaven."

This is one individual unit of Scripture which, you will have noted, overlaps the end of a chapter! The basic idea holding the unit together is that of instructions given by Paul to specific groups, not to the whole church. Though not of equal length, it has six subsections (three groups of two), Paul's instructions to wives and husbands, children and fathers, and finally slaves and masters.

Beforehand and in the verses which follow, Paul's words are to be applied to everyone in the church, not to specific groups. As such they

---

2. Rather than being too dogmatic about where individual units and main sections start and finish in a Bible book, it's helpful to remember Deuteronomy 29:29 and allow for others to have different ideas. The important thing is to consider the structure, for in the process of doing that we will often be given helpful insights.

are different, so what lies before and afterwards form parts of different units. Having said that, they are all units of application. This links them together as part of a main section of the book. In chapter 4:7 however, there is a significant change in content. Here Paul moves from application to sending greetings, so signifying the start of a new main section.

## Helpful Questions

Two questions are helpful for identifying the various building blocks of a Bible book:

### 1. Where does the content change?

This is the most important question to ask. Above all, it is an author's change in content that determines the beginning and end of a building block of structure. It may be a change of theme, argument or subject matter. It may be a change of location, or a new person speaking in the text. It may be a new audience being addressed or new application.

Whatever it is, once identified, we need to ask: How significant is this change? Does it signify the start of a new individual unit or just a subsection of a unit? Perhaps it is a bridging section forming the end of one idea and the beginning of the next. Or is the change considerable, suggesting the start of a new main section?

### 2. Are there any connecting words to help divide the text?

In the last chapter we noted the importance of connecting words, such as "then", "therefore", "so", "because", "but", "for", "afterwards" etc. These words will often mark the beginning and end of the building blocks of Scripture. Having identified them, just as with a change in content, we need to ask: How big a change do they alert us to? Is the connecting word just taking us on to another verse or subsection, or is it taking us to the next unit, or even to a new main section of the book?

## A helpful exercise – Summary Statements

Once a text has been divided into its component parts, it is often helpful to come up with a short title or summary statement for each part. This process helps check that the division is correct. If something can't be summarised it may need further division. Once completed, these summary statements will be helpful for the second task when considering structure - that of working out how the pieces fit together.

## A Worked Example

Below is Psalm 1, an individual unit of Scripture. Before reading on, take some time and ask: How would you divide it up into subsections? Look for changes in content and connecting words. Once you have a structure, try to summarise the whole unit (the whole psalm) and each subsection, using a title or short statement.

"[1]Blessed is the one who does not walk in step with the wicked or stand in the way that sinners take or sit in the company of mockers, [2]but whose delight is in the law of the LORD, and who meditates on his law day and night. [3]That person is like a tree planted by streams of water, which yields its fruit in season and whose leaf does not wither - whatever they do prospers. [4]Not so the wicked! They are like the chaff which the wind blows away. [5]Therefore the wicked will not stand in the judgement, nor sinners in the assembly of the righteous. [6]For the LORD watches over the way of the righteous, but the way of the wicked leads to destruction."

Looking through the psalm, there are three notable sub-sections in content. These are v1-3 (all about a godly person), v4-5 (all about the wicked) and v6 (which mentions both the righteous and the wicked).

v1-3:  The godly person

v4-5:  The wicked

v6:    Both righteous and wicked

In addition, there are a number of connecting words: "or" (v1 twice), "but" (v2), "therefore" (v5), "for" (v6) and "but" (v6).

Combining these observations, the psalm can be divided as below. Then a summary statement can be given to each subsection and the whole psalm given a title:

*Psalm 1: Two contrasting ways to live with two contrasting results*

v1-3: The godly person:
A statement of blessing (v1a)
Three things he[3] doesn't do (v1)
**But**… his delight and what he does (v2)
An image, a fruitful tree, to represent the godly person (v3)

v4-5: The "wicked":
A statement of contrast (v4a)
An image, chaff, to represent the wicked (v4b)
**Therefore**…wicked/ sinners will not stand in judgement

v6: Both righteous and wicked:
**For**… the LORD watches over the righteous
**But**… way of the wicked leads to destruction

## Task 2: Consider the Structure of each Individual Unit

Once the component parts have been identified, our next task is to work out how these building blocks fit together. In the next chapter we will look at the wider structure - that is the architecture of how individual units connect to form main sections, and how main sections come together to form the books of the Bible. First however, we need to consider the structure of each individual unit. Although there are variations, there are three common types of structure.

### 1. Linear

This type of structural design, the line, is often used in writing today. A story progresses from one situation to another along a line. It moves on, step by step, until it reaches an end. Similarly, a logical reasoned argument moves along a line with each step of thought connected to the one before.

---

3. I use "he" here (rather than "she" or "they") following the original Hebrew for "man" in v1, for a good reason. This is explained in the suggested thoughts for the exercises for chapter 8 (page 282).

Throughout the Bible these linear structures are also common. Whether it is the progression of an Old Testament story or that of an argument in one of the Prophets or New Testament letters; the progression is linear, from a beginning to an end.

### Purpose of Linear Structure

The purpose of linear structure is twofold. First it conveys the process of movement, and secondly it draws our attention to the end.

Consider Jesus' parable in Luke 15:8-10, a good example of linear structure:

[8]"Or suppose a woman has ten silver coins and loses one. Doesn't she light a lamp, sweep the house and search carefully until she finds it? [9]And when she finds it, she calls her friends and neighbours and says, 'Rejoice with me; I have found my lost coin.' [10]In the same way, I tell you, there is rejoicing in the presence of the angels of God over one sinner who repents."

Looking for changes in content, this passage can be divided as follows:

Suppose a woman loses a coin
> Doesn't she search until she finds it?
   > And when she finds it she rejoices
     > In the same way, there is rejoicing in heaven
      when one sinner repents

Here the linear structure moves both the story and the logical argument forward. It then draws our attention to the conclusion of both the story and the argument. Rejoicing is the right response.[4]

### 2. Comparison /Contrast

Comparison or contrast is another structural tool that is used by today's authors and is commonplace throughout the Bible.

---

4. This is the middle of three lost and found parables all with a linear structure, all concluding with rejoicing. This repetition adds to Jesus' point. There are many wonderful truths in Luke 15, but the structure highlights the importance of rejoicing over sinners that repent.

In Psalm 1 that we have just considered, there is contrast between the godly person of v1-3 and the wicked of v4-5. The psalm then concludes with a repeat of that contrast: "For the LORD watches over the way of the righteous, but the way of the wicked leads to destruction."

Contrasts may be between many things, such as sides of an argument, events or people. Think of Jesus comparing Mary's and Martha's attitudes (Luke 10:38-42) or Paul comparing Hagar and Sarah (Galatians 4:21-31) and many of Jesus' parables such as the two builders (Matthew 7:24-27) and the parable of the Pharisee and the tax collector (Luke 18:9-14). Examples in the Old Testament include the comparison between Naomi's two daughters-in-law Ruth and Orpah (Ruth 1:8-18) and later in the same book, Boaz and another kingsman-redeemer (Ruth 4:1-10).

## Purpose of Comparison / Contrast

Have you ever looked at a picture of an animal that has excellent camouflage? It merges with its background so well that it can hardly be seen. But put that animal against a contrasting background and it is easily spotted.

In just the same way, the Bible often teaches its truths using contrast. Our sight of the truth is limited, so rather than just teaching the positive, the negative is taught as well. Consider Isaiah 1:18b:

"Though your sins are like scarlet, they shall be as white as snow; though they are red as crimson, they shall be like wool."

If instead the verse simply said, "your sins shall be as white as snow;" the truth would have been conveyed. But the contrast with the bright red of scarlet, not to mention the repetition, brings home the point.

## 3. Mirror Structures

Unlike the first two types of structural design, the mirror structure[5] is rarely used today. It is, however, very common throughout the Bible.

---

5. The academic name for this structure is a "chiasm" or "chiasmus". This is the term commonly used in books, but I prefer "mirror structure" as it is easier to remember and describes the structure.

The mirror structure is best understood by looking at an instance when it is used. Consider Jesus' well know teaching in **Matthew 6:24**:

    A - No-one can serve two masters.

      B - Either you will hate the one

        C - and love the other

          or                                                    **- Mirror line**

        C'- you will be devoted to the one

      B'- and despise the other.

    A'- You cannot serve both God and Money.

The structure – the way in which the verse is put together – is as if there is a mirror line across its centre. A corresponds to A', B to B' etc. with a turning point in the centre, between C and C'.

For individual units the various lines A, B, C etc. will usually be subsections such as in the examples below:

**Mark 1:21-28:**

    A - Introduction (v21)

      B - Crowds amazed at Jesus' authoritative teaching (v22)

        C - Unclean spirit cries out (v23-24)

          D - Jesus' rebuke shows His authority (v25)    **- Mirror Line**

        C'- Unclean spirit cries out (v26)

      B'- Crowds amazed at Jesus' authoritative teaching (v27)

    A'- Conclusion (v28)

**Isaiah 52:13-53:12:**

    A - God's servant lifted up and exalted (52:13-15)

      B - God's servant despised, rejected and suffering (53:1-3)

        C - God's servant's suffering explained (53:4-6)  **- Mirror Line**

      B'- God's servant despised, rejected and suffering (53:7-9)

    A'- God's servant lifted up and exalted (53:10-12)

## The Purpose of Mirror Structure

The purpose of mirror structure depends on its length. When short, the purpose may simply be to add impact and aid memory. Consider a couple of lines from Jesus' teaching:

Mark 2:27:     "The Sabbath
                   was made for man,
                   not man for
                the Sabbath."

Matthew 23:12:  "For those who exalt themselves
                   will be humbled,
                   and
                   those who humble themselves
                will be exalted."

The mirror structure adds impact and aids memory.

But when the mirror structure is longer, with a greater number of parts either side of the mirror line, the mirror structure now has additional purpose. In particular, it draws attention to the central turning point or mirror line.

Consider Matthew 6:24, the example given on the previous page. If this verse were a linear structure the emphasis would fall on the last line: "You cannot serve both God and money" and the take-home point would be the need to serve God, not money. But the mirror structure changes that. Now the emphasis instead lies at the central turning point, the idea of what we "love" or are "devoted" to. As a result, the take-home point is what we love is of supreme importance, even more important than the act of service. It's not serve God leading to his love, but love God leading to his service. (Spot the mirror!)

## Introductory and Concluding Statements

In addition to these three common structures for individual units, it is always helpful to look for introductory and concluding statements. These provide important clues for understanding the units themselves.

In Luke 18:1 we are informed: "Then Jesus told his disciples a parable to show them that they should always pray and not give up."

This statement introduces the parable which follows (Luke 18:2-8), and it is helpful for understanding. If we come away after studying the parable motivated to pray and not give up, that is a very good sign we have understood it correctly. If we come away with any other application, we probably need to go back and think again!

Likewise, concluding statements should be noted. To put this into practice, here are some concluding statements for when thinking about "S for Structure":

---

**In studying the structure of a Bible passage:**

**First - Identity the component parts.**
We do this by asking:

1. Where does the content change?
2. Are there any connecting words to help divide the text?

Each unit is held together by one unifying idea (though they may have subsections).
For each subsection, try to write a summary statement or provide a title.

**Second - Consider the structure of individual units.**
There are three common types of structure for individual units:

1. Linear - to convey movement and bring emphasis to the end.
2. Contrast - to bring out the truth of what is being taught.
3. Mirror line - with emphasis at the mirror line.

Look out for helpful introductory and concluding statements.
For each unit, try to write a summary statement or provide a title.

---

"My printed-out Bible passage is now covered in colour!" exclaimed Rachel.

"Yes, I've got scribbles all over my text too," added Joe. "I'm also running out of space for the questions I've been writing down."

"They look great," replied Mrs Wise, "and no need to worry about space, as you have finished the observe stage. Well almost. Now, for the really important bit."

Mrs Wise went on to remind Rachel and Joe that all the different things they had looked at were simply ways authors used to get their readers' attention. "A memorable phrase, a repetition, a surprise all grab our attention," she continued, "as do quoted and added words, images and structure." She paused to fill up Joe's empty teacup.

"Now," she announced, "we need to ask the most important question."

Mrs Wise paused. Rachel leaned forward to make sure she could hear.

Joe broke the silence: "The recipe for these delicious cakes?" he suggested.

"Oh Joe!" exclaimed Rachel.

"He's not too far off you know," replied Mrs Wise. "So far we have looked at the different ingredients. Now we have to put them all together and ask: 'What is the emphasis in what the author is saying?'"

## E is for Emphasis

The final part of "Observe" needs careful thought. Up until now, as we "read, read and read again" the passage, the focus has been on observation, asking questions and looking for things in the text. Now we need to pause. What is the emphasis in what the author is saying?

It is important to realise that the author's emphasis in an individual unit is not the same as what connects the material in that unit. As we have seen, a unit may be held together in a variety of ways. It may be a section of application or logical argument, a scene in a story or a section of poetry with the same subject matter, or anything else that unites the text together.

In contrast, the emphasis of a unit is what the author wants to draw our attention to within the text.

Sometimes the author's emphasis and what holds together the unit are the same. In Psalm 1, which we looked at earlier, my suggested summary title was "Two contrasting ways to live with two contrasting results." The author's emphasis is identical, the sharp contrast which is highlighted throughout the psalm.

But consider Colossians 3:18-4:1 which we also looked at. Whereas the text is unified in that it is all application to specific groups within the church, the emphasis is very different. Here the emphasis is on serving the Lord. This is clear from the repetition. Wives are to do what is "fitting in the Lord," children what "pleases the Lord," slaves with "reverence for the Lord" and masters are to remember that they "have a Master in heaven". v23-24 summarise all this perfectly with yet more repetition: "Whatever you do, work at it with all your heart, as working for the Lord, not for human masters, since that you know you will receive an inheritance from the Lord as a reward. It is the Lord Christ you are serving."

## Be specific

In thinking through emphasis, it is important to be as specific as we can. What one particular thing is the author stressing? Each passage in the Bible is unique. That is not to say that two passages can't teach the same point, but no two passages teach the same point in exactly the same way. Earlier we read Jesus' parable of the woman who lost a silver coin (Luke 15:8-10). Rather than saying the emphasis in on "rejoicing," it is better to make it as specific to that passage as possible. "The importance of rejoicing over one sinner who repents" is much better as it brings out the unique emphasis of that passage.

Perhaps after consideration, rather than one particular thing, two or more possible points of emphasis will emerge from the text. That is fine. It may be that the author intends that. On the other hand, it may be that as we reflect further one emphasis becomes more pronounced. The important thing is to write down our ideas to take on to the next stage of Bible interpretation - "Understand".

## END OF CHAPTER EXERCISES

For each of these exercises, once you have read the text, aim to spend a few minutes thinking through your answers. Once you have drawn your conclusions, compare them with the suggested thoughts on page 261-265.

### Old Testament Exercise

**Read Judges 3:12-30**

**What is the structure of these verses?**
(HELP: Divide the text into scenes as the action changes (as if in a film) and look for connecting words. Write a short summary statement for each scene. When done, think through the whole structure.)

**What unifies these verses?** What title would you give them?

**What is the emphasis in the passage?**
(HELP: Consider what is memorable / repeated / surprising / the words / images and the structure.)

### New Testament Exercise

**Read Matthew 7:7-12**

**What is the structure in these verses?**
- Look for changes in content to help split up the passage.
- Look for connecting words to divide up the passage.
- What is odd about v12?

**What unifies these verses?** Write a summary statement or title for them.

**What is the emphasis in the passage?**
(HELP: Consider what is memorable / repeated / surprising / the words / images and the structure.)

# STAGE 2: UNDERSTAND

"The Bible is a supernatural book and can be
understood only by supernatural aid."
**A.W. Tozer**

# INTRODUCTION TO UNDERSTAND

---

*"Desire without knowledge is not good -*
*how much more will hasty feet miss the way."*
**Proverbs 19:2**

"Don't yield to Satan's lie that you don't have time to study the Scriptures. Choose to take time to study them. Feasting on the Word of God each day is more important than sleep, school, work, television shows, video games, or social media. You may need to reorganise your priorities to provide time for the study of the Word of God. If so, do it!"
**Richard G. Scott**

---

"Thank you so much for joining me on a short walk," explained Mrs Wise, "I find it so helpful for my old joints."

She stopped for breath. The view across the lake was spectacular, as was the sound of the birds in the reeds. "So beautiful isn't it?"

"Yes. It sure is!" replied Joe. "And thank you for helping us with our Bible reading."

"I've been so excited," added Rachel. That passage we looked at this morning. "I now see clearly, how it applies to me."

"Ah…beware of the crocodiles!" Mrs Wise announced with all seriousness.

"You what!?" exclaimed Joe. He really wasn't expecting that. The lake was beautiful, but had she really said 'crocodiles'? Was she feeling alright?

"We need to avoid the crocodiles," repeated Mrs Wise, "in the great sea."

Far from losing her mind, Mrs Wise went on to remind Rachel and Joe that they were on a journey. They were in Bible Land listening to the Bible as originally heard. Soon they would travel back to Today's World, but in between there was a great sea.

"Oh yes, I remember now," said Joe, "the sea between us today and the original readers, representing changes in time, culture, language and how God relates to us."

"Yes," said Mrs Wise, "and in that sea there are crocodiles! If we apply the text too early, without proper thought, it's like walking into the sea - trying to get home without a bridge." She paused as if remembering something. "There are all kinds of dangers if we conclude how it applies too early, particularly with the Old Testament. I've sadly seen too many Christians eaten by crocodiles."

Rachel looked horrified.

"So what comes next?" asked Joe.

### Next is "Understand"

Having observed the text carefully, we now have a good idea of what the author wants to say and their particular emphasis. But rather than jumping ahead to application, we need first to understand.

"Understand" comes in two parts. First: "What did the text mean then?" (to the original hearers). Then, once that has been grasped, second: "What does the text mean now?" (to us today). To answer that second question, we will need to build a bridge back to Today's World across the sea. More on that in chapter 8. For now note that the order is:

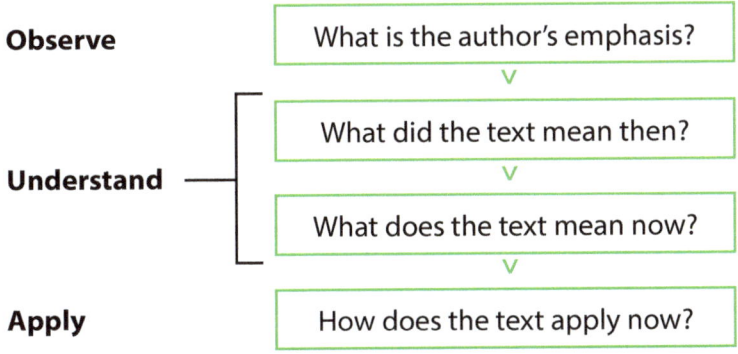

**Observe** — What is the author's emphasis?

**Understand** — What did the text mean then? / What does the text mean now?

**Apply** — How does the text apply now?

"So how do we understand?" asked Joe.

"Do you remember the key to 'Observe'?" asked Mrs Wise.

"Read, read and read again." Joe and Rachel replied together with perfect timing.

"Good memory," replied Mrs. Wise. "Now it is: 'Ask questions again and again'. And as you keep asking questions, remember what I do, what in fact we all should do."

"What's that?" inquired Rachel.

"Carefully study," replied Mrs Wise. "Remember, '"MRS WISE Carefully Studies.'"

"Oh I see," replied Joe.

"I think the 'C' in 'Carefully' and the 'S' in 'Studies' stand for something," added Rachel.

"You two are catching on!" replied Mrs Wise with a warm smile.

# UNDERSTAND PART 1

## WHAT DID THE TEXT MEAN THEN?

"The clarity of Scripture means that the Bible is written in such a way that its teachings are able to be understood by all who will read it seeking God's help and being willing to follow it."

**Wayne Grudem**

# CHAPTER 5

## CONTEXT (PART 1)
## IMMEDIATE AND BOOK CONTEXT

---

*"Reflect on what I am saying, for the Lord
will give you insight into all this."*
**2 Timothy 2:7**

"I can do all things through a verse taken out of context!"
**Anon**

---

Mrs Wise turned the key to unlock the front door to her house after their walk. "Sorry I am not so fast on my feet these days."

"Oh. Not a problem," replied Joe.

"I think," Mrs Wise continued pausing for breath, "I now need to take a seat." She put down her walking stick. "It's been a long time since I ran a marathon!"

Rachel tried hard to imagine Mrs Wise running a marathon.

"Though, I think I'd be up for some work on my jigsaw," she continued, "with a cup of tea of course. Would you two like to join me?"

Mrs Wise proceeded enthusiastically to show Rachel and Joe her latest jigsaw project. It was a beautiful landscape, about half completed.

"Oh I love jigsaws," declared Rachel picking up a piece of what looked like cloud in the sky. "Wonderful to see how each piece with its little picture fits alongside its neighbours."

"Yes, and then those moments when whole areas of the jigsaw suddenly come together," added Joe, "to gradually form the big picture."

"Each piece has its context, is what I think you are saying," replied Mrs Wise. "The key is placing each piece in its context."

### C (of "Carefully") is for Context

Context, put simply, is how something connects with what surrounds it.

In a jigsaw puzzle each individual piece fits in. It connects to the pieces around it, which in turn connect to other pieces to build up the overall picture.

The Bible is the same. Every sentence, individual unit and main section connects to those around it and working out this context is crucial for understanding. Where there is more than one possible understanding of a text, context is where to go. Context is king.

Consider two phrases: "I can't see a bear in that tree" and "I can't bear the sight of that man." In both phrases the word "bear" is used, but in the two sentences we know the word means two completely different things. This is because the context controls the meaning. Taking a Bible word, phrase or a whole passage away from its context is therefore a dangerous thing to do. As someone has said, "Take text out of context and you are left with a con" (a deception). Remove the context and the meaning of the text can change.

Think about Matthew 7:1 where Jesus says these words: "Do not judge, or you too will be judged."

This verse is commonly used to teach that we should never judge other people in any way. But does it mean that? Only if the verse is taken away from its context.

Putting the verse back into context, we read in Matthew 7:4-5:

"⁴How can you say to your brother, 'Let me take the speck out of your eye,' when all the time there is a plank in your own eye? ⁵You hypocrite, first take the plank out of your own eye, and then you will see clearly to remove the speck from your brother's eye."

Here we read that Jesus teaches that we *should* judge. After all, how can we take a plank out of our own eye or remove a speck from our brother's eye without judging it to be a plank or a speck? In v6 Jesus repeats the need to make judgements: "Do not give dogs what is sacred; do not throw your pearls to pigs." What's more in the verses which follow (Matthew 7:13-27) Jesus again and again instructs us to judge between two different things.

The context therefore corrects misunderstanding. In Matthew 7:1 Jesus is not teaching that we should never judge others - just that we should always judge ourselves and see our faults, before we judge others.

### The levels of context

In chapter 4, under "S for Structure," we saw how the Bible is divided into books and how each book can be divided into main sections and individual units, with each unit containing one basic idea. Having this structure in mind is helpful for considering the context, which can be thought of at three different levels:

Context:

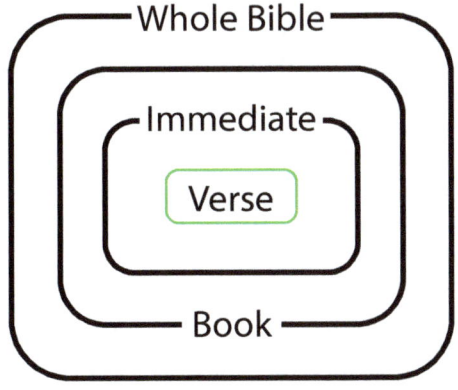

### A. Immediate Context

To consider the immediate context for any individual unit of Scripture we need to ask two basic questions:

- How does this unit connect to the passage which comes before it?
- How does this unit connect to the passage which comes after it?

Previously, we may have observed a change of content with the surrounding passages, now we must understand how the unit being studied fits in.

Sometimes the answer to this question will be very straightforward. The connection is a change of scene in a story for example. Sometimes, however, it needs more thought.

Remember the key to "Understand" is "Ask questions, again and again". To connect an individual unit to what comes before and after, here are some helpful questions to ask:

- Are there any identical words, phrases or ideas that connect the passages?
- Are there any contrasts which connect the passages?
- Why does this individual unit come here and not elsewhere?
- What would happen if this passage were removed from the Bible text?
- What possible misunderstandings might come by what is being taught? Are these corrected by neighbouring units?

Let's return to Matthew 7:7-12, which we looked at as an exercise in chapter 4:

[7] "Ask and it shall be given to you; seek and you shall find; knock and the door will be opened to you. [8] For everyone who asks receives; the one who seeks finds; and to the one who knocks, the door will be opened.

[9] Which of you, if your son asks for bread, will give him a stone? [10] Or if he asks for a fish, will give him a snake? [11] If you then, though you are evil, know how to give good gifts to your children, how much more will your Father in heaven give good gifts to those who ask him! [12] So in everything, do to others what you would have them do to you, for this sums up the Law and the Prophets."

Looking at these verses, we saw that they formed an individual unit of Jesus' teaching on prayer. We noted an emphasis on the confidence we can have in prayer and that Jesus gave a promise in v11.

"And it's a wonderful promise from the very lips of Jesus Christ himself! If we ask, we will receive good gifts! You may be poor, but your heavenly Father is rich, and he loves to give. If only we would ask more. The reason so many Christians don't enjoy more wealth and more possessions, is that they don't ask. Ask and it will be given to you! Seek and you will find! So many riches are waiting for you Christian - good gifts your heavenly Father longs to give you!"

Perhaps you have heard something like this before. What do you think? Is that conclusion correct? How can we tell? The answer comes from the context.

The key question is: What are the "good gifts" that Jesus promises? Perhaps it is material wealth, but equally, perhaps it is not. The context will tell us. Context is king.

The passage just before this encouragement to pray is the text we looked at earlier in the chapter - Jesus' teaching on not judging others before we have judged ourselves. So how does this passage on prayer for good gifts follow on? The answer is not immediately clear.

What about the passage which follows? This is about two gates, a narrow gate which leads to life and a broad gate which leads to destruction. How is this passage connected? Again, the answer is not immediately obvious.

Rather than give up, we need to persevere. The human Bible writers, let alone the divine author behind them, didn't put these teachings together at random. There is order. We just have to find it!

B. Book Context

When struggling to work out how a particular unit of Scripture fits in with its surroundings, the answer often comes by considering the wider book context. Understanding the book as a whole, will often unlock its individual parts.

So how do we understand a Bible book as a whole?

To start, we need to read the entire Bible book, or at the very least, the chapters surrounding the passage being studied.

This may take time, particularly if it is a long Bible book, but it is important. If we were to receive a personal handwritten letter from a good friend, would we read just a few lines from the middle of the letter and then put it down? Would we conclude that those few lines didn't make sense? Surely not. We would read the whole letter and then the meaning of those lines, set in context, is likely to become clear.

> **ADDITIONAL TIP**
>
> Study Bibles and good commentaries can be very helpful for understanding Book Context. Another excellent source of help is produced by the Bible Project (https://bibleproject.com/) whose series of videos provide very helpful outlines for each book of the Bible.
>
> Before reaching for these though, I recommend reading the whole Bible book concerned at least once, seeking to answer the questions below. Once we are familiar with the book, then we will be better equipped to understand, and read the commentaries / watch the videos with discernment.

As we read through a whole Bible book, just as when we read through a short passage, there is one crucial question to answer: What is the author's purpose in writing? Once understood, that will always shed light on each individual passage within the book.

Three questions are helpful for working out the author's purpose in writing their book. As we read, it's a good idea to keep asking these questions again and again and note our answers:

## 1. Are there any key verses in the book?

A "key verse" is a verse which tells us something about the author's purpose or priority in writing. John 20:30-31 is a good example:

"Jesus performed many other signs in the presence of his disciples, which are not recorded in this book. But these are written that you may believe that Jesus is the Messiah, the Son of God, and that by believing you may have life in his name."

This verse is "key" for understanding the book of John. Near the end of his gospel, it tells us why he has written his book, for he says, "these things are written so that..." (and then he gives his purpose) "...you may believe that Jesus is the Messiah, the Son of God, and that by believing you may have life in his name."

In studying any passage of John's gospel, it is therefore helpful to ask how the passage fits in with this overall purpose in writing. Does the passage provide evidence? Does it teach us about believing, or teach us about Jesus as Messiah or Son of God? Does it instead instruct us about "life in his name"? Why not read through John's gospel slowly looking for answers to these questions. The answers are there; indeed, every part of John's gospel is addressing these things, for John tells us that is why he wrote.

There are many varieties of key verse, but all types tell us something of the author's purpose or priorities. They may:

- **Give clear purpose for the book.**
  (E.g. John 20:30-31 (as above); Exodus 29:46; Luke 1:1-4; 1 John 5:13)

- **Sum up the application of the book.**
  (E.g. Deuteronomy 10:12-13; Malachi 3:7; 1 Corinthians 15:58)

- **Summarise what God is doing.**
  (E.g. Genesis 12:1-3; Exodus 3:7,10; 2 Kings 17:7-20; Jeremiah 31:31-33; Acts 1:8; Revelation 1:1)

- **Summarise teaching about God's character.**
  (E.g. Exodus 29:46; Daniel 2:20-22; Micah 7:18)

- **Be picked up as key by the New Testament or later in the Old Testament.**
  (E.g. Habakkuk 2:4 with Romans 1:17 and Galatians 3:11; Joel 3:28-32 with Acts 2:17-21; Exodus 34:6-7 with Nehemiah 9:17,31; Psalms 86:15 and 103:8 with Jonah 4:2 and Joel 2:13)

## 2. What are the repeated themes of the book?

Just as authors may use repetition in a short passage to draw our attention to what is being said, they use repeated themes throughout whole Bible books to do the same. Such a theme may be connected to a key verse and then repeated. For instance, Proverbs 1:7 introduces the "fear of the LORD" as a key theme. This is then repeated (in 1:29, 2:5, 8:13, 9:10, 10:27, 14:27, 15:16,33, 16:6, 19:23, 22:4, 23:17, 24:21 and 29:25) to draw our attention throughout the book. Whether an author uses an introductory key verse or not, noticing repetition of a theme is important for understanding a book. Reading through the book of Daniel the sovereignty of God is reiterated time and time again. Reading Colossians should leave us totally thrilled by Jesus as he is repeatedly exalted. The author's purpose is made through repetition.

## 3. What is the wider structure of the book?

In chapter 4 we began to look at structure by examining how individual units are put together. Now as the "book context" is considered, we need to look at how those individual units come together to form main sections and how main sections fit together to form the books of the Bible.

## Types of Architecture

Like a city skyline with multiple different types of architecture, the Bible contains a wonderful array of structural designs, ways in which component parts are put together.

When considering individual units in chapter 4, we looked at the three most common types - linear, comparison and mirror structures.

These designs are also commonly used for main sections of books and for whole Bible books.

## Linear

The whole book of Ruth is a good example of linear structure.

The story starts with death (that of Naomi's husband and sons), yet by the end arrives at life with the birth of Obed and his descendants. It starts with despair and ends in hope, from being barren to fruitfulness.

This overall linear structure then draws our attention to the conclusion, the birth of Obed with its associated joy. Obed, we are told, is the grandfather of the great King David (Ruth 4:22). Having taken us forward with its linear structure, the book concludes by pointing us even further forward, with yet more joy, to the birth of David.

## Comparison

Again, comparison is often used by the Bible authors to construct Bible books or sections of larger Bible books.

The book of Jonah presents a comparison between the first two and last two chapters:

| Chapters 1 and 2: | Chapters 3 and 4: |
|---|---|
| Jonah's outward rebellion | Jonah's inward rebellion |
| 1:1: God's Word comes to Jonah | 3:1: God's Word comes to Jonah |
| 1:2: God's message: Preach to Nineveh | 3:2: God's message: Preach to Nineveh |
| 1:3: Jonah's response (runs away) | 3:3: Jonah's response (goes) |
| 1:4: A warning - the storm | 3:4: A warning - the message |
| 1:5-15: Humble response of unbelievers - faith in God | 3:5: Humble response of unbelievers - faith in God |
| 1:16: God's mercy | 3:10: God's mercy |
| 2:1-10: God teaches grace to Jonah using a fish | 4:1-11: God teaches grace to Jonah using a plant |

Other examples of comparison are the contrast between Judah and Joseph (Genesis 38 and 39), the two battles with the Philistines (1 Samuel 4:1a-11 and 1 Samuel 7:2a-17) and the contrast between Nicodemus the Pharisee and the woman by the well (John 3 and 4).

## Mirror Structure

Mirror structures are also frequently used to hold together sections of Bible books. Instead of phrases for these larger mirror structures, it is the individual units which mirror each other:

**Mark 1:14-2:17:**

**A** - 1:14-1:20 - Jesus by the Sea of Galilee preaching and calling people with instant obedience.

    **B** - 1:21-1:28 - Jesus in Capernaum teaching, healing with a word. Amazement in the crowd.

        **C** - 1:29-1:34 - Jesus heals by reaching out with a touch with mobbing of the crowd.

            **D** - 1:35-39 - Jesus' priority is to preach   **- Mirror line**

        **C'** - 1:40-1:45 - Jesus heals by reaching out with a touch with mobbing of the crowd.

    **B'** - 2:1-2:12 - Jesus in Capernaum preaching, healing with a word. Amazement in the crowd.

**A'** - 2:13-17 - Jesus by the Sea of Galilee teaching and calling Levi with instant obedience.

Here the various stories (individual units) each form a line in the construction and are linked together based on what Jesus does, where he is at the time and the response of others. The mirror line then contains a separate idea. As we have seen, the purpose of this structure is to bring emphasis to what is at the mirror line, in this case Jesus' priority to preach.

At first sight, because of the repetition, the emphasis in Mark 1:14-2:12 might appear to be Jesus' healing miracles. It would be easy to conclude that healing was the main reason for his coming. But the central verses on the mirror line (1:35-39) correct that idea. Here Jesus clearly rejects further opportunities to heal and declares, "Let us go somewhere else - to the nearby villages - so that I can preach there also. That is why I have come." (1:38).

Jesus' priority is to preach[1], and our author has gone to great lengths to arrange his structure so that we understand this. Take a moment to reflect on that. Is that your priority?

---

1. In Mark 1:39 repetition adds weight to preaching as Jesus' priority.  A surprise however is that we are also told that his activity continued to be "driving out demons". Preaching is therefore linked to driving out demons. The advance of the kingdom of God and the defeat of the demonic come primarily as the gospel is preached!

Sometimes mirror line patterns are built around who is speaking, what is taught or what is done. This is the case in the account of what happened in the Garden of Eden recalled in **Genesis 2:5-3:24**:

**A** - 2:5-17 Narrative - God the sole actor; man present but passive
    **B** - 2:18-25 Narrative - God main actor, man minor role,
        woman and animals passive
        **C** - 3:1-5 Dialogue - Snake and woman
            **D** - 3:6-8 Narrative - Man and woman      **- Mirror Line**
        **C'** - 3:9-13 Dialogue - God, man, and woman
    **B'** - 3:14-21 Narrative - God main actor, man minor role,
        woman and snake passive
**A'** - 3:22-24 Narrative - God sole actor, man passive[2]

Here again, each line in the structure is an individual unit of Scripture, in this case a scene in the story, based on who is in the scene, whether it is action or speech and who is the main actor. Again, the central point at the mirror line is what is most important, the eating of the forbidden fruit.

Finally, mirror line structure can be used for the arrangement of main sections of a book or even for an entire Book. Here are Daniel chapters 2-7 and the book of Leviticus laid out showing their mirror lines:

**Daniel Chapters 2-7:**

**A** - Four Kingdoms then the Kingdom of God (Dan 2)
    **B** - Persecution of God's people (Dan 3)
        **C** - King humbled, God glorified (Dan 4)
                     **- Mirror line**
        **C'** - King humbled, God glorified (Dan 5)
    **B'** - Persecution of God's people (Dan 6)
**A'** - Four Kingdoms then the Kingdom of God (Dan 7)

---

2. See Gordon Wenham, Genesis, Word Biblical Commentary Vol. 1, pp. 50

**Leviticus:**

**A** - Ritual (Lev 1-7)

    **B** - Priesthood (Lev 8-10)

        **C** - Purity (Lev 11-15)

            **D** - Day of Atonement (Lev 16)        - **Mirror line**

        **C'** - Purity (Lev 17-20)

    **B'**- Priesthood (Lev 21-22)

**A'**- Ritual (Lev 23-27)

---

**DANGER TO AVOID (and a word of encouragement)**

Finding mirror structures is not easy and requires a great deal of careful observation. Commentaries will sometimes point them out, but a good clue comes when you notice repetition which, at first sight, doesn't appear to be needed. Always ask: Could this be part of a mirror structure?

When finding a possible mirror structure, it's important to put it to the test. Just like a nervous walker all alone on a dark night, it's easy to see things that aren't actually there!

Two questions should be asked. First, do the two sides of the mirror really match or not? Don't see something that isn't there! The second test is to ask whether the teaching on the mirror line is consistent with the emphasis being drawn by other factors in the passage. The Holy Spirit, as we have seen, has no shortage of methods for drawing emphasis in a passage. When all these come together to suggest a main point, then we can have confidence we are on the right path.

But the importance of finding mirror structures can be overemphasised and there can be an overemphasis on finding mirror structures as important. Take the mirror structure in my last sentence. Does it really matter if you missed it? The understanding was conveyed in the words, as is nearly always the case for what the mirror structures teach in the Bible.

> A careful reading of Mark 1:14-2:12 would not conclude that Jesus' priority was to heal, because his priority to preach is clear from his words in 1:35-39. We shouldn't worry too much about missing a mirror structure; but if one is spotted, it can give additional confidence in knowing the emphasis of a passage.

In addition to the three common types of structure mentioned already, the Bible also contains some other less common arrangements in Book Context. These include:

## Spiral Structure

Imagine a great, spiral staircase. It climbs up several floors of a magnificent palace with large paintings on the walls and fine pieces of artwork positioned for you to admire as you climb.

This is the spiral structure. As we progress, rather than a linear, logical view of something, we start at the base on which the staircase is built and then climb to see the same beautiful objects again and again, but from different angles. The truths are restated and re-applied, and the view gets more and more wonderful until we reach the top.

The purpose of such a structure is to convey the same message again and again from different angles, leading to a climax. The letter of 1 John and the book of Revelation contain examples where this structure is used.

## Repeated Sequence

The repeated sequence is a development of the comparison structure. Here a basic pattern is given and then repeated one or more times. The repeated plagues in Exodus 7:10-12:30 are a good example, as is the repeated pattern in the book of Judges first laid out in Judges 2:11-19 which is repeated seven times in the book. In the New Testament the repetition of a series of events in Mark 6:30-8:26 (feed a crowd, cross the sea, argue with the Pharisees, discuss bread, heal someone's senses) is a further example.

This repetition on a grand scale allows comparison to be made between the various repeating cycles.

In the repeated sequence of the book of Judges, the pattern always ends with the death of the judge - that is, except for Deborah. This time, instead of the judge's death, we are told of the defeat and then the gradual further weakening of Jabin the arch-enemy until he is destroyed (Judges 4:23-24), followed by a great victory song (Judges 5). This break from the normal sequence is deliberate on the part of the author and we are meant to notice it. The judge (ruler) we need will not die, but rather defeat our arch-enemy and subdue him until he is finally defeated. Then, we too can sing a great victory song.

## Acrostic

The acrostic, like the mirror line, is rarely used today. In this structure, each line (or group of lines) begins with the next letter of the (Hebrew) alphabet. This gives what is written a certain beauty in the original language and made it easier for the original readers to remember - so important in the days before printing.

Unfortunately, with translation the acrostic nature is lost in English versions, but footnotes in many modern Bibles will highlight an acrostic structure. Acrostics are most commonly found in the psalms, with Psalms 9-10 (together they are an acrostic) 25, 34, 37, 111 ,112, 119 and 145 being examples.

The purpose of an acrostic, beyond aiding memory and beauty, is not clear, but almost certainly it has something to do with showing a sense of completeness and perfection. So Psalm 119 shows us the completeness of the Word of God for life, and Psalm 145 the perfection of God's character.

## Combinations

Sometimes, rather than having just one of these structure types, the Bible authors combine them. A common combination is a linear structure with a mirror line within it. This draws emphasis to a central point as well as allowing progression to a conclusion.

One of the most extraordinary structures in the Bible is that of the book of Lamentations. It contains five distinct poems, corresponding to the five chapters we have in our Bibles. Chapters 1, 2 and 4 are acrostics each with 22 verses, one for each letter of the Hebrew alphabet. Chapter 3 is also acrostic, but in this chapter each letter has three verses. As such our attention is drawn to it. Chapter 5 is surprising in that, although it also has 22 lines, it is not written in the acrostic pattern as we might expect. This again draws our attention to its content.

In addition to this framework is a mirror structure - again highlighting the centre:

**Chap 1:** Mourning after Jerusalem's destruction
because of the sins of the people
  **Chap 2:** The anger of God
    **Chap 3:** Author's response + God's compassion - **Mirror Line**
  **Chap 4:** The anger of God
**Chap 5:** Mourning and repentance for their sins,
pleading for forgiveness

The book as a whole is about sin and God's righteous anger against sin. But our skilful author won't let us drown in our sin and in our fear of the consequences. Through these carefully laid down structures, our attention is drawn away from our sin and God's anger to the need for our repentance and God's wonderful compassion. Right at the very centre of the middle chapter on God's compassion we read these wonderful lines:

"For the Lord will not cast off forever, but, though he cause grief, he will have compassion according to the abundance of his steadfast love; for he does not afflict from his heart[3] or grieve the children of men." (Lamentations 3:31-33- ESV).

What amazing words, so beautifully placed, to encourage us to repent when we have sinned!

---

3. The ESV is closer to the Hebrew here than the NIV's "he does not willingly bring affliction". That implies something outside of God is making him do something he is not willing to do. The truth, however, is that causing affliction and grief has its place in the expression of God's justice against sin, but more central to God's nature, from his heart is "the abundance of his steadfast love" (3:32).

## ADDITIONAL TIPS

Three other things to look for as we consider structure are:

### Introductory comments

These introduce a new unit or a new main section in a book. Paul begins 1 Corinthians 7 with the line: "Now for the matters you wrote about:" This clearly starts something different, so commencing a new section in his letter where Paul will reply to specific issues raised by a letter they wrote to him. Indeed, Paul then repeats the phrase "Now about…" in 7:25, 8:1, 12:1, 16:1 as further introductory markers.

### End markers

End markers are conclusive statements that signal the completion of a unit or main section. In Job 31:40 we read: "The words of Job are ended" and in Psalm 72:20: "This concludes the prayers of David son of Jesse." These statements help divide up their respective books.

### Bookends

Another method used to divide up Bible books is to put the same phrase at the beginning and end of the unit or main section, just like a pair of bookends[4].

Identifying the bookend phrase is helpful, not just for structure, but because the phrase itself gives important clues to the teaching of what lies in between.

As an example, consider the story of Joseph and Potiphar's wife in Genesis 39. In v2 we are told, "The LORD was with Joseph so that he prospered" and in v23 "…the Lord was with Joseph and gave him success in whatever he did."

These phrases are bookends. They not only tell us that this is a separate unit of the text of Genesis, but they also point to a major teaching point from the episode, namely that the LORD was with Joseph and gave him success.

---

4. The technical term which you may read in commentaries for this bookend technique is an "inclusio".

> The key thing is careful observation. The Bible authors don't repeat without a reason. A careful reading of Matthew's gospel will note a repeated verse in chapter 4:23 and 9:35:
>
> 4:23: "Jesus went throughout Galilee, teaching in their synagogues, proclaiming the good news of the kingdom, and healing every disease and illness among the people."
>
> 9:35: "Jesus went through all the towns and villages, teaching in their synagogues, proclaiming the good news of the kingdom, and healing every disease and illness."
>
> Matthew's repetition is deliberate, for he didn't need to say the same thing twice. In using these bookends, he is identifying a main section in his gospel (Matthew 4:23-9:35). Furthermore, he is summarising and repeating its main content. Contained within the bookends is some teaching of Jesus on the good news of the kingdom and some accompanying healings to demonstrate the power of the kingdom.

**Our unanswered question**

Let's now return to the question raised earlier as to what Jesus meant by "good gifts" promised in his teaching on prayer in Matthew 7:7-12. Rather than jumping to conclusions, Book Context contains the answer.

In the exercise in chapter 4, we noted that Matthew 7:12 is a strange verse in that it doesn't seem to connect to what has immediately come before:

"So in everything, do to others what you would have them do to you, for this sums up the Law and the Prophets."

This is not about prayer but introduces an entirely new subject - that of summing up the Law and the Prophets.

So why is it there?

Reading through Matthew up to this point reveals that "the Law and the Prophets" have been mentioned before in the gospel: "Do not think I have come to abolish the Law or the Prophets; I have not come to abolish them but to fulfil them." (5:17). Putting these two verses together, we have an "introductory comment" - Jesus has come to fulfil the Law and the Prophets - and a "concluding statement" - this sums up the Law and the Prophets. They are in fact bookends with the same basic content. They mark the beginning and end of a whole section in Matthew's gospel, with Jesus' teaching on prayer (Matthew 7:7-11) coming at its close. So how does Jesus' teaching on prayer conclude this section of Matthew's gospel?

Reading through the section (Matthew 5:18-7:11), no-one can miss the incredibly high standards of the teaching. Jesus starts by affirming the ongoing importance of the Old Testament (5:18). The law is to be taught and practised (5:19), for "unless your righteousness surpasses that of the Pharisees and teachers of the law, you will certainly not enter the kingdom of heaven." (5:20).

Jesus then spells out what he means. To enter the kingdom of heaven, the righteousness required is not like that of the Pharisees, an outward obedience to the Bible's commands that an observer can see, but a greater, inner righteousness that God can see. This righteousness involves transformed emotions and desires (5:22,28), truthfulness in our words (5:31,37), kindness (5:42) and love for enemies (5:44). This righteousness involves looking only to God for our rewards as we give, pray and fast (6:1-18), and having hearts characterised by love for God (6:19-24), trust in God (6:25-34) and humility (7:1-6).

By the end of the section, Jesus' teaching leaves us exposed, guilty and fearful. If this is what it is to be right before God, how can we ever enter the kingdom of heaven? Our only hope is that God will forgive us for our failings and then give us transformed hearts and the ability to obey. But is God willing? Will he give us these good gifts? Jesus' answer is this teaching on prayer.

We cannot in ourselves keep to these high standards, but we can pray and ask our heavenly Father for them. The "good gifts" of 7:11 are the righteousness, sincerity, purity and love expected of Jesus' followers. By considering the "good gifts" of 7:11 in their context, we come to a very different understanding from the preacher who promises material wealth[5] - and far better "good gifts" they are too.

C. Whole Bible Context[6]

To complete a jigsaw, each individual piece has to fit into its overall picture. Only this allows for a full understanding of the individual piece. Similarly, along with connecting a Bible passage to its immediate surroundings and into its book, we need to appreciate where it fits into the overall picture or storyline of the Bible.

In our example, the words of Jesus "this sums up the Law and the Prophets" helpfully point us to the much wider context. The "good gifts" are what the Law and the Prophets have long demanded. Now, with the coming of Jesus, they are promised for those who ask in prayer.

**The Bible's Overall Storyline**

At the very simplest level, the Bible moves from creation to new creation. An introduction (Genesis 1-11) sets the stage and launches the main themes of what follows. First, the story of Israel with its climax in Jesus and then the story of the church, before the Bible's glorious conclusion and that of all history, in the new creation.

**Creation** ⟶ **New Creation**

Genesis 1    Genesis 12                                    Revelation 21-22

| Introduction | Story of Israel | Jesus | Story of the church |

---

5. Jesus' teaching is not a promise that we will always receive the exact good gifts for which we ask now. Ultimately, a "good gift" is what we need, and our supreme need now before we die is to stay completely dependent on Jesus for our salvation. Better this side of heaven to stay humble, acknowledging our need as we fight against ongoing sin, than become proud and independent because we have received so much "righteousness" in answer to prayer. By using the analogy of a father's gifts to a son, Jesus reminds us that it is the goodness of the Father that leads to his good gifts, not the works of the son (including the work of prayer). We are by nature "evil" (7:11). That's a surprising word to use unless it is something we must never forget.
6. In academic books "Whole Bible Context" is sometimes referred to as "Canonical Context" as the "canon" describes all the books of the Bible.

Although Appendix 2 presents an outline to show where the content of the Old Testament books fit in, it is beyond the scope of this book to provide a more detailed overview of the entire storyline of the Bible. Consequently, if you are not familiar with the overall plot of the Bible, understanding how it all fits together as one unified book, I offer some recommendations in the footnote below.[7]

In the next chapter we will see that fitting the passage into the Bible's storyline is simply the start of understanding the "Whole Bible Context". It is however a crucial start, for as we will see, where a passage falls in this overall storyline greatly affects how we are to understand it and make its application to us today.

## END OF CHAPTER EXERCISES

Before reading the next chapter, it will be important to be familiar with Genesis 12:10-20. As a minimum, look at this passage and its associated questions before moving on to chapter 6. Once you have read the text, enjoy spending time thinking through each of the exercises. Suggested thoughts by way of answers are on page 265-271.

### Old Testament Exercise

**Read Genesis 12:10-20**

**Work through the observation questions of MRS WISE.** (What is memorable, repeated or surprising? Consider the words. Are there any images? What is the structure? Where is the emphasis in the passage?)

**Consider the immediate context**:

**Read Genesis 12:1-9.** What does God promise in these verses? How does this connect to what follows in 12:10-20?

**Read 13:1-4.** Compare this with 12:8-9. What do you notice? Where are Abram and Sarai by 13:5?

**Read 13:5-18.** What does this passage have in common with 12:1-7? How does 12:10-20 fill the gap between the two passages?

7. I recommend reading either "God's Big Picture" by Vaughan Roberts (IVP 2004) or "Remaking a Broken World" by Christopher Ash (The Good Book Company 2010). Alternatively, if you prefer a more interactive learning style, "The Bible Course" by Andrew Ollerton (Bible Society) is extremely helpful with its series of videos and questions for discussion.

**Read Matthew 6:22-23**

On their own these verses are difficult to understand and could mean many things. But they are not alone.

**Consider the Immediate Context:**
**Read Matthew 6:19-24**

What do v19-21 and v24 have in common?
(HELP: v24 was mentioned in chapter 4, pages 80 and 81)

The image in v22-23 connects to this immediate context. What therefore do "eyes" represent? (Check your answer with the wider context of 5:28-29.)

Two important questions remain though: What do "light" and "darkness" represent? And what does v23b mean: "If then the light within you is darkness, how great is that darkness!"?

**Consider the wider Book Context:**
**Read Matthew 5:17 and Matthew 7:12.**

What is the significance of these verses? (HELP: See page 112-113)

**Read Matthew 6:1-18 (especially v1-2, v5 and v16).** How do the warnings in these verses fit with the warning of Matthew 6:19?

**Read Matthew 6:25-34.** How does this passage follow on?
(HELP: Note the connecting word in v25, but especially note v32-33. How does this help us to understand "light" and "darkness" and "If then the light within you is darkness, how great is that darkness!"?
Is your body full of light?)

# CONTEXT (PART 2)
# WHOLE BIBLE CONTEXT

---

*"Do your best to present yourself to God as one approved,*
*a worker who does not need to be ashamed and*
*who correctly handles the word of truth."*
**2 Timothy 2:15**

"Any part of the human body can only be properly explained in reference to the whole body. And any part of the Bible can only be properly explained in reference to the whole Bible."
**F.F. Bruce**

---

Mrs Wise reappeared. She had been gone for some time, but now walked back into the living room holding something under her arm.

"The jigsaw is all but completed," announced Rachel inserting what was almost the last piece into the sky. "Look Joe's finished the trees."

"Oh. What a lovely picture!" replied Mrs Wise, clearly delighted.

"We left you the last pieces," added Joe.

Mrs Wise added the last few pieces and the three of them spent a few moments admiring the picture, pointing out some of the details they had all noticed.

"Just like the Bible," continued Mrs Wise. "So much to notice in each small piece, and then you work out how it all fits together."

Rachel and Joe listened on attentively.

"A jigsaw is the first way to think about whole Bible context," continued Mrs Wise, "but there is another way, and for that I have something to show you!"

Mrs Wise then revealed what she was holding.

It was another beautiful picture, but rather than being made up of pieces, it was formed by what seemed to be hundreds of small, coloured threads which had been carefully woven through some fabric.

"It's called cross-stitch," she announced. "Have either of you come across it before?"

Rachel and Joe looked equally blank.

"As you can see," continued Mrs Wise, "the picture is put together by weaving coloured threads in and out of the fabric. The same thread appears in one place on the picture then disappears round the back of the fabric and reappears elsewhere on the picture to continue that colour.

Mrs Wise turned over the picture to reveal a jumbled mess of coloured threads.

"It takes time," continued Mrs Wise. "But do you see how it works? Each colour enters the picture at one place, then having gone in and out a few times there, jumps to another place to put in another appearance and then comes up somewhere else. Eventually, with all the threads in place, you have one glorious picture."

"That looks like a lot of work," commented Joe.

"Yes, it is. But you know the good thing - it helps you appreciate each and every thread of colour."

"And the Bible is like that?" asked Joe.

"Yes. Exactly like that," replied Mrs Wise.

## Whole Bible Context – The Second Task

As described at the end of the last chapter, our first task in considering whole Bible context is to position our passage in the Bible's overall storyline, just as a piece is located in a jigsaw.

Our second task is to think through which threads of colour our particular Bible passage picks up. Like a cross-stitch picture, the Bible contains a great number of different coloured threads. These threads connect together different parts of the Bible that are not directly alongside each other, but they work together to create the overall picture. As we saw in chapter 1, the overall picture is that of the Lord Jesus Christ. Each thread therefore reveals something of him.[1]

The threads can be of four main types:

1. Words (Including quotes, phrases and images)
2. Promises (and their fulfilment)
3. Patterns
4. Themes

Each of these types of thread can be seen in a wide range of colours - each separate colour representing a different individual word, promise, pattern or theme.

Importantly though, all four types of Bible thread, each with its many different colours, share one thing in common. They all run in the same direction.

---

1. In academic books "Whole Bible Context" is sometimes referred to as "Christological Context" for it describes how the text being studied fits into the context of the gradual, progressive revelation of Jesus Christ.

### Progressive Revelation

God's teaching in the Bible is not given all at once, but gradually, progressively over many centuries of history. As such, each thread of the Bible (whether it is a word, promise, pattern or theme) is revealed slowly, a bit at a time, with our understanding of each thread deepening as we read from Genesis to Revelation.

To "Understand" as we have seen, starts in Bible Land. It starts with asking the important question: "What did this text mean *then* to the original hearers?" In considering the threads of the Bible, the question becomes: "What did this *thread* mean *then* to the original hearers?"

The rest of this chapter is devoted to explaining this more clearly. It's a long chapter so please take your time as we examine each one of the four different types of thread in turn.

## 1. Words (Including quotes, phrases and images)

The most basic thread of all is that of words. Each Bible word is introduced at some point in the Bible and then, like a coloured thread in a cross-stitch pattern, disappears for a while before re-entering the Bible text later on. Some words will only appear a few times, others hundreds of times, but with each new appearance of a word our understanding of that word becomes richer.

The same is true for phrases in the Bible's text. Consider Jesus' common description of himself as "the Son of Man".

If today (with no knowledge of the Old Testament) we read "the Son of Man" as Jesus' description of himself, we are likely to be confused or perhaps even offended; was he not also the son of woman?

The people of Jesus' day, however, would have immediately recognised the "Son of Man" Bible thread.

Up until the prophet Daniel, the phrase "son of man" was used to emphasise mere humanity in contrast to God (e.g. Job 25:6; Psalm 8:4; Ezekiel 2:3). In Daniel 7:13-14, however, this phrase is assigned to a great figure who "was given authority, glory and sovereign power; all nations and peoples of every language worshipped him... and his kingdom is one that will never be destroyed." Here is a figure with sovereign power to be worshipped. By tracing this Bible thread, we can appreciate that Jesus' description of himself perfectly describes his humanity, but also indicates that he is God.

In the same way, images in the Bible can form threads when they are repeated. So when Jesus teaches about a mustard seed growing with "such big branches that the birds can perch in its shade" (Mark 4:32) he is picking up an image used in Ezekiel 17:23 and 31:6. Jesus didn't need to add that image, but does so to make a point. In Ezekiel the emphasis is on restoration of Israel and God's blessing to the nations. It is no co-incidence that immediately after this teaching in Mark, Jesus travels to the other said of the lake (Mark 4:35), the Gentile side, where he brings blessing to the nations. The use of an image in one part of the Bible provides important clues for how it is probably being used elsewhere.

---

**ADDITIONAL TIP**

Tracing the threads of images is, on the whole, more difficult than tracing the threads for individual words. However, a useful resource to help us understand Biblical images is available in the "Dictionary of Biblical Imagery" (Inter-Varsity Press). As the name suggests, this excellent book lists and explores the various images that the Bible uses, providing helpful cross references and explanation for approximately 850 of the Bible's images.

---

Finally, quoted words are another variation of the "words-thread". Here one or more whole verses of Scripture reappear at a later stage in the progressive revelation, so connecting two or more otherwise very separate passages in the Bible.[2]

---

2. When comparing quoted verses with their original source, it is not uncommon to find differences in the words used. Rather than misquoting the Bible, these differences are virtually always down to the fact that the Greek translation of the Hebrew Old Testament (called the "Septuagint") was commonly read and so quoted in the 1st century. Non-Jewish writers such as Luke would have known Greek better than Hebrew, so the Septuagint would have been his Bible. Some of the Bible writers themselves depended on a translation, just as we do today.

**How to investigate a "words-thread"**

To study a particular word, phrase, image or quote in its whole Bible context, three things are vital to remember: Translation, Timing and Context.

## TRANSLATION – Use at least two good modern translations.

A great starting place for investigating a words-thread is to have access to at least two good modern Bible translations.[3]

Comparing the text being studied in different versions draws our attention to the exact words that are used and so identifies where the translators differ.

With just one Bible translation, it is easy to assume that, because two or more English words in our translation are the same, the words in the original language are also the same. But sometimes English Bibles translate two different Greek or Hebrew words with the same English word. Making matters even more complicated, sometimes they translate the same Greek or Hebrew word with two different English words. This may be because the translators are keen for their version to have a more readable style. Alternatively, it may be because the different English words capture slightly different aspects of the original, and so the translation provides more accuracy.

Rather than despair and conclude that the only answer is to become an expert in the Bible's languages, we can compare at least two modern English translations. Where these agree, we can have a high degree of confidence in the words used.

Where the translations don't agree or we wish to check further, the free resource Scripture Tools for Every Person (STEP) - mentioned on page 50 - will identify which exact words were first used in Greek or Hebrew.

Once identified, we can then study the thread of that original word very easily again using STEP. A click on the word, and all the times it appears in the Bible are displayed with its English translations. This

---

3. More than two versions can be helpful, but it's more important that they are good versions for study. See pages 41-42 for some comments on the various Bible translations available.

enables the use of the original Greek or Hebrew word to be examined with the immediate context for each use also being provided.

## TIMING – Ask: What did it mean then?

| Abraham | Judges | David | Exile | Acts |
|---------|--------|-------|-------|------|

When considering word threads, it is necessary to remember that the meaning of a word can change over time. The word "awful" today means terrible or bad. But, two hundred years ago, it meant to be "full of awe". Awe is a sense of wonder and amazement (we still have that sense today in the word "awesome"), but "awful" has changed. "God is awful" written in the 1800s could easily be misunderstood today.

Not only do words change in their meaning, but their associations also change. "Salvation" for the reader in David's day would immediately bring to mind the Exodus. For them, Jesus dying on the cross was still in the future.

Time changes meaning. Consequently, we need to be careful and consider timing by putting ourselves into the shoes of the original hearers.

---

**DANGERS TO AVOID**
**Using a later meaning to understand a word.**
Today, the word "saint" is rarely used. But when it is, it is most often associated with a person (usually elderly) of outstanding, godly character. Someone might say, "My neighbour is a real saint," and we immediately picture someone like Mrs Wise - old, kind and gracious.

---

To impose this modern understanding of "saint" onto 1 Corinthians, however, where Paul addresses people as "saints" would lead to misunderstanding. When he uses "saints" it is simply to describe ordinary (messed up) believers. In Paul's understanding, *every* Christian is a "saint".

This trap of timing gets even more deadly when we add in a change of language. So the English word dynamite comes from the Greek word *dunamis*, meaning power. This Greek word is found in Romans 1:16, but that doesn't mean we can re-translate that verse: "I am not ashamed of the gospel, for it is the *dynamite* of God for salvation for everyone who believes." That is to use a later meaning of the word. Did Paul, writing in the 1st century, really have dynamite in his mind as he penned these words? Besides, dynamite destroys things whereas the power of the gospel brings life - quite the opposite of the 19th-century explosive.

**Using an earlier meaning to understand a word.**
This is the opposite error of the above. Here the wrong understanding of a word comes from bringing in an earlier meaning of the word from history. In ancient Greek the word for "head" (*kephalē*) could be used to mean "source" or "origin", but by New Testament times that use of the word had all but disappeared. It is therefore not right to impose this meaning onto the word in the New Testament. In Ephesians 5:23 Paul writes: "...the husband is the head of the wife as Christ is the head of the church." By then, the understanding of *kephalē* was almost completely limited to the head of a body, or headship associated with authority. It is therefore not correct to conclude that Paul's point is that Christ is the head (source) of the church - he is talking of authority.[4]

---

4. Furthermore, to argue that Christ is the head (source) of the Church, doesn't make sense when Paul has just said that the husband is the head of the wife, for he is clearly not saying that the husband is the source of his wife.

## CONTEXT – Never forget, context is king.

Whether studying a particular word or phrase, poetic image or quotation, each instance should never be separated from its context. This is of first importance.

### Using context to understand a Bible word

Let's now work through an example of how to use context to better understand a Bible word. In John 3:16 John famously wrote: "God so loved the world that he gave his only Son...". How might we study the word for "world" in this verse?

First, we need to look up the Greek word behind this translation using something like STEP (see page 50). This is the Greek word *kosmos*.

Then we need to work out how our word (*kosmos*) fits into its "jigsaw context," (immediate, book and whole Bible) that we considered in the last chapter.

Once that is done, we can consider its "words-thread" context. This is done by using STEP or a similar tool, to identify the other uses of the word *kosmos* in the Bible and then examining how that word *kosmos* is used elsewhere. This then throws light on it's meaning in John 3:16.

Such a search reveals 4 other uses in John chapter 3, a further 72 uses in the rest of John's gospel and a further 80 uses in the rest of the New Testament.

By examining these, remembering to consider each example in its individual "jigsaw context" a good understanding of the meaning of *kosmos* can be reached.

But such a study will also reveal a problem. The word *kosmos* is used in more than one way. It may describe:

- the whole physical earth (Matthew 4:8, 13:35)
- a system opposed to God (John 7:7, 8:23)
- the origin of a set of principles (Colossians 2:8, 20)
- the non-Jewish people (Romans 11:12)

So how do we know in which way it is being used in John 3:16?

To decide between different possibilities in meaning for any word, we need to consider:

1. Which understanding best fits with the jigsaw context?
2. The weight of influence we give to each of the other uses of the word found elsewhere.

## The weight of influence

If the same original word is used elsewhere and we can understand it there in its context, it helps us understand the word in the passage we are studying. However, the weight of influence from our understanding of that word elsewhere, depends on how far removed, is that other use of the word.

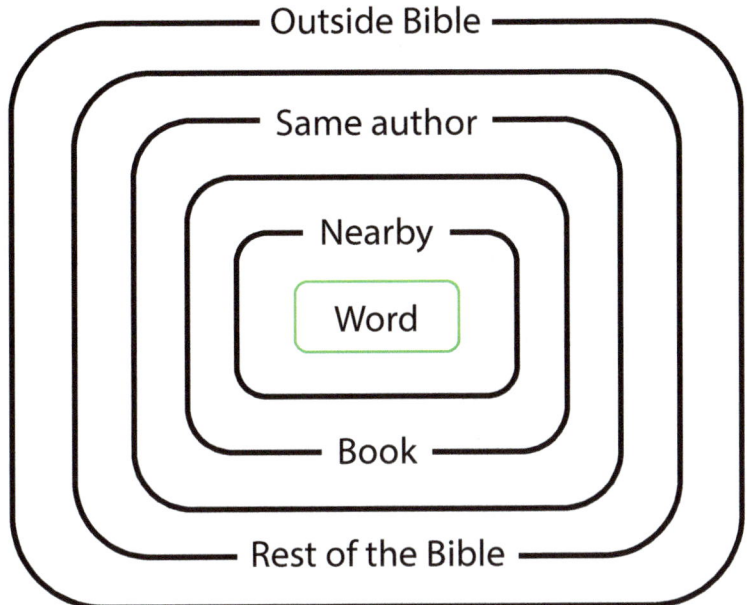

The diagram above demonstrates that another use of the same original word can influence our understanding of the word we are studying to varying degrees.

If the word is nearby, it carries the most weight for understanding the word in question. Of next importance is the use of the word in the same book. So, the 4 other uses of *kosmos* in John 3 are most important, followed by the other 72 uses in John. Beyond the same book, the way a word functions is more likely to be the same if the author is the same. Therefore, John's use in his letters is more likely to be in keeping with his use in John 3 compared with Paul's or Luke's use of *kosmos*. Having less weight still is the use of the word by non-Biblical authors from the same time period, but when there are only a few examples of a word with which to work, these sources can be helpful.[5]

In our example, John's use of *kosmos* in John 3 (and in the rest of his gospel) mostly describes the world in opposition to God. That is not to say that John doesn't rarely use *kosmos* in other ways (e.g. John

---

5. For Greek words, the Greek translation of the Old Testament known as the Septuagint is often helpful as are other ancient Greek manuscripts. STEP again helps by giving reference to these sources.

17:24) - but, because this is his dominant use, repeated many times and above all because it fits well with the "jigsaw context" of John 3:16, we can be confident that is his meaning.

In conclusion, John 3:16 is not saying God so loved the physical world, much as we might love the beauty of his creation; nor is it saying that God so loved the people he had made, but God so loved the world, the sinful world in opposition to him, that he gave his one and only Son.

## Go back to the original text

Once this process of investigating the "words-thread" is complete, we need to return to the passage we are studying. Excitement from our deeper understanding of a particular word, phrase, image or quote must not distract us from our chief task - that of understanding the passage in front of us. Now, equipped with our new insights, we need to return to the text and ask two questions:

1. How does this add to our *understanding* of what the author is saying?
2. How does this affect the *impact* of what the author is saying?

This second question is particularly important to ask when considering images and quotes, for (as we have seen) these are a great way for an author to add emphasis.

Let's ask that second question now. What impact was meant by John when he used the word *kosmos*? It is surely to bring home the truly remarkable nature of God's love - God so loved the world (the sinful world in opposition to him) that he gave his only Son. Incredible!

### DANGERS TO AVOID

To ask "What impact was meant by this image, word or quote?" is not quite the same as "What impact does this image, word or quote have on me?" The feelings produced in us may be the same, but they may also be very different from those produced in the original hearers.

Asking how a Bible passage impacts us is a good question to ask, but we must never forget the danger of leaving Bible Land too quickly. We must always first ask: What was the impact on them?

**FURTHER DANGERS TO AVOID**

**Beware of modern associations with words and images.**

Along with changes of meaning, over time the feelings or ideas associated with words and images can also change.

In James 1:14 we are told: "but each person is tempted when they are dragged away by their own evil desire and enticed."

The word "enticed" translates very accurately the Greek word (*deleazō*). But "enticed" today is often associated with sexual desire. As such it may be concluded that the evil desire James has in mind is that of sexual lust. But the Greek word for "enticed" is taken from the world of fishing where bait entices a fish. It is therefore an error to conclude James is speaking particularly of sexual sin.

**Beware of determining the meaning of a word from its root or components.**

Sometimes commentaries will suggest that the meaning of a particular word can be determined by examining the word or words from which it comes - that is its root or components. This is often helpful. In English "deca…" (meaning "ten" in Greek) is a component of words such as "decade" and "decathlon" (meaning ten years and ten contests). Indeed, in the Biblical languages cases of this are more common than in English, but it is an error to assume that it is always the case. Just as a "pineapple" isn't an apple-like fruit that grows on pines (!), so in the Biblical languages many words don't fit neatly with their components. As ever, considering the context for understanding is most important - context is king.

## 2. Promises

The second type of thread connecting different parts of the Bible is that of promises and their fulfilment. God's promises made in one part of the Bible are connected to their fulfilment later on.

As such, an important task when reading any Bible text is to identify any promises made and to ask whether any promises are being fulfilled.

Sometimes this type of Bible thread will only have two appearances, the promise and the fulfilment (e.g. 1 Samuel 2:31-34 with 1 Samuel 22:18 or Joshua 2:26 with 1 Kings 16:34), but more often the thread of a promise will have many appearances. These occur as the promise is made and is then expanded. Later the thread re-appears as the promise is gradually fulfilled to different degrees, until final completion.

By way of example, think of one of the great promises God made to Abram in Genesis 12:2: "I will make you into a great nation". Let's trace that promise-fulfilment thread up until the end of 2 Samuel.

The first re-appearance of this thread is in Genesis 13:16:

"I will make your offspring like the dust of the earth, so that if anyone could count the dust, then your offspring could be counted."

As Bible readers we need to recognise the thread and note its development. This is not a simple repetition, but an expansion of the promise. Rather than just "offspring" Abram's offspring are described as "the dust of the earth". This is more than just a few!

In Genesis 15:1-6 the promise appears again.

---

**EXERCISE**

Take a look at Genesis 15:1-6. What does this new appearance of the thread of the promise to Abram add to our understanding?

---

Along with the new illustration of stars in the sky for the great number of offspring to come for Abram, God states that the nation will come through Abram's son, his own flesh and blood. This is not through his servant, as Abram had been thinking. Every addition to the promise is given for a reason. We should ask: What difference does it make?

The importance is in what follows: "Abram believed the LORD and he credited it to him as righteousness." (Genesis 15:6).

Righteousness has come to Abram, because of his faith - a point picked up in the New Testament (Romans 4:3,20-24; Galatians 3:6; James 2:23). But hasn't Abram had faith before? Has he not already left his homeland trusting God (12:4), allowed Lot to pick the best of the land (13:9), given a tenth of everything to Melchizedek (14:20) and refused the goods of the king of Sodom (14:22-23)? Abram has trusted in God before. Why then is it only now, that it is credited to him as righteousness?

The answer comes when we consider the content of his faith. Now with the promise expanded, for the first time Abram believes in a "son from his own flesh and blood". Abram has faith in a "son" and it is credited to him as righteousness. We are being taught something very important about the promise.[6]

Continuing to trace the thread of this promise, it then appears in Genesis 17:5-6 with further expansion, "I will make nations of you and many kings will come from you."

Next comes some fulfilment: Isaac is born, then Jacob and Esau, but they are just the beginning. By the end of Genesis there are 70 descendants (Exodus 1:5) and in Egypt they "became so numerous that the land was filled with them" (Exodus 1:7). Fulfilment is taking place, but still there is no nation and no kings have yet come from Abram's line.

For that fulfilment, the land of Canaan had to be provided. Then the Judges had to give way to King Saul and King David, but eventually the promise is fulfilled, for David reigns over a great nation.

But is it fulfilled? Just then, as the promise seems to be complete, we are given a surprise as the coloured thread appears again. God adds yet further detail in an expansion of the promise to David:

"Your house and your kingdom shall endure forever before me, your throne shall be established forever" (2 Samuel 7:16).

This is speaking of someone greater than David (for David dies), and so the coloured thread continues.

---

6. Salvation in the Old Testament comes in exactly the same way as in the New Testament, through faith in Jesus Christ. Abram's righteousness comes the moment he trusts in the son that will come through his family line. He doesn't know his name, but Abram is believing in Jesus and it is credited to him as righteousness.

### Identifying Promise-Fulfilment threads

In chapter 8 we will see how these promise-fulfilment threads all find their fulfilment in Jesus, but how do we identify them?

Helpfully, Bible authors themselves often identify them for us, and study Bibles frequently assist us with cross references. There is however, no real substitute for personal reading of the Bible.[7]

As we read, looking out for promises and their fulfilment, it's also good to identify any apparent failure of promise fulfilment. This too is to see part of the coloured thread. After the exile, when the nation of Israel is ruled by a foreign power, the promise to Abram of a great nation, let alone a throne to be established forever, seems dead. But by noticing this apparent failure of the earlier promise, we are also being taught that God's promise of a great nation is far richer than the kingdom of Israel on earth… and so the coloured thread moves on.[8]

## 3. Patterns

As human beings we love patterns, we love their order and their beauty. Whether it's a pattern on the clothes we wear or in the clouds in the sky, or in the music we listen to, we notice and enjoy patterns.

And this is important, for the recognition of patterns is vital for learning. Everything we see is a pattern of shapes and movement which we have learned to associate with a word - the name we give to it. Then we learn that a dark sky means rain is coming, a set of symptoms mean a medical illness, a cruel character leads to likely behaviour etc. And this recognition of patterns is an exciting component in how God communicates with us in the Bible.

In chapters 3 and 5 we have already noted the importance of Biblical patterns when considering structure. Mirror lines, repeated sequence, spirals, acrostics are all patterns of structure. But patterns are also used by God as coloured threads connecting otherwise unconnected parts of the Bible.

---

7. There are many helpful Bible reading schedules readily available on the internet. See for example: https://www.biblegateway.com/reading-plans/
8. The thread of this promise to Abram of a great nation is taken up again in chapter 8.

There are two types of these "pattern" coloured threads:
1. Patterns of association.
2. Foreshadows.

## Patterns of Association

Have you ever played those word association games? In them, one person says a word and you have to think of other words that they might associate with it. So, if I say "Cambridge", the place where I am currently sitting to write, you might say "university" or "learning".

But why would you say those words rather than "mining" or "mountains"? The reason is obvious: Cambridge has a world-famous university. It has been a centre of learning for over 800 years, but it has never been known for its mining or mountains!

Because of repeated linking in our experience, the word "Cambridge" has become associated with "university" and "learning". This is so much so that, if we heard about a young man "who's made it into Cambridge," we would immediately conclude that he had been accepted to study at the university in Cambridge.

The Bible is full of these associations. A pattern is repeated again and again so that one thing becomes associated with another.

By way of an example, let's return to Abram. As we have seen, God appeared to him and gave him great promises. Included was a promise of land, but then, as we saw in the exercise at the end of the last chapter, there was a severe famine. Rather than trusting in God, Abram and Sarai travelled down to Egypt, and in doing so they start a Biblical pattern.

Imagine yourself as an original reader of Genesis, an Israelite sometime after the Exodus. You are familiar with the history of Israel. What would be brought to your mind as you read Abram and Sarai going down to Egypt because of a famine? What would come to your mind as you read "the LORD inflicted serious diseases on Pharaoh and his household"? What about Pharaoh's words "Take her and go!"? or the fact that Abram left with a large number of possessions?

The whole episode is a pattern of the Exodus. Jacob went down to Egypt with his family at a time of great famine. Living in Egypt brought great trouble as it did for Abram, but God sent plagues and rescued his people. Likewise, the people leave to the sound of Pharaoh's voice "take and go" with an abundance of possessions (Exodus 12:35).

The Bible is full of patterns like this, coloured threads which move through the Bible and carry with them teaching for us today. In chapter 9 we will look at this in much more detail. For now, we simply need to recognise the importance of patterns and that virtually anything can be associated with them. A place, a person, a role, an object, an action, or even a number may be associated with a pattern. Time now for you to consider an example.

---

### EXERCISE

A repeated pattern is developed in the Bible using the time period of 40 days.[9]

**By examining the pattern, what is associated with the time period of 40 days?**

To answer the question:

Look up **Genesis 7:4,12,17**

What happened after that period of time? (Genesis 9:21)

Look up **Exodus 24:18**

What happened after that period of time? (Exodus 32:1-6)

Look up **Numbers 13:2,25**

What happened after that period of time? (Numbers 14:1-4)

Once you have completed the exercise, compare your answer with the suggested thoughts on page 271.

---

### Foreshadows

The other sort of pattern which acts as a coloured thread in the Bible, is the foreshadow. To understand what is meant by this, consider the picture opposite. What do you see?

---

9. The time period of 40 *years* is also associated with a pattern. The pattern is a period of God's humbling discipline for the sins of Israel (Numbers14:33-34; Deuteronomy 8:2; Judges 13:1; Ezekiel 4:6), but also a time where God sustains his people (Exodus 16:35 Deuteronomy 29:5; Nehemiah 9:21).

Do you see a boy holding a ball? The answer is both "yes" and "no". Strictly speaking, what we see is a shadow or a pattern of a boy holding a ball. At the same time however, we do see something of the reality of what is round the corner. We know from the shadow what is coming.

In the Old Testament there are many patterns or shadows like this. They are not the real thing, but they "foreshadow" the real thing; they point to a greater reality which is coming.[10] Think of David as he fought Goliath. David appeared weak, but he trusted in God and so brought salvation for God's people through the defeat of Goliath. This foreshadows Jesus, who also appeared weak but brought salvation to God's people through the defeat of sin, Satan and death.

In chapter 8 we will return to foreshadows as they are extremely important for when we consider "What does the text mean now?" Meanwhile we should note their existence and, just as with patterns of association, that virtually anything (a place, a person, a position, an event etc.) can act as a foreshadow pointing forward to a greater reality in the New Testament - the greater reality that comes with Jesus.

---

10. In books these shadows are usually referred to as "types" and their study is called "typology". The "type" is the shadow, the "anti-type" is the greater reality to which it points.

## 4. Themes

The final type of coloured thread to consider is that of themes.

A theme is a Bible topic - it is any subject on which the Bible teaches. Whereas promises are fulfilled and patterns are repeated, themes are developed. Typically, themes start near the beginning of the Bible and are developed gradually as God reveals more and more about them progressively over the pages of the Bible from Genesis to Revelation.[11]

There are an enormous number of Bible themes, but three are of primary importance.

### The three great themes of the Bible[12]

<u>God</u>

Above all the Bible is God teaching us about God. There are many sub-themes. We learn of God's character, God's attributes, God's will and his actions in the world and in his coming kingdom. This is the greatest theme of the Bible.

Consequently, asking the question "What does this teach about God?" is one of the very best questions we can ask of any Bible text.

> **DANGER TO AVOID**
>
> Because the Bible is first and foremost about God, there is a real danger if we start with looking for a message for ourselves. The Bible has plenty to say to us, but only in the context of its revelation of God. Only when God is central, only when he is seen as the all-powerful, all-wise, all-loving, all-sufficient eternal majesty, can we begin to hear the Bible's message to us. "The fear of the LORD is the beginning of knowledge." (Proverbs 1:7)

---

11. A Bible theme covers everything on a particular topic. As such, when tracing a Bible theme through the Bible it will often overlap with promises and patterns where these contribute to the topic being examined.
12. To help remember these three great themes (**G**od, **P**eople and **R**elationships) the memory aid "MRS WISE Carefully Studies Jesus CHRIST" can be extended to "MRS WISE Carefully Studies **G**od's **P**erfect **R**evelation of Jesus CHRIST".

## People

The second great theme of the Bible is people. Men and women created in the image of God are the climax of God's creation. Positively we learn how important people are, how we should be and how we should act. But negatively, because of sin, we also learn of the darker side of who we are. As a result, much of what the Bible has to teach about people is hard to hear and accept: our weakness, our failings and the sheer depth of our sin. A second great question to ask therefore of any Bible passage is, "What does this teach about people?"

## Relationships

The third great theme of the Bible is relationships. God as Trinity implies relationship within the Godhead, God relates to us and God relates to his creation. In turn we relate to God, to each other, to those who love us and to our enemies. We relate in families, in communities and we too relate to creation. All these relationships are taught in the Bible. So, the third great question to ask of any Bible passage is: "What does this teach about relationships?"

### The theme of sacrifice

To further understand the idea of a Bible theme as it weaves like a coloured thread through the Bible, consider the theme of sacrifice. This is a sub-theme of relationships, for it describes an important aspect of what is necessary for God to relate to sinful people.

The first mention of sacrifice[13] in the Bible is in Genesis 3:21 when God provides garments of animal skin for Adam and Eve to cover their nakedness. This introduces the theme. In contrast to Adam and Eve's attempts to cover up with fig leaves, God is showing that his provision of a sacrifice is needed to cover sin.

At this early stage, the theme has only just begun. If that was all

---

13. For themes, if we search on just one specific word in the original languages, such as "sacrifice" there is a danger. The word "sacrifice" is not present in Genesis 3:21, but the theme is clearly mentioned. Nothing fully substitutes for reading through the whole Bible and thinking about a theme, but help comes from examining other closely associated words which carry the same idea and so contribute to the theme. STEP helpfully lists associated words so that these too can be explored as we trace a theme through the Bible.

we had on the subject, our understanding would be very poor. So the theme is developed.

Sacrifices are again mentioned in Genesis, most notably in Genesis 15 and Genesis 22. In chapter 15, sacrifice is first connected with God's promise (v12-16), God's covenant (v18) and God's presence, for a "smoking brazier and blazing torch" pass through the sacrifice, two things later associated with God himself (Exodus 13:21, 19:18).[14]

In Genesis 22 the idea of God as the great provider of the sacrifice is repeated (v14) with just a hint of the sacrifice being a substitute (v13). By Exodus 12 at the Passover, the sacrifice of a lamb in the place of each firstborn son is much clearer. Then the whole sacrificial system in Leviticus (particularly chapter 16) develops our understanding much further - a sacrifice is needed for the forgiveness of sins.

The theme of sacrifice continues in the Prophets, but again is developed. Isaiah 53:4-12 speaks, not of an animal, but of a servant, a human person, who is "led like a lamb to the slaughter" (v7) and "the LORD makes his life an offering for sin" (v10). This points forward to the Lord Jesus Christ, the "Lamb of God who takes away the sin of the world" (John 1:29). He is "our Passover Lamb" who "has been sacrificed" (1 Corinthians 5:7) so, "Just as people are destined to die once and after that to face judgement, so Christ was sacrificed once to take away the sins of many" (Hebrews 9:27-28).

The theme of sacrifice moves like a coloured thread from the Garden of Eden to the cross and is developed all the time.

Following the cross, no sacrifice for sins is needed, but "in view of God's mercy" Paul calls us "to offer your bodies as living sacrifices, holy and pleasing to God" (Romans 12:1). We are now to live sacrificial lives for the risen Jesus who continues to bear the marks of his sacrifice in glory (John 20:27).

That's a very quick tracing of the coloured thread of sacrifice through the Bible, with many appearances omitted. If we were studying John

---

14. This association of God with smoke and fire is a "pattern of association". Note that the covenant is unilateral - only those things associated with God's presence pass between the cut pieces of the sacrifice, Abram does not. The covenant is a one-sided provision of grace: it all depends on God Himself.

1:29 (where John the Baptist sees Jesus and declares, "Look the Lamb of God, who takes away the sin of the world!") an understanding of this thread adds a great deal of weight to what John says.

By using the word "lamb", John is not saying that Jesus is gentle and friendly. By "takes away the sin of the world" John doesn't just mean he removes sin for a short period of time. Instead, because of the thread, the words are packed full with much greater meaning. It is as if John says, "Look! See this man Jesus. He is God's perfect provision for the whole world. His is the one true sacrifice to pay for sin. He is the one who will die in our place, die our death and turn away God's wrath, so that by trusting in him all your sin is forever paid. He is the Lamb of God who takes away the sin of the world!"

"That's amazing!" exclaimed Rachel.

Joe thought for a while and added: "Are you saying that they all point to Jesus, every promise, pattern and theme? So, way back in Genesis when God provided those animal skins for Adam and Eve, it was pointing to Jesus?"

"Yes, I am," replied Mrs Wise. "In some way or another, promises are fulfilled, patterns are repeated, and themes are developed, and they all point to Jesus."

"So how do they all point to Jesus?" asked Rachel.

"We'll get there," replied Mrs Wise. "But before then, there is one last thing we need to consider for good Bible understanding."

## END OF CHAPTER EXERCISES

Once you have read the text, think carefully through each exercise. If you are pushed for time, the New Testament task is much shorter as most of the text work has been done, so providing an example of what to do. Suggested thoughts by way of answers are on page 271-275.

### Old Testament Exercise

**Genesis 12:10-20**

In the exercise at the end of the last chapter, we began to look at this passage. Let's now consider its whole Bible context by examining the different coloured threads which run through it.

Word-Threads

As part of "Observe" we noted the repetition of "seeing" Sarai's beauty, mentioned three times (vv12,14,15).

The Hebrew word for seeing is extremely common in the Bible (over 1200 times) but, if our search is limited to just the first part of the book of Genesis and to seeing something desirable, there are only two appearances of this thread.

**Read Genesis 3:6 and 6:2.** What do these verses and Genesis 12:14-15 have in common? What pattern is repeated? Why do you think the author of Genesis provides this threefold repetition of seeing Sarai in Genesis 12:10-20?

The three-fold repetition of Pharaoh's question summed up as "What have you done?" also draws our attention.

**Read Genesis 3:13 and 4:10** where the exact same phrase is repeated. What is the author of Genesis teaching us by this repetition?

Promise fulfilment

This was considered as we examined the immediate context for this passage on page 115 and suggested thoughts on p267-268. Rather than trusting in God's promises (Genesis 12:1-3,7), Abram leaves the promised land. Instead of being a blessing to the nations, Abram is the opposite.

## Patterns

As we saw on page 133, this episode sets up a Biblical pattern. Jacob too travels to Egypt at a time of famine and faces trouble in Egypt, later to be rescued by God sending plagues so that, at the Exodus, God's people leave Egypt with a great number of possessions.

## Themes

**Putting everything together, which Bible themes are in this passage?**

HELP: What do we learn about God? What do we learn about People? What do we learn about Relationships?

## New Testament Exercise

In chapter 3 we looked at **Romans 12:20**:

"If your enemy is hungry, feed him; if he is thirsty, give him something to drink. In doing this you will heap burning coals on his head."

We noted that the phrase "heap burning coals on his head" was difficult to understand.

### Examine the context

Take a look at the context of Romans 12:17-21. What negative understanding of "heap burning coals on his head" can be ruled out by the context?

### Examine the words

The footnotes in most modern English Bible translations tell us that the words of Romans 12:20 are a quotation from Proverbs 25:21-22. Unfortunately, the context in Proverbs (a list of various proverbs) doesn't appear to help our understanding. There is, however, one small thing to note at the end of v22. If we give our enemy food to eat and water to drink, along with the mysterious "you will heap burning coals on his head", we are told that "the LORD will reward you." In other words, "heap burning coals on his head" must be something that has the approval of God.

The Greek word for "head" is the normal word for a person's head, the place of the mind. "Coals" simply mean the coals in a fire and "burning" is a word that means fire. In Paul's thinking, fire can be associated with testing (1 Corinthians 3:13).

What about the Greek word for "heap"? This is found just here and in one other place in the Bible, by the same author, Paul. **Look up 2 Timothy 3:6**: How is the word translated?
(HELP: It is the word which comes before the word translated "sins" in virtually every modern English translation.)

With this new understanding for the word translated "heap", what might Paul mean by the phrase "heap burning coals on their head"?

## Whole Bible Exercise

The aim of this exercise is to trace a Bible theme (God's curse) from Genesis to Deuteronomy. Later, in the exercises for chapter 10, we'll return to the same theme and explore how the thread develops in the rest of the Bible.

Look up the references below (not a complete list). How is the theme of God's curse gradually developed?

**Genesis 3:14-19, 4:11** - What is cursed and why?
**Genesis 5:29 and 8:21** - What is different about Noah?
**Genesis 12:1-3** - What now brings a curse or a blessing?
**Genesis 27:29** - To whom is this promise repeated here?
**Deuteronomy 27:12-26 (especially v26)** - Who will be cursed?
**Deuteronomy 28:15-30, 38-41, 45-48, 53-61** - What does it mean to be cursed?
**How are we left by the end of Deuteronomy as we consider this theme in the Bible?**

# CHAPTER 7


# SITUATION

---

*"How much better to get wisdom than gold,*
*to get insight rather than silver."*
**Proverbs 16:16**

"The aim is never to become a master of the Word,
but to be mastered by it."
**Don Carson**

---

Mrs Wise returned to the living room. "We've been wondering," explained Rachel, "about this photograph."

Joe and Rachel had both been drawn to a beautifully framed picture on the sideboard. The words: "Mama Wise. Thanks from us all!" were written in bold ink across the top left-hand corner. It was signed "Dr Joseph Odhiambo."

"We assume this lady is you. But why were you being thanked?" asked Joe.

Instead of answering, Mrs Wise thought for a while and then replied. "See if you can work it out. What do you think?"

"Well, it looks like you are in Africa," suggested Joe.

"We were actually wondering whether it was Kenya from the clothes the people are wearing," added Rachel "and the fact that Odhiambo is a common Kenyan name."

Mrs. Wise looked impressed and nodded her head.

"Joe and I met in Kenya you know. We served at a school out there."

"And from what you are wearing, were you a nurse?" questioned Joe.

"Not quite," replied Mrs Wise. "What do you notice about the people?"

Joe looked again. There were eight women all seated in a long row with a few small children playing nearby.

"They are all holding a baby!" remarked Rachel.

"So, you were a midwife in Kenya?" suggested Joe. "And I think you have just delivered all these babies."

"Yes! All in one night!" exclaimed Mrs Wise. "Though Dr Joseph was the real hero. He took the photo."

Rachel and Joe fell silent.

"That was excellent," Mrs Wise reflected. "You worked out the exact situation. Now you know why I was thanked. The text takes on more meaning when you understand the situation."

### S (Studies) is for Situation - What is the Situation?

To understand any writing well we need to understand the situation in which it is written. This is known as the "situational context" and it can greatly affect the meaning.

At a simple level think about the phrase, "She is amazing." Imagine that being said at a party, on the sports field or on a hospital ward. There is overlap in meaning, but the exact sense of "amazing" varies, because of when and where it is said.

The writing in the Bible is no different. Consider Jesus' well-known parable of the Pharisee and the tax collector, where two people go to the temple to pray (Luke 18:9-14). Today (in the UK at least) tax collectors are generally regarded as law abiding and decent people. Pharisees on the other hand are known to have been the bad guys in Jesus' time. So in our situational context, Jesus' conclusion to his parable sounds reasonable - the good tax collector, rather than the bad Pharisee went home justified before God.

But in Jesus' day the situation was very different, for the Pharisees were regarded as good people, indeed the best. They were committed to God and lived excellent moral lives. Tax collectors on the other hand, were hated. They worked for the Romans, the oppressive enemy, and so were anything but good.

So, Jesus' conclusion to his parable is actually shocking. The hated, corrupt tax collector goes home justified before God! Whereas the good, upright Pharisee does not!

### The need for a time machine

The example of the Pharisee and the tax collector demonstrates the importance of imagining ourselves into the shoes of the original hearers. We need to start in Bible Land. To let our modern viewpoint determine our understanding is a mistake.

To start in Bible Land, picture a time machine, such as that in the popular television series Dr Who.

To travel in time, first we need to step inside the machine. That involves leaving behind our current world with its reasoning, culture, science and experiences. These things can no longer be in our thinking.

Next, once in the machine, we will need to programme the computer and select the time in history to which we are travelling.

Sometimes this is easy because a Bible book tells us when it was written. Most of the Prophets fit into this category, as do some of the Psalms with helpful introductory comments locating them in history (e.g. Psalm 3, 18, 34, 51, 52 etc.).

Other books can be dated to within a few years, such as most of the New Testament, but sometimes dating a book is much harder. Take 2 Samuel. When was the time period for the original hearers? It must have been written after the events described, but beyond that we are simply not told.

Rather than speculating, or worrying that we can't therefore understand 2 Samuel, we can instead take great comfort in God's sovereignty. If we needed to know more about the time of writing, we would have been informed (Deuteronomy 29:29). The rough time period we have, is all that is needed.

Once we arrive in the "time machine" of our minds, our last task is to leave the machine and explore where we are.

### Seven aspects to "situation"

So how do we explore? How do we step into the shoes of the original hearers and so understand what they would have understood by the text?

A useful starting place is to consider seven aspects of situational context. For most passages only one or two of these will apply, but having them as a check list can be helpful.

As a memory aid, each has been linked to a small picture and, for those who find it useful, the seven aspects follow the English alphabet from C to I:

 **Culture** - How would any cultural or religious practices be understood by the original hearers? (Are there any cultural or religious practices that we therefore need to understand?)

 **Dangers** - Does the text say anything about dangers and difficulties being faced? How would the original hearers relate to what is being said?

 **Emotions** - What is the tone of the words? How would the original hearers be feeling about what is written?

 **False Teaching** - Does the text tell us about false teaching or idolatry? If so, what is it? What can the original hearers learn from what is written?

 **Geography** - Where is the action in the text taking place? Is this place name, river, mountain or other aspect of geography important to the original hearers? Have other events also occurred here to provide significance?

 **History** - What, if anything, are we told about the historical situation of the hearers? How would the original hearers relate to the historical situation in the text? Who is the ruler at the time? Are they a good or a bad ruler? Is this a period of economic prosperity or hardship? Is this a period of faithfulness to God or rebellion against God?

 **International Relations** - Does the text mention other nations? If so, what is the relationship with them in the text? Is it peace, tension or war? How does this impact the meaning of the text?

## Working out the Situation

Equipped with these seven aspects of situation in our minds we can now leave the time machine and explore. But we need to be careful with where we look for insight. As we will see, non-Biblical sources can be useful, but we must always start with the Bible itself, for the Bible alone is the inspired, living Word of God.

There are three stages to using the Bible to gain a good understanding of "situation" - the same three stages as when considering context. In each we can look for information. Once that has been considered, additional clues from outside the Bible may enrich understanding.

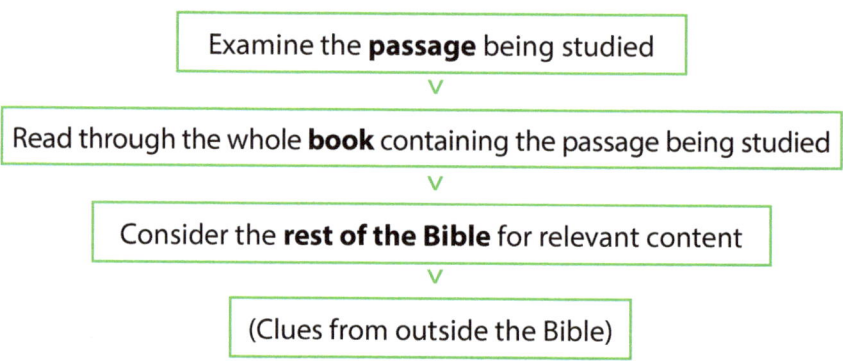

Examine the **passage** being studied

V

Read through the whole **book** containing the passage being studied

V

Consider the **rest of the Bible** for relevant content

V

(Clues from outside the Bible)

## Examine the passage being studied

The first place to look for clues about the situation is the passage itself. Every detail provided by the text has a purpose. That purpose may be to provide emphasis as we saw in chapter 2, but often a detail is deliberately given so that we might better understand the situation. Key to this process, as for all understanding, is to "ask questions again and again". Why is this detail given? What significance would this place name have? What would it have felt like to hear this back then? The seven-fold checklist with its questions should prove helpful.

## Read through the whole book containing the passage

Next, if we are to understand the situational context well, we should read the whole book containing the passage being studied and look for further clues.

Are there areas of overlap in the rest of the book with the passage being studied? Are further things revealed about the situation of the author, hearers or characters in the text? The seven-fold checklist should again prove useful.

## Consider the rest of the Bible for relevant content

After looking for clues in the passage and the whole book in which it is found, further insight can often be gained from the rest of the Bible. The book of Acts, for example, contains some very useful background information on the places to which many of the New Testament letters were written.

A study Bible with cross references may help, linking the passage to other relevant Bible texts. Alternatively, a search on a location or a particular Bible character may reveal another text where they are mentioned and so provide further details on their history.

> **ADDITIONAL TIP**
> A useful resource for understanding "situation" is a Bible Dictionary.[1] These books provide an alphabetical list of Bible objects, themes, names, places, maps and other relevant information. For each entry, background facts and Bible references are given.

## Clues from outside the Bible

Finally, once our study of the Bible text is done, further light may be shed on the text from sources outside the Bible. Such sources include other writings from the same period of history, archaeology and books written later in time reflecting on past events. A good Bible commentary, Bible dictionary or other helps such as a Bible atlas, should provide such information. Where the sources agree with each other, a degree of confidence can be built up regarding the situation in a given text.

---

1. An excellent example is the "New Bible Dictionary Third Edition" (IVP 1996) ISBN: 9780851106595.

In the letter to the church at Laodicea in the book of Revelation Jesus says, "I know your deeds, that you are neither cold nor hot. I wish you were one or the other! So, because you are lukewarm - neither hot nor cold - I am about to spit you out of my mouth." (Revelation 3:15-16).

How are we to understand this text? It is often taken to mean that the church in Laodicea was half-hearted in their commitment: they were lukewarm. They weren't completely cold, but neither were they hot for the sake of Jesus and the gospel. As such, Jesus is displeased and about to spit them out of his mouth.

But understanding from archaeology corrects this. We know that in Laodicea there was no good water supply. The result was that water was piped in from two nearby towns. Hierapolis had hot medicinal springs and Colossae had cold, refreshing drinking water. But by the time the water had travelled down the pipes, it had either cooled down from Hierapolis or warmed up from Colossae. Either way, on reaching Laodicea it had become an unpleasant, lukewarm liquid. Drinking it made you feel sick.

So taking their water supply as an illustration, Jesus makes his point - how he wishes they could be likened to the hot or cold water (both good) found at the neighbouring towns. Instead their deeds, like their foul water, meant he was about to spit them out of his mouth.

---

**DANGER TO AVOID**

Information from non-Biblical sources can be useful to add further colour to what may otherwise be a relatively black and white picture, but it should never change the picture itself. The picture, the principal teaching of the passage, is what we need to know. The Bible is sufficient for all our spiritual needs[2] (2 Peter 1:3-4). As such, we must avoid jumping to a conclusion that is different from that we would come to, if we simply had the Scriptures for our understanding.

---

2. Occasionally additional "situation" information is needed for us to understand, but then the Biblical authors provide the material we need (e.g. Ruth 4:7; Mark 7:3,11,19).

**Putting it into Practice**

Let's now think about three passages of Scripture. For each we will look into the situation. The first considers culture, the second history and the third geography. For each passage we will see how grasping the situation opens the door to a richer understanding of the text.

## A woman who loves much – Considering Culture

"[36]When one of the Pharisees invited Jesus to have dinner with him, he went to the Pharisee's house and reclined at the table. [37]A woman in that town who lived a sinful life learned that Jesus was eating at the Pharisee's house, so she came there with an alabaster jar of perfume. [38]As she stood behind him at his feet weeping, she began to wet his feet with her tears. Then she wiped them with her hair, kissed then and poured perfume on them. [39]When the Pharisee who had invited him saw this, he said to himself, 'If this man were a prophet, he would know who is touching him and what kind of woman she is - that she is a sinner.'" (Luke 7:36-39)

With descriptive skill Luke introduces us to a scene. The location is the house of a Pharisee (a fact repeated four times), and a woman is present. She is known to have "lived a sinful life" and "is a sinner," so we can imagine a woman with a reputation.

She comes with a jar of perfume, having heard that Jesus was there. From this we can assume that she had met Jesus, or at least heard Jesus beforehand.

Next, we learn that, standing behind Jesus, she begins to cry. She then washes his feet with her tears, dries them with her hair and anoints them with perfume.

Remember at this stage of "understand" our first task is to ask: "What did the text mean then?" We need to imagine we are in Bible Land as original hearers. How would they have understood the text? As we have seen, key to that understanding is to ask questions, "Ask questions again and again."

Why does this woman come and why does she bring a jar of

perfume? Why does she cry? Then why does she wash Jesus' feet and why does she apply perfume to them? Why does she dry his feet with her hair? Perhaps a towel was not available, but why does she not use the folds of her dress or other clothing?

These are situational questions and the kind of questions we should be asking. Later in Luke's account of what happened we are given some clues:

"⁴⁴Then he [Jesus] turned towards the woman and said to Simon, 'Do you see this woman? I came into your house. You did not give me any water for my feet, but she wet my feet with her tears and wiped them with her hair. ⁴⁵You did not give me a kiss, but this woman from the time I entered, has not stopped kissing my feet. ⁴⁶You did not put oil on my head, but she has poured perfume on my feet. ⁴⁷Therefore I tell you, her many sins have been forgiven - as her great love has shown. But whoever has been forgiven little loves little.'

⁴⁸Then Jesus said to her, 'Your sins are forgiven.'

⁴⁹The other guests began to say among themselves, 'Who is this who even forgives sins?'

⁵⁰Jesus said to the woman, 'Your faith has saved you; go in peace.'"

## Examine the passage being studied

From this text we now learn that, on entering the house, Jesus was not provided with water to wash his feet or oil to anoint his head or a welcome kiss.

Reading this today, these cultural practices may appear strange, but the text is telling us something about the situation. These things were clearly normal in that culture then, but in this instance, they were not provided.

By asking why they were not provided and putting ourselves into the shoes of the original hearers, we grasp the significance.

In every culture there are normal things which happen when a guest arrives at a house. In my own culture in the UK it is a greeting: "So good to see you!" followed by "Please come in" and "What would you like to drink?" Leaving out one of these things might be an oversight, but not to say any of them - that would be offensive. Simon's intention with Jesus, was a deliberate insult.

In v47 we are given more information. Jesus tells us her many sins have been forgiven as her great love has shown. This then is why she has come with her jar of perfume. It's because she loves him.

On entering, however, she notices Jesus' feet have not been washed. He has been insulted. How can this man be treated like this? It's terrible. And then she cries. Suddenly, she realises she can use her tears as water. Being behind him, she has access to his feet, so she washes, dries and kisses them and applies her perfume. Even if the hosts have not provided the usual cultural welcome, she will.

## Read through the whole book containing the passage

The next stage for gaining situational context clues is to read the whole book containing the passage that is being studied. In this example, Luke's gospel has two other instances of Jesus dining at the house of a Pharisee (11:37-54 and 14:1-24). And on each occasion there is a clash between the Pharisees and Jesus.

On the other hand, within Luke, there are two further passages (5:29-32 and 19:7-10) where Jesus dines with Levi and Zacchaeus, tax collectors. These are people rejected by society, but in contrast to the Pharisees, these Jesus comforts.

As original hearers, the message is being repeated. The supposedly good Pharisees were opposed to Jesus, and he was opposed to them. Their insistence on obeying rules clashed with his message of grace to sinners. But in contrast, Jesus welcomed those who welcomed him, even if they were rejected by society, like tax collectors and this woman.

## Consider the rest of the Bible for relevant content

It appears from what we have seen so far that Jesus was insulted. But was the welcome given to Jesus by Simon the Pharisee really that insulting? What does the rest of the Bible say about Jewish culture for welcoming guests?

Although many years beforehand, in Genesis 18:1-8 Abraham has guests, so what happened then? In v2 we are told, "When he saw them, he hurried from the entrance to his tent to meet them and bowed low to the ground." Then in v4-5: "'Let a little water be brought, and then you may all wash your feet and rest under this tree. Let me get you something to eat, so that you can be refreshed and then go on your way - now that you have come to your servant.'"

Abraham then rushes off to ask Sarah to bake fresh bread whilst he selects a calf to eat. The guests eat as Abraham stands nearby under a tree, waiting in case they require anything else. This gives us some insight into how guests were treated in Bible times. Not providing water for Jesus to wash his feet was insulting.

## Clues from outside the Bible

From the Bible text alone, most of our questions have now been answered, but what about the use of this woman's hair? Why did she dry his feet with her hair, rather than with the folds of her dress or some other piece of clothing?

A good Bible commentary may throw light on this puzzle. For example, it might inform us that, in the Babylonian Talmud (an ancient Jewish writing), the teachings of a second-century man called Rabbi Meir are recorded. He speaks about what a man should do if he sees his wife "go out with her hair unfastened". He states, "Such a one, it is a religious duty to divorce."[3]

The reason, again provided by the Babylonian Talmud, was because a woman's hair was considered to be a "sexual incitement"[4]. In public a woman's hair was therefore to be kept up and covered.[5] The only place for a woman to let down her hair was at home with her husband; this was part of her loyalty to him.

Understanding this cultural view of a woman letting down her hair, enables us to better understand what this text would have meant to an original hearer. By letting her hair down this woman is doing something very unusual. It is clearly not making a sexual gesture, for

---

3. Babylonian Talmud Gittin 90a-b
4. Rabbi Shesheth in Babylonian Talmud Berakhot 24a quoting Song of Songs 4:1
5. In 1 Corinthians 11:5 Paul refers to this cultural practice at the time.

she is behind Jesus dealing with his dirty feet. So what is she doing? She is making a great pledge of loyalty to Jesus.

She knows how others will regard her for doing this, but that doesn't matter to her - she loves Jesus, and he has been insulted. By using her hair, she is certainly taking a risk, for what would Jesus make of it? She could have used her clothing, but she wanted to make a statement. In direct contrast to the attitude of her hosts, she is loyal, she is devoted to Jesus.[6]

So, what will Jesus do? That would be the big question in the minds of the original hearers. Will he ask for her to be removed as would have been expected? Will he politely ask her to stop, explaining that she had gone too far and embarrassed him, or might he accept her? Instead, what he does is even more remarkable.

Following her actions, the hatred of the Pharisees towards this woman would have greatly increased. Their insult had badly backfired. Rather than putting Jesus down as intended, Jesus had now been greatly honoured. His feet had been washed, with tears no less, dried with unfastened hair and then perfumed at great expense - all because of this sinful woman.

And then Jesus turns to her and says (v48): "Your sins are forgiven." Not only would this have been wonderfully comforting to her, but in saying these words Jesus knew he would get the attention of the Pharisees, for only God could forgive sins (Mark 2:7). Was Jesus claiming to be God?

And so it did gain their attention (v49). They were angry at her, so Jesus deliberately turns the anger of the guests away from her and onto himself. The woman has stood by him, and he now stands by her. He didn't need to say what he did, but in a remarkable act of sacrificial love for her he does. Now she can "go in peace" (v50).

6. I am grateful to David Moore for pointing out the probable allusion here to 2 Samuel 6:13-23, where David makes a spectacle of himself out of love for the Lord. If so, the Pharisees are being compared with the barren Michal.

## Another woman who loved much – Considering History

Time now for you to look at a text. It's from the book of Ruth, another woman who loved much.

---

**EXERCISE**

Ruth 1:1: "In the days when the judges ruled, there was famine in the land, and a man from Bethlehem in Judah, together with his wife and sons, went to live for a while in the land of Moab."

**List what this verse tells us about the "situation" at the beginning of the book of Ruth.**

**What is the significance of each one of these things?**

HELP: Imagine you are an Israelite reading this at the time of King David. What associations do these things have? (See Deuteronomy 23:2-4; Judges 2:10-19, 3:12-30, 19:1-2,22-30)

---

The first verse of Ruth provides a very important introduction to the book, telling us a great deal about the situational context.

The story starts at a time of great hardship. It is "In the days when the judges ruled," a period of huge uncertainty and lawlessness in the history of Israel. To make matters worse there was a famine in the land.

A man from Bethlehem in Judah[7] is then introduced with his wife and sons. Living in the 21st Century, when we hear of Bethlehem, we immediately think of the birthplace of Jesus. That's not wrong, but for the first part of "understand" we need to remember to leave our knowledge behind and imagine ourselves as the original hearers. What would Bethlehem have meant to them? Bethlehem means "house of bread", but now there is no bread in the house of bread. Worse, there had been recent violence to one of its people. In Judges 19 a young

---

7. To the Israelite reader the mention of a man from Judah would also bring Genesis 49:8-12 to mind and with it some hope. Could this man be the promised king to rule over the nations? He soon dies, but by the end of the book the hope has increased, for Boaz (also from Judah) is blessed, "Through the offspring (the word picks up Genesis 3:15) the LORD gives you by this young woman, may your family be like that of Perez, whom Tamar bore to Judah." (4:12). The book ends with the family line of Perez leading to David (4:22).

woman from Bethlehem had been brutally raped and murdered. The situation of this family was bad, so bad that they leave the promised land and move to Moab, one of Israel's enemies.

Within one verse the author has provided us with a great deal of situational context. The circumstances for this family are terrible, and in v5 things become even worse, for by then only Naomi (the man's wife) is left alive of all those who left Bethlehem. "Don't call me Naomi" (meaning pleasant), she says in 1:20, "Call me Mara (meaning bitter) because the Almighty has made my life very bitter."

That is her situation, a terrible place to be. She describes it as "empty" because "the LORD has afflicted me" (1:21). But Naomi is about to receive God's grace. By the end of the book, instead of being empty, her lap will be full with a child; instead of being afflicted she will be blessed (4:16). The situation will have been transformed from death to life, from despair to hope; but to appreciate this remarkable work of God in its fullness, understanding the situational context is key.

## The mention of a mountain – Considering Geography

Genesis 22:1-19 contains the heart moving story of God testing Abraham. Abraham is instructed by God to go to a certain place and sacrifice his only son, Isaac. It's confusing, for Isaac was the son God had promised, and it's extremely moving. Only at the very last minute does God intervene and provide a ram as a substitute. (If you don't know the story, please read it through now.)

The situational context is important if we are to fully understand this story. The emotional situation is clear enough. This must have been so traumatic for Abraham. Our author brings this home with additional and repeated words. God doesn't simply say, "take Isaac and go" but "'Take your son, your only son, whom you love - Isaac - and go to the region of Moriah. Sacrifice him there as a burnt offering on a mountain that I will show you.'"

So emotional. But why the added detail of "to the region of Moriah" and "on a mountain I will show you"? This geographical note is not strictly necessary for the telling of the story. Clearly however it is important, for he repeats the reference to the mountain in v14:

"So Abraham called that place The LORD Will Provide. And to this day it is said. 'On the mountain of the LORD it will be provided."

Why does the author add in this extra point? What is so special about a mountain in the region of Moriah?

For the answer we need to trace the thread of Mount Moriah through the Bible. Genesis 22 is its first mention, but this same mountain reappears in 2 Chronicles 3:1:

"Then Solomon began to build the temple of the LORD in Jerusalem on Mount Moriah, where the LORD had appeared to his father David. It was on the threshing floor of Araunah the Jebusite, the place provided by David."

This verse tells us that Mount Moriah is the very place where Solomon built the temple, the place of sacrifice. All those years earlier God had deliberately taken Abraham to Moriah for his sacrifice, for God intended that later the temple would be built on that same mountain.

What is more, we are told it was the place where the LORD had appeared to David "on the threshing floor of Araunah the Jebusite". This is a reference to 2 Samuel 24:10-25 where there had been a terrible plague sent by God. 70,000 people had died because of sin but, in response to God's command, David had bought a threshing floor, built and altar on it and offered sacrifices. Then because of the sacrifice, at that exact spot on the mountain, the plague had stopped.

This mountain was therefore special. It was the mountain of sacrifice and so Abraham was taken there. But Abraham himself was not to provide the sacrifice, for "The LORD Will Provide" (22:14). Isaac, Abraham's only son, whom he loved, would go free, but only because God would provide a substitute. Initially at Moriah that was a ram, then at the threshing floor burnt and fellowship offerings, then in the temple countless sacrificed animals; but these all pointed forward to the perfect sacrifice that God would provide - his only son whom he loved, Jesus.

By noticing the added detail in Genesis 22 and considering the geography, we gain a greater insight into the majesty of God.

## END OF CHAPTER EXERCISES

If you only have time for one exercise, please look at the Old Testament passage as we will return to this in chapter 10. Once you have drawn your conclusions, compare them with the suggested thoughts on pages 275-276.

### Old Testament Exercise

**Read 2 Kings 2:19-24**

This passage contains two strange episodes in the life of Elisha. Understanding the situational context is key.

**Summarise in ten words or fewer what happens in each episode. Where does each of these events occur?**

**What is the history of the places mentioned**?

(HELP: See Joshua 6:20-21,26 with 1 Kings 16:34 and Genesis 28:10-22 with 1 Kings 12:25-33.)

**How does what happened in history compare with what happens in this passage?**

Additional Question: What would the original hearers have thought when they heard of "unproductive land" or "wild animals killing children"?

(HELP: Trace the threads of these things in the Bible. See Genesis 3:17-18; Deuteronomy 29:23-27 and Leviticus 26:22. How does this add to our understanding of 2 Kings 2:19-24?)

### New Testament Exercise

**Read Matthew 8:1-3**

By putting ourselves into the shoes of the original hearers, this miracle has a far richer meaning than a simple display of Jesus' power to heal.

**What was the significance of leprosy (a skin disease) to an Israelite living at this time?**

(HELP: Consider the theme of leprosy in the Bible. See: Leviticus 13:45-46; 2 Kings 5:7,27; Numbers 5:2, 12:9-12.)

**What point is being made by the details provided in how Jesus heals him?**

## UNDERSTAND PART 2

## WHAT DOES THE TEXT MEAN NOW?

"Ignorance of Scripture is ignorance of Christ"

**Jerome**

# JESUS (PART 1) – PROMISES

---

*"For no matter how many promises God has made,*
*they are 'Yes' in Christ."*
**2 Corinthians 1:20**

"The stars may fall, but God's promises
will stand and be fulfilled."
**J.I. Packer**

---

So far, in our study of how to read the Bible, we have thought about "Observe" and the first part of "Understand". We have seen that we start "Understand" by asking "What did the text mean then?" to the original hearers. We took in the significance of "jigsaw" (literary) context placing each verse in its immediate, book and whole Bible context.

Then within whole Bible context, we noted that there are various things which like coloured threads, connect otherwise unconnected passages. We observed how words, quotes, images, promises, patterns and themes can all form these connections. Lastly, we saw the importance of the situational context. By putting ourselves into the shoes of the original hearers our understanding grows as we consider their culture, dangers faced, emotions, false teaching, geography, history and international relations.

Having worked through all this, we should now have a fairly good idea of what the text meant then to the original hearers. We ended "Observe" with the important question: "Where is the author's emphasis in what they wrote?" Now, with our deeper understanding, we should be able to answer: "What did the author want their original hearers to understand?"

But we are not original hearers! We live in the 21st Century. This is long after the death and resurrection of Jesus and the completion of the New Testament, not to mention the events of the Old Testament. So what does the text mean now, to us?

### Crossing the Divide

To answer the crucial question of what the text means to us, we need to take our understanding of the author's purpose for his original hearers in Bible Land and pack that into our bag. Then, we have a journey to make. We must cross the great sea of culture, situation and time between Bible Land and Today's World.

That journey is what the next three chapters will describe - how to find a good bridge from any passage in the Bible and cross over in safety, without falling into error.

## The centrality of Jesus

In chapter 1 we listened to some incredible teaching by Jesus:

"And beginning with Moses and all the Prophets, he explained to them what was said in all the Scriptures concerning himself." (Luke 24:27)

"If you believed Moses, you would believe me, for he wrote about me." (John 5:46).

And to the Pharisees he said:

"You study the Scriptures diligently because you think that in them you have eternal life. These are the very Scriptures that testify about me." (John 5:39).[1]

Jesus was clear that the whole Bible was written about him. As a result, wherever we are in the Bible, seeing the connection with Jesus is crucial if we are to find a good bridge from Bible Land to Today's World.

Finding a connection with Jesus in the New Testament is usually easy. The gospels describe his life and teachings on earth, the book of Acts his ongoing work by the Holy Spirit (Acts 1:1-2) and the New Testament letters continue his teaching. Nevertheless, asking, "Where is the connection with Jesus?" is still an excellent question to ask. A focus on Jesus keeps us away from a central focus on ourselves, which is never healthy. But what about the Old Testament - how do we see Jesus there?

## Jesus in the Old Testament

To understand how the Old Testament reveals Jesus, we need to listen to some remarkable teaching in the New Testament (emphasis mine):

"For everything that was written in the past was written to teach us, so that through the endurance taught in the Scriptures and the encouragement they provide we might have hope." (Romans 15:4).

Or listen to Paul in 1 Corinthians 10:6, referring back to various Old Testament events:

"Now these things occurred as examples to keep us from setting our hearts on evil things as they did."

And again in 1 Corinthians 10:11:

"These things happened to them as examples and were written down

---

1. This teaching of Jesus was also repeated by the apostles e.g. Peter in Acts 10:43.

as warnings for *us*, on whom the culmination of the ages has come."

Peter writes "It was revealed to them (the Old Testament prophets) that they were not serving themselves but *you*, when they spoke of the things that have now been told you by those who have preached the gospel to you by the Holy Spirit sent from heaven." (1 Peter 1:12).

These verses teach that the Old Testament was written with Christians in mind, not just Old Testament hearers. Behind the human authors, God himself was at work as the supreme author, to make it particularly relevant for people living after Jesus. God made sure that there was a fullness of meaning in the text, a fullness that would only be understood later by Christians. This fullness concerns how the Old Testament points to and reveals Jesus.

"So, as Christians, do we understand the Old Testament better than they did?" questioned Rachel.

"Paul teaches that exact point," replied Mrs Wise. She opened her well-worn Bible at 2 Corinthians 3:14. "But their minds were made dull, for to this day the same veil remains when the old covenant is read. It has not been removed, because only in Christ is it taken away."

Rachel and Joe spent a moment taking this in.

"That's not to say that Old Testament believers didn't understand anything of what was being said about Jesus," added Mrs Wise, "they did, but not nearly as well as we understand it."

"So how does this work?" asked Joe, "I mean, how do we understand the Old Testament better than they did?"

Mrs Wise thought for a while. "Have you ever watched one of those detective films?" she replied. "You know the kind of thing. Someone is found dead and there are a number of possible explanations. Was the death natural or suicide, or was it murder? A detective is called in and you watch the film trying to solve the mystery yourself. You pick up on clues, or what you think are clues, and try to put them together. Finally, all is revealed at the end."

"And if you are like me, you realise you had it completely wrong!" added Joe.

"Oh. I'm the same," replied Mrs Wise, "but here is the important point. When you watch the film a second time it is a whole different experience."

"Yes - you know how it ends!" laughed Joe.

"Exactly!" replied Mrs Wise. "So knowing the end, you start to see new things when you watch it a second time. You see clues in the story you hadn't noticed the first time you watched the film." She paused, "The clues not only point to the end, but knowing the end unlocks the clues."

There was a silence as Rachel and Joe put this together with Bible reading.

"Oh! Now I see what you are saying," burst out Rachel.

"We know how it ends, so we know who to look for - Jesus. So when we read the Old Testament, unlike the Israelites, we see the clues - we see the pointers to Jesus, because we know where it is all going."

## Making the Journey

Having completed the first part of "Understand - What did the text mean then?" we are now ready to leave Bible Land. We stand at the edge of the great sea with Today's World in the distance. Our hard work on the text is done and our bag is full with the understanding of the original hearers. We are ready to cross over. But to cross the sea we first need to find a bridge - that is a connection with Jesus, for all the Scriptures testify about him.

There are three principal ways to do this using the coloured threads we looked at in chapter 6: Promises, Patterns and Bible Themes.[2]

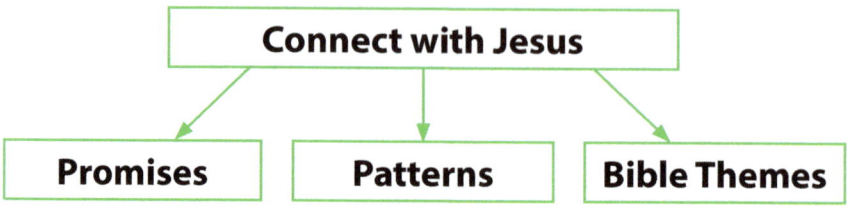

In this chapter we will start by considering "Promises". How "Patterns" and "Bible Themes" connect to Jesus will be the subject of the next two chapters.

---

**ADDITIONAL TIP**

As we think about each of these possible connections in turn, sometimes a passage will contain more than one type of connection. If so, that makes a strong link. At other times there will be no apparent connection with Jesus. When this occurs, we should focus on Bible Themes, for often when considering these, the link with Jesus then becomes clear.

---

**PROMISES – Is there a promise that is fulfilled in Jesus?**

In chapter 6 we saw how promises, like coloured threads, run through the Bible connecting one part with another. At that stage we asked the question: "What did the text mean then?" To do this we learned how to trace coloured threads back in time, looking for previous appearances to make sense of them to the original hearers.

At this point, as we consider "What does the text mean now?" we need to take up those coloured threads again, but this time trace them forward to Jesus. To do that we need to listen carefully to the apostle

---

2. In addition, (although this is disputed by some), most Christians believe that Jesus occasionally appeared in the Old Testament in what are known as "christophanies". These are often associated with the "angel of the LORD". Examples of christophanies are in Genesis 16:7-13; Genesis 32:22-32; Exodus 3:2-6; Joshua 5:13-15 with Exodus 3:5 and Revelation 19:10; Judges 6:11-24; 13:3-23; Isaiah 6:1-10 with John 12:41; Daniel 3:24-25.

Paul in 2 Corinthians 1:20:

"For no matter how many promises God has made, they are 'Yes' in Christ."

This truth is crucial for our understanding. All the promises God has made find their "Yes" in Jesus. He is the one of whom all the Scriptures speak. So, every promise points to Jesus and finds its fulfilment in Jesus.

But "fulfilment in Jesus" can be in several different ways. Some fulfilment has already happened during Jesus' life on earth, some may be ongoing in his body (the church) and some may be in the future, fulfilled only in glory in the new creation. Jesus is always central to all the promises God has made, but how each particular promise works out varies and needs some thought.

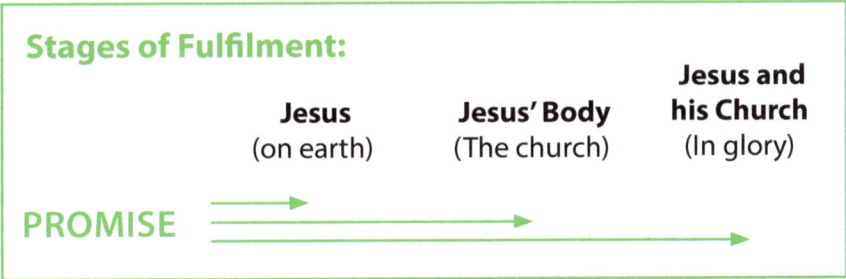

As the diagram above shows, promises can be fulfilled at any one of the three levels, or partially at more than one level.

### Fulfilment at one level

Micah 5:2 speaks of a ruler coming from Bethlehem. This was completely fulfilled when Jesus was born (Matthew 2:6). His birth will never happen again so there are no further fulfilments. Similarly, some of the promises describing Jesus' death on the cross (e.g. John 19:24,36,37) are fulfilled completely at that specific event in history.

Isaiah 11:6-9 on the other hand, (which we looked at in chapter 3) contains the promises that the "wolf will live with the lamb" and "the lion will eat straw like the ox". Here the promises are also only fulfilled at one level, but this time their fulfilment occurs in the new creation.

## Fulfilment at multiple levels

But other promises are partially fulfilled in Jesus' earthly lifetime and then continue in the life of the church. Take Isaiah 49:6:

"he [God] says: 'It is too small a thing for you to be my servant to restore the tribes of Jacob and bring back those of Israel I have kept. I will also make you a light for the Gentiles, that my salvation may reach to the ends of the earth.'"

This promise speaks of a servant, a key figure in the latter part of Isaiah, who will suffer and bring God's salvation. It clearly points to Jesus, as several New Testament texts confirm (Mathew 8:17, 12:18-21; Luke 22:37; John 8:12; Acts 8:32; Romans 15:21). Jesus on earth is the "light for the Gentiles".

But in Acts 13:46-47 we read something surprising. Paul and Barnabas are addressing a Jewish crowd in Pisidian Antioch: (emphasis mine)

"We had to speak the word of God to you first. Since you reject it and do not consider yourselves worthy of eternal life, we now turn to the Gentiles. For this is what the Lord has commanded *us*: 'I have made you a light for the Gentiles, that you [singular] may bring salvation to the ends of the earth.'"

This is astonishing. Paul and Barnabas take the very words of Isaiah that apply to Jesus, and then they apply the text to themselves! This is not because they had misunderstood Isaiah. No - they realised that Jesus continues to be a light to the Gentiles through his body, the church. Christians today are the means through whom Jesus continues to bring light to the Gentiles, that he may bring salvation to the ends of the earth. The work of evangelism is not primarily our efforts, but Jesus' light shining through us.

## God's Promise to Abram

With this in mind, let's finally take another look at God's promise to Abram which we considered in chapter 6: "I will make you into a great nation" (Genesis 12:2). Previously, we traced that promise through to the end of 2 Samuel. We noted that just as the promise appeared to be fulfilled with King David ruling over a great nation, God expanded the promise. He declared to David: "Your house and your kingdom shall endure forever before me, your throne shall be established for ever." (2 Samuel 7:16).

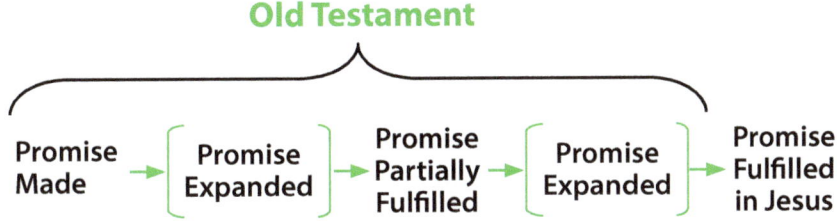

If we were studying a later part of the Old Testament we would need to go on and trace the thread forward to that point. But to answer, "What does the text mean now?" in Today's World, we need to follow that thread even further forward into the New Testament.

So where in the New Testament do we see a reference made to the promise to Abram? A key verse is Galatians 3:16:

"The promises were spoken to Abraham and to his seed. Scripture[3] does not say 'and to seeds' meaning many people, but 'and to your seed' meaning one person, who is Christ."

This is remarkable. What Paul is saying is that the promises made to Abraham (Abram) some 2,000 or so years beforehand, were supremely made concerning Jesus. Jesus is ultimately the one from whom a great nation will come. Jesus is the king from Abram's line. Jesus is the one whose "kingdom shall endure forever" and whose "throne shall be established for ever." All the promises that God has made find their 'Yes' in him.

So, the promise to Abram is fulfilled at multiple levels. First the Old Testament kings in Abram's line are a partial fulfilment. This is particularly true for those kings like David who ruled well. But these kings also point forward to the great king, the Lord Jesus. He fulfilled the promise whilst here on earth announcing: "the kingdom has come" (Matthew 12:28). But that didn't complete the fulfilment, for

---

3. Referring to Genesis 12:7, 13:15 and 24:7

God's kingdom is still being built in the lives of his people, the church. The church is the "great nation", the "holy nation" (1 Peter 2:9) which continues to grow day by day.

And one day it will become "a great multitude that no-one could count, from every nation, tribe, people and language standing before the throne and before the Lamb" (Revelation 7:9). This is the final fulfilment, with Jesus on the throne, ruling over a perfected great nation. This is where the coloured thread ends, where the original promise of a great nation first made in Genesis 12:2 is completely fulfilled. God keeps his promises.

## END OF CHAPTER EXERCISES

Rather than look at some passages in depth, the exercise for this chapter is to consider how each of the texts below connects to Jesus. Read the verses and look out for promises that are fulfilled in Jesus. Some references to help are provided.[4]

Suggested thoughts are given on page 276-278.

### Genesis 3:15

(HELP: Judges 4:21; 1 Samuel 17:49; Matthew 1:25; 1 John 3:8; Romans 16:20; Colossians 2:15; Hebrews 2:14; Revelation 12:9,17.)

### Psalm 2:7-9

(HELP: Matthew 17:5; Acts 13:32-34; Romans 1:4; Hebrews 1:5; Revelation 2:26-27, 19:15.)

---

4. If you would have struggled to think of these references yourself, Appendix 5 can be used. It lists many of the connections between the Old and New Testaments.

# CHAPTER 9

# JESUS (PART 2) – PATTERNS

---

*"These are a shadow of the things that were to come;
the reality, however, is found in Christ."*
**Colossians 2:17**

"The Bible is to us what the star was to the wise men;
but if we spend all our time in gazing upon it, observing its motions,
and admiring its splendour, without being led to Christ by it,
the use of it will be lost to us."
**Thomas Adams**

---

In the last chapter we began to look at the process of finding a bridge from the Old Testament text to Jesus. We considered promises and saw the usefulness of asking: "Is there a promise that is fulfilled in Jesus?" Then, if the text contains such a promise, we need to work out on what level or levels it is fulfilled.

Promises pointing forward to Jesus are, however, fairly rare. But that is not the case for the second type of bridge - that of patterns.

### Patterns – Is there a pattern that points to Jesus?

In chapter 6 we saw that patterns are another type of coloured thread linking together different parts of the Bible. First, there are patterns which develop an association, and second there are foreshadows. For both types of patterns, the key question to ask as we look for a bridge to Jesus is: "Does this pattern reoccur in the New Testament?"

### Patterns which develop an association

Let's ask that question now for the time period of 40 days which we considered in chapter 6. In the Old Testament we realised that this was associated with a period of testing and failure for the people of God. Does that pattern recur in the New Testament? Is a period of 40 days mentioned?

The answer is yes. In Luke 4:1-14 we read that Jesus was "led by the Spirit into the wilderness, where for 40 days he was tested by the devil."

Because there is an established pattern (40 days means testing and failure), we expect the same result, failure, for Jesus. Instead, Jesus passes the test by perfectly resisting the devil. We are therefore being taught that Jesus is very different from all those that have come before him.[1]

What about the pattern of "going down to Egypt", which we also noted in chapter 6? Abram and later the people of Israel go down to Egypt and on both occasions there are bad associations. It's the same further on in Israel's history (1 Kings 3:1, 10:28, 11:18; Isaiah 31:1; Jeremiah 42:15-17, 44:12-14). Egypt is a place where trouble comes, and a place from which God has to rescue his people.

So, does this pattern recur in the New Testament? If so, who goes down to Egypt?

The surprising answer is Jesus! (Matthew 2:13-18). We'd expect Egypt to be the last place where Jesus would go because the Old Testament has set this up as a bad thing to do. But things have changed. King Herod of Israel was brutally murdering baby boys (Matthew 2:16). This picks up another pattern, for Pharaoh in Egypt had previously murdered baby boys (Exodus 1:16). Herod, in effect, has become the new Pharaoh. Previously God had to rescue from Egypt, now God has to rescue from Israel! Even Egypt, the terrible place, is relatively safe compared with Israel. It's a powerful teaching point - a point that can only be made with force because of the pattern of "going down to Egypt" and its associations.

---

1. 40 days is also the period of time that Jesus appeared to his disciples after his resurrection (Acts 1:3). Instead of a period of testing this was a period when he "presented himself to them and gave many convincing proofs that he was alive." Testing (God's apparent absence) has been replaced by the blessing of his appearance.

## Foreshadows

"We come now to the most amazing way in which the Old Testament reveals Jesus," explained Mrs Wise. "It's also the most common way."

"Do you remember that illustration I gave you of a boy carrying a ball round the corner? You couldn't see him, but you could see his shadow?"

"Yes. I remember," replied Rachel. "Seeing the shadow meant you knew something of what was coming."

"That's right. And these shadows of Jesus, telling us something about him are all over the Old Testament. In fact, I'd go so far as to say that pretty much everything in the whole Old Testament either promises something about Jesus or in some way foreshadows Jesus."

Rachel and Joe sat stunned by what had just been said.

"What everything?" asked Joe.

"Yes - sometimes it's not so obvious, but every picture that the Old Testament paints is a shadow that points to Jesus."

There was a pause as Rachel and Joe thought this through.

"Let me explain from Ephesians chapter five," Mrs Wise continued. She read with seriousness in her voice: "This is what Paul wrote: 'For this reason a man will leave his father and mother and be united to his wife, and the two will become one flesh.' This is a profound mystery - but I am talking about Christ and the church."

"We had that verse at our wedding," added Rachel.

"It's a great verse," replied Mrs Wise with a smile, "but did you notice what it says?

Paul is quoting Genesis 2:24. It refers to the very first human marriage, and Paul says that marriage points to the relationship between Jesus and the church."

"Yes," replied Joe. "Marriages have Jesus and the church as a great example to follow."

"That's true," replied Mrs Wise, "but there is so much more to it than that! You see, in God's mind, the relationship between Jesus and his church came first. And to teach us about that relationship he created marriage. Marriage was created as a shadow (what Paul calls a 'mystery' as it doesn't reveal everything) so that we could begin to see something of the greater reality that was coming, the relationship between Jesus and his church."

"So, marriage was created as a shadow," reflected Rachel slowly, "before Jesus came, to teach us about the relationship between Jesus and his church?"

"Yes," continued Mrs Wise, "and the amazing thing is that everything is like that. The whole of Old Testament history was written by God with the coming of Jesus in mind. All of it happens in order to form shadows pointing ahead to what we see much more clearly in the New Testament."

"In other words, God wrote the whole of Bible history, not just in words, but in actual events to teach us about Jesus?"

"Exactly!" replied Mrs Wise. She then smiled, "God is God after all!"

## Finding a safe connection to Jesus

Understanding the Old Testament as a series of shadows all pointing to Jesus presents a few questions, but there are two in particular which are very important to answer if we are to find a safe connection to Jesus.

## Question 1: Shadow or Imagination?

First, how can we be sure that an idea that we have, a shadow that we have seen, is a true shadow pointing to Jesus?

Being confident here is vital. After all, to see a connection with Jesus that is not real is to find a false and dangerous bridge.

## Testing a bridge we have found

To test the safety of a possible bridge, our natural tendency maybe to want a method, a dependable technique that will guarantee us safety. Searching for such a method may take us to the New Testament where we try to work out the means by which the New Testament authors understood the Old Testament. But it is important to realise that the New Testament is not a textbook on how to understand the Old Testament. It is instead written by people who had met with Jesus and seen his glory at the cross and resurrection and so wanted to preach him to the world.

Having heard Jesus' teaching that the Old Testament was all about him, the disciples then read the Old Testament looking for him and they saw him, not because they were uniquely given divine insight, but because the light of Jesus as revealed in the New Testament shines brightly on the Old Testament for all to see - they were watching the film again, now knowing the end.

Seeing Jesus in the Old Testament is like looking for a good friend in a crowd. When you see your friend, you immediately recognise them. It's not like looking for a stranger we have never met - we know Jesus, so we don't need to go through the steps of a fail-safe method to recognise him.

That is not to say we can't make a mistake - we can initially think we have seen our friend, only later to realise it wasn't them after all. That realisation comes when we take a closer look. So, for increased confidence there are a few tests that we can (and should) apply to any possible shadow of Jesus in the Old Testament. These tests provide assurance that the shadow is real or open our eyes to our mistake.

### The Test of the Original Reader

Think about the difference between seeing a person in two dimensions, such as in a photograph, and seeing them in three dimensions, that is face to face. In the Old Testament the original readers only had a two-dimensional understanding of the text so far as it reveals Jesus - they only saw shadows. But two-dimensional seeing is still good seeing, it is not wrong.

As such, our understanding of an Old Testament text can never go against the understanding that an original reader would have had. This is the first test we should apply. What is revealed by a person's photograph never goes against recognising them in real life.

By way of example, imagine concluding that, because the whole Bible points to Jesus, the tree of the knowledge of good and evil in the Garden of Eden is a shadow of Jesus. As such eating its fruit is symbolic of becoming a Christian, because once eaten, we then understand the difference between good and evil.

This teaching is wrong because an original reader of the Old Testament could never conclude that. Genesis 3 clearly teaches that eating the fruit was to go against God's command. Consequently, eating its fruit cannot be pointing to becoming a Christian.

What about the teaching that Jesus is foreshadowed in Genesis 2:21-24? In these verses God causes Adam to fall into a deep sleep. He then takes one of Adam's ribs from his side and closes up the wound with flesh. Then from the rib, God makes the first woman, to be united to Adam as his bride, much to Adam's joy.

There is no specific reference elsewhere to inform us that this foreshadows Jesus, but there is a pattern. Adam "dies" (falls asleep) as Jesus did, and a wound is made in his side (John 19:34). From his death, a bride is created, Eve for Adam and the church for Jesus. This leads to union (Ephesians 5:31-32) and great joy (John 3:29).

Is that a safe connection with Jesus? Our first test is to ask, how would an original reader have understood it?

In asking this question, it is clear that an original reader would not have understood these verses as pointing to Jesus - they weren't familiar with the end of the film so wouldn't have seen the pattern. But, at the same time, there would have been nothing in their understanding which would have opposed that pattern - their photograph fits the reality.

If elsewhere the Bible taught that deep sleep is not a picture of death, that would contradict the photograph, but instead the Bible affirms sleep as a picture of death (1 Thessalonians 4:13).[2]

This test of the original reader is of great importance. The fuller meaning of any Old Testament text cannot contradict the meaning it would have had for the original hearers. It may add to their understanding, just as seeing the real person adds to the seeing from a photograph, but it never goes against it.

---

2. The association of "deep sleep" with death provides insight to another foreshadow of Jesus in Genesis 15:12-21. Here deep sleep and darkness descending on Abram foreshadow Jesus dying (Matthew 27:45).

## The test of the rest of the Old Testament

Another test we can apply to a possible shadow of Jesus is to ask whether later Old Testament texts, such as the Psalms or Prophets, contradict or support the possible shadow.

To help think this through, consider Gideon. Was Gideon a shadow of Jesus?

In Judges 7:7-25 Gideon defeated the Midianites. In the middle of the night his men approach the enemy camp. Then suddenly they blow on trumpets and smash clay jars to release light so terrifying the enemy that they start to attack each other and run away in panic. Does this foreshadow Jesus' victory over his enemies?

A reading of Isaiah 9:4 is instructive: "For as in the days of Midian's defeat, you have shattered the yoke that burdens them, the bar across their shoulders, the rod of their oppressor."

Isaiah 9:1-7 is the well-known Christmas passage where Jesus is promised as a "great light". In v7 we are told: "He will reign on David's throne and over his kingdom," so there can be no doubt this refers to Jesus.

In v4 the reference to Midian's defeat under Gideon[3] therefore links Gideon to Jesus. Jesus' victory is "as in the days of Midian's defeat" - it fulfils a pattern of victory, light defeating darkness, and so confirms the shadow as correct.

If instead Isaiah had said, "unlike in the days of Midian's defeat," the Old Testament test would reject Gideon as a shadow of Jesus. Likewise, if Isaiah had linked Midian's defeat to winning a battle using sinful means, there would be a clear break with the pattern with Jesus and the shadow should be rejected.

On finding a possible shadow of Jesus, always ask: "Is there anything taught elsewhere in the Old Testament that supports or goes against this shadow of Jesus?" If there is a contradiction, don't cross the bridge - it is dangerous.

---

3. Isaiah 10:26 also refers to the defeat of Midian and adds "at the rock of Oreb" linking back to Judges 7:25. This differentiates this defeat of Midian from their defeat in Numbers 31.

## The test of the New Testament

Confidence that we are on the right track with a possible shadow of Jesus, (or the realisation that we have taken the wrong path), most clearly comes from the New Testament.

When a New Testament text contradicts the possible shadow of Jesus with what it teaches, the dangerous bridge is revealed. God, the supreme author of the Bible, never disagrees with himself. A good question to ask therefore is: "Does the New Testament teach something contrary to the possible shadow we have seen?"

More positively, the New Testament often confirms a possible shadow as real. As we have seen, the New Testament is not a textbook for how to see shadows of Jesus, but it does show us some of the shadows to look for. Where the teaching of the New Testament overlaps with a shadow we have found, we can have great confidence in our understanding.

Broadly there are three types of shadow in the Old Testament which point to Jesus, which are affirmed by the New Testament:

1. Shadows relating to the nature of Jesus.
2. Shadows relating to the role of Jesus.
3. Shadows of an object relating to Jesus.

## Shadows relating to the nature of Jesus

Jesus is both fully God and fully man, unspoilt by sin. This nature of Jesus, both divine and human, is regularly revealed by the Old Testament in shadow form.

The Old Testament Law doesn't just teach what righteousness is, but points us to the righteousness of Jesus (Romans 10:4; 1 John 2:1). The wisdom of Proverbs (particularly Proverbs 8:1-9,12) is not just helpful advice for us, but points to Jesus as "the wisdom of God" (1 Corinthians 1:24). Wherever we read of an act of mercy or grace in the Old Testament we see a shadow of Jesus. Where we see worship (psalms) or dependence on God (prayer) we are seeing something of Jesus, the perfect man in worship or prayer.

## Shadows relating to the role of Jesus

Throughout the Old Testament there are a large number of roles taken up by various characters. Many of these point forward to Jesus.

The role of king is a good example. Whether it's King David or King Solomon or any other king, there is something in their role as king, ruling with authority, which points to Jesus as the King of kings. The same is true for the roles of prophet (bringing God's Word), priest (bringing restored relationship with God), shepherd (leading God's people), saviour, son, suffering servant and many more. In all these roles there is a shadow pointing to Jesus.

Appendix 3 lists the most important roles that are confirmed by the New Testament as pointing to Jesus. For each, examples are provided of relevant Old Testament passages where the shadow can be seen.

---

**EXERCISE**

In chapter 4 we looked at the story of Ehud the left-handed man and his defeat of King Eglon and the Moabites (Judges 3:12-30). Find a bridge from this passage to Jesus.

(The table in Appendix 3 should help if needed)

Suggested thoughts by way of an answer are given on page 279.

---

## Shadows of an object relating to Jesus

Less frequently, an object in the Old Testament may foreshadow Jesus. These shadows are different from shadows of nature or role. Their difference is that, instead of a direct pattern (such as righteousness pointing to Jesus' righteousness or kingly rule pointing to Jesus' kingly rule), their pattern comes through the significance of the object.

Each object has meaning in its Old Testament setting. Consider manna in the desert (Exodus 16), food given by God to sustain life. This significance - its sustaining of life - links the object to Jesus. Jesus is the spiritual "bread of life" (John 6:48) which "anyone may eat and not die" (John 6:50). God's provision of manna in the desert therefore is a shadow of God's provision of Jesus - what is supremely needed to sustain life.

Another example is the Old Testament temple. Its significance is the place of sacrifice and the place of God's presence living in relationship with his people. This links it to Jesus' body, the ultimate temple of God (John 2:19-21), for it is here that God lives with his people (John 1:14) and where the perfect sacrifice is offered (Hebrews 10:14).

Appendix 3 also lists the most important objects supported by the New Testament as pointers to Jesus. For each, there is a summary of its significance.

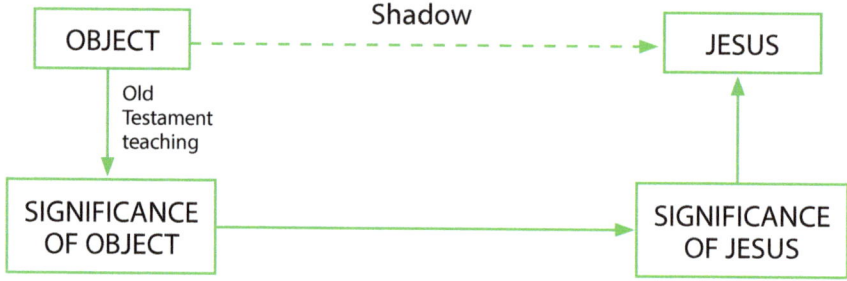

**DANGER TO AVOID**

Having something in common is not the same as being a shadow. To build the tabernacle, Moses is told to use acacia wood (Exodus 26:15). Is this requirement of wood because it points to the wooden cross of Jesus?

To conclude that would be wrong. The error is to forget that a shadow isn't defined by having the same substance as what comes later - a shadow is defined by being a pattern of what is yet to come or being an object with a significance pointing forwards.

In contrast, the altar in the tabernacle, though made of stone, does pattern the cross. Throughout the Old Testament altars are repeatedly, without contradiction, the place of sacrifice - that is their significance. As such they point to the great place of sacrifice, the cross of Jesus.

### Learning from the shadow

Finding a shadow of Jesus in the Old Testament is exciting and it comes with an opportunity. For the shadow itself does more than point to the Jesus we already know; it is given that we might know Jesus better.

Seeing Jesus in the Old Testament is like seeing a photograph of a much older brother, taken before we were born. As we examine the photograph we can recognise our brother, for we know him, but the photograph also teaches us something new about our older brother that we had not known before and could never have known without the photograph.

This is the case with seeing Jesus in the Old Testament. The text doesn't just repeat our understanding - the photograph adds something. Neither is the Old Testament suddenly made irrelevant now that Jesus is revealed. Instead, the Old Testament, like the old photo, helps us to know Jesus better and appreciate him more.

Consequently, when reading the Old Testament, we need to focus on what that text teaches us about Jesus. We must not leave the passage as soon as we see the connection with Jesus, but instead study the old photograph carefully, because that will teach us something new.

This is why all the steps of "MRS WISE Carefully Studies Jesus" are important. They are not just about connecting the passage with Jesus, but about revealing him more clearly. Every passage contains something unique. Even if the teaching is essentially the same, it is never exactly the same. Perhaps it is given in a different way or addresses something from a different angle. The glory of Jesus is infinite and each passage has its own special, unique place in revealing that glory.

In conclusion, the New Testament revelation of Jesus opens our eyes to recognise him in the Old Testament. But at the same time, our new vision of Jesus in the Old Testament sheds light on our previous understanding of him. Understanding Jesus is therefore a glorious and ever-increasing spiral. The two testaments work together with ever increasing clarity.

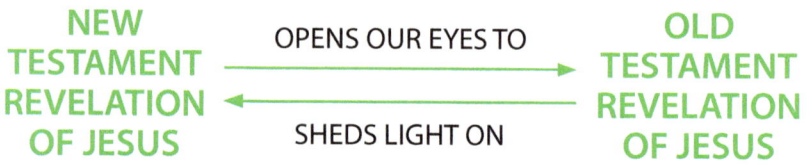

## Question 2: What to do when the shadow doesn't match the reality?

If our first question was how to tell the difference between a true shadow of Jesus and a product of our imagination, our second question has to do with shadows which are true, but appear to point to a very different Jesus.

David, the great king of the Old Testament is a shadow of King Jesus. But what about David's adultery with Bathsheba or his murder of Uriah, her husband? Samson may have been a shadow of Jesus in the moment of his death as he brought a great salvation (Judges 16:27-30), but what about the rest of Samson's life which was characterised by violence and lust? That wasn't anything like Jesus' life. What do we do with such strangely shaped shadows?

The first thing to grasp is that just because something acts a shadow of Jesus in one way, it does not mean it acts a shadow of Jesus in every respect. Where an aspect of a shadow goes against clear teaching elsewhere, that aspect of the shadow can be rejected. But, incredibly, even these contradictions can point to Jesus - not directly, but as negatives of a film.

A film's negative is the exact opposite of the film itself - white appears black and black appears white. On finding a shadow that appears to go wrong therefore, a good question to ask is: "Does this still shadow Jesus, but as a negative? Does it point forward to the need for the exact opposite?"

This is the case with David's acts of adultery and murder. Along with teaching a great deal about sin and the damage sin causes, these events also reveal the need for a much better king. In this strange way they also point forward. What David did serves as a contrast, a negative to what Jesus later does. Instead of a king who selfishly lusts, Jesus selflessly loves. Instead of a king who uses his power to kill and take, Jesus denies his power and lays down his life to give. Even the darkest episodes in the Old Testament point forward to Jesus - these are the Scriptures that testify about him.

### Foreshadows and Fulfilment

Once we have seen and tested a shadow it's important to realise that just as with promises (though less commonly) shadows can have one or more stages of fulfilment. Therefore, on finding a shadow, we need to think through which stage, or stages of fulfilment, it is particularly pointing to.

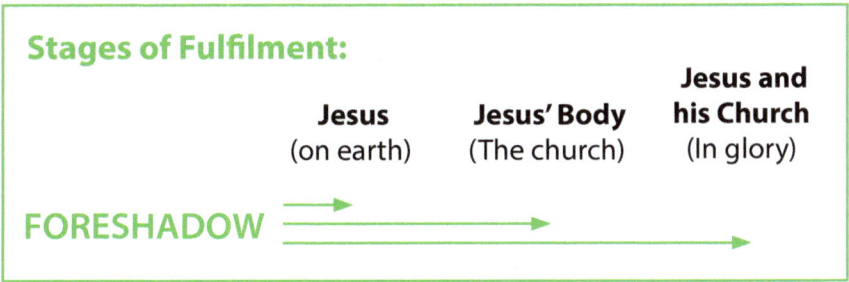

A good example, where multiple levels of fulfilment can be seen, is with the Old Testament temple. Standing in the temple courts, Jesus declares to those nearby (John 2:19):

"Destroy this temple and I will raise it again in three days."

Not surprisingly, on hearing this, the Jews are confused:

"It has taken forty-six years to build this temple, and you are going to raise it in three days?" But we are then told by John: "But the temple he had spoken of was his body."

In this instance, Jesus sees the physical temple as a shadow of his physical body whilst on earth (first stage of fulfilment) for that is where God is present. If the Jews destroy him, he will be raised in three days.

But elsewhere, the temple is a shadow of Jesus' body - the church (second stage of fulfilment), for Jesus is present in the church (Romans 8:9-11). What is more, each member's body is a "temple of the Holy Spirit" (1 Corinthians 6:19) and is being built as "living stones" into a "spiritual house" (1 Peter 2:4-5).

Finally, in Revelation 22:22 we read: "I did not see a temple in the city because the Lord God Almighty and the Lamb are its temple."

This is the end of the coloured thread, the third stage of fulfilment, where the shadow supremely gives way to reality. Here in the heavenly city there is no temple, for there is no need for sacrifice or walls to separate people from God. And yet there is a temple - the Lord God Almighty and the Lamb - the glorious, accessible and eternal presence of God.

## END OF CHAPTER EXERCISES

As in the last chapter, the aim of these exercises is to consider how each of the texts below connects with Jesus. Read the verses and look for patterns that are fulfilled in Jesus. If you need help, refer to Appendix 3. Suggested thoughts are given on pages 279-283.

**Numbers 21:4-9**
**1 Samuel 16**
**Psalm 1:1-3**

# JESUS (PART 3) - BIBLE THEMES

---

*"Oh, the depth of the riches of the wisdom and knowledge of God!*
*How unsearchable his judgements, and his paths beyond tracing out!"*
**Romans 11:33**

"We shall not benefit from reading the Old Testament unless we
look for and meditate on the glory of Christ in its pages."
**John Owen**

---

"Being honest," said Joe with some loss of heart in his voice, "I'm still finding Bible study difficult."

"Me too," added Rachel. "Mrs Wise - you have been so helpful and we are really thankful, but neither of us could find a connection with Jesus in that passage. Bible study is just hard."

The old lady smiled. "That all sounds very normal," she replied, "and very healthy."

Rachel and Joe looked up.

"You have to remember," she continued, "Bible study is not the same as learning maths or science or history. Bible study is about relationship."

She looked intently at the young couple. "We don't read for head knowledge, but to relate to Jesus and meet with him.

Sometimes we forget that and he allows us to struggle so that we come back to him and pray. Spiritual things are spiritually discerned remember, not by following a method or having a superior intellect."

"So it's OK to struggle?" asked Rachel.

"Better than OK!" replied Mrs Wise. "It's beautiful - it shows you want the relationship. It's a good thing. Only, make sure you struggle with his help, depending on him, not on your own abilities!"

---

**DANGER TO AVOID**

When struggling to understand a passage, it can be tempting to allow ourselves to determine what it means. We may do this by asking "What does it mean to me?" rather than by working hard, prayerfully, at what the author meant by the passage.

This "reader response" approach is OK in some modern-day poetry, when the author may intend us to come to our own understanding, but not with the authoritative Word of God. This is God's communication, and we are not at liberty to understand it as we choose. To do so is to ignore God and instead twist God's purpose into our own self-centred ends.

### No need to despair

Having considered promises and patterns in the text, we may now have made a connection with Jesus, or we may have found a possible connection with Jesus that needs testing. Alternatively, like for Rachel and Joe, the passage may have left us completely puzzled.

Regardless, there is no need to despair. The way forward is to continue prayerfully and consider Bible themes which we began to look at in chapter 6. In doing this we will virtually always make progress. Whether it is to confirm an idea as correct, or to find an entirely new bridge, Bible themes are a great way to travel from Bible Land to Today's World and so help answer the crucial question: "What does the text mean now?"

### Bible Themes – Jesus at the centre

As we saw in chapter 6, there are an enormous number of Bible themes, but three are of particular importance: God, People and Relationships. Just as with promises and patterns, Jesus is always central.

For the theme of God, Jesus is the supreme revelation of God. He is "Immanuel", meaning "God with us" (Matthew 1:23). "Anyone who has seen me has seen the Father," declared Jesus (John 14:9).

The same is true for the theme of People. Jesus perfectly reveals humanity. He is the faultless person, the unspoilt image of God, as men and women should be.

Furthermore, Jesus is key to the theme of Relationships. He eternally relates to the Father and the Spirit in the Trinity. Jesus is our means of relationship with God through his saving sacrifice. Jesus is the perfect king ruling over us, the perfect priest representing us to God and the perfect prophet teaching us about God. Jesus is Lord, judge, shepherd, mediator, friend, brother and even husband. Jesus is the perfect model to follow in all our relationships. All themes centre on Jesus.

### How to consider a Bible theme

Back in chapter 6 we began the process of considering a Bible theme. We saw how Bible themes, like coloured threads, weave their way through the Bible and that any event or teaching in a text can make up part of a Bible theme.

Then, our focus was to trace the theme backwards. Our aim was to understand how the theme would have been understood by an original hearer so that we could answer: "What did the text mean then?"

As an example, we saw how "salvation" to an Israelite living at the time of King David, would not have called to mind Jesus' death and resurrection. For them, at that time, those things had not yet happened. "Salvation" would instead have recalled their rescue from Egypt.

At this point, as we consider "What does the text mean now?" we need instead to leave Bible Land. We need to cross the bridge from the specific event or teaching in the text then, to its teaching today. How to do that for Bible themes will be the subject of this chapter.

## Crossing the Bridge with a Bible Theme

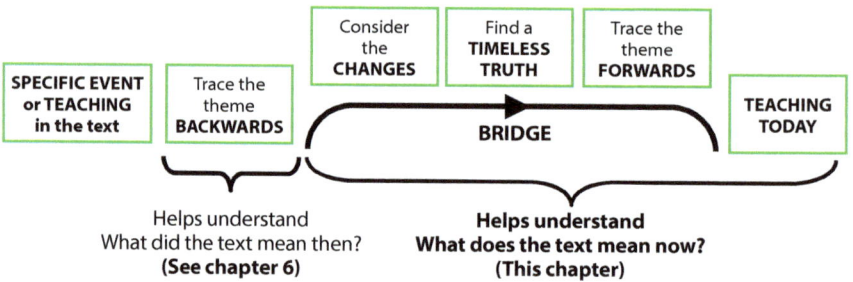

The diagram above describes how to trace a Bible theme that has been identified in a passage, to its teaching today. Don't worry if at first it looks a bit complicated, for with a bit of practice all will become clear.

Let's start on the left-hand side. A specific teaching in the text is something like "God heard the Israelites when they cried out to him, suffering in Egypt" (Exodus 3:7) or "Jesus taught his disciples to pray with 'Our Father in heaven...' etc." (Luke 11:1-4). It is something specific in time and location, described in the text we are looking at.

The first step before we cross the bridge was covered in chapter 6 - we need to "Trace the theme backwards". As we saw in that chapter, this involves understanding what the text meant then, to its original hearers, by examining the teaching or event in the passage in its context, bearing in mind what comes before it.

Once that is done, we can begin to cross the bridge. To do this, first we need to "Consider the changes". This is to ask what has changed between when the Bible was written, back then, and now, in our world today.

Next, we need to "Find a timeless truth" that relates to the content in our passage. This is something taught in the Bible as true over all of time. In the example from Exodus: "God hears his people when they cry out to him under suffering" is a timeless truth, for it never changes over time.

To help in the process of finding a timeless truth, or (once found) to check that our timeless truth is faithful to the Bible, the last step is to "Trace the theme forwards".

This final step effectively tests the bridge. It determines whether our timeless truth makes the bridge safe to cross. Only if it is safe should we cross over. Otherwise, we need to stop, go back and find a better bridge.

### Tracing a Theme Forwards (Checking a Timeless Truth)

So how do we "Trace the theme forwards" and so check the safety of our bridge (the timeless truth)? We need to ask two simple questions:

**1. What does the rest of the Bible teach on this theme?**
In particular: Are there any passages which confirm or contradict the "timeless truth"?

## Confirmation

Sometimes another passage in the Bible will directly reference the text we are studying. A study Bible will often assist in identifying such passages. Help is also provided in Appendix 5 which lists references where the Old Testament is picked up by the New Testament.

In our example of "God hearing the Israelites when they cried out to him under suffering" there are a number of passages which refer to this episode (Numbers 20:16, Deuteronomy 26:7, Acts 7:34). These all confirm that God heard the Israelites as they cried out to him.

Much more often, the rest of the Bible will either teach or repeat our "timeless truth" without directly referring to the passage we are looking at. That "God hears his people when they cry out to him under suffering" is both taught elsewhere as a principle (Exodus 22:23; Luke 18:7-8) and is illustrated in other episodes (Judges 2:18; Psalm 107:6).

Such texts provide confirmation that the bridge is safe to cross.

## Contradiction

If ever the rest of the Bible contradicts the "timeless truth", however, the bridge is revealed as unsafe to cross.

So, what about our example of "God hears his people when they cry out to him under suffering"? Is that ever contradicted? The answer is "yes"! Texts such as 1 Samuel 8:18, Isaiah 1:15 and Micah 3:4 speak of God *not* listening to the prayers of his people and so should make us think hard. A careful look at those passages, though, confirms that the reason God did not hear them was because of their persistent, severe and unrepentant sin. Now, we might want to change the wording of our timeless truth slightly: "God hears his people when they cry out to him under suffering provided, they are not persistently sinning with unrepentant hearts."

---

**ADDITIONAL TIP**

If we can't find a contradiction or confirmation for our "timeless truth" elsewhere in the Bible, a good rule is to keep on looking for these things rather than to jump to a conclusion. Certainly, if something is not confirmed as true by God, it cannot be of great significance, for otherwise God would have revealed it clearly. Even if it is true, we do well not to overstate its importance.

---

**2. How is the theme fulfilled in Jesus?**

This is the most important question to ask, and just as with promises and patterns, Bible themes can be fulfilled in Jesus at number of levels.

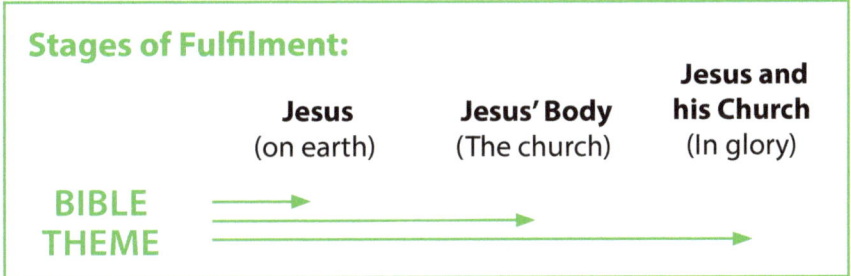

Whilst Jesus was on earth, the theme of crying out to God under suffering, reaches its climax on the cross:

"And at three in the afternoon Jesus cried out in a loud voice 'Eloi, Eloi, lema sabachthani?' (which means 'My God, my God, why have you forsaken me?')" (Mark 15:34).

In quoting Psalm 22:1 Jesus provides insight into the suffering he experienced, and because of a later verse in the psalm, confirms to us that God heard his cry:

"Save me from the lion's mouth, from the horns of the wild oxen. You answered me!" (Psalm 22:21 - CSV).

Today in the church this theme continues. Every time a Christian cries out to God under suffering they are echoing Jesus' cry on the cross and all those cries before him.

Does God hear their cries? Yes indeed, for the whole Bible testifies to the truth that God hears the cries of his people, and that one day in glory, "There will be no more death or mourning or crying or pain, for the old order of things has passed away." (Revelation 21:4). Then suffering will end and rather than calling out to God at a distance "we shall see him face to face" (1 Corinthians 13:12). That is where the coloured thread of this Bible theme ends.

Once we have completed these steps, we have in effect crossed the bridge from Bible Land to Today's World and so answered the question "What does the text mean now?"

### The Three Great Bible themes

Before we conclude the stage of "Understand", for the rest of this chapter we will consider the three great Bible themes. For each, we will take specific teaching points or events in a text and then demonstrate how to cross the bridge to their teaching today.

### The theme of "God"

With the theme of God, the step of "Consider the changes" is simple, because there are no changes. God's character and attributes (such as his power, wisdom, love etc.) never change with time (Malachi 3:6; Hebrews 13:8; James 1:17).

This means that if we learn something about God from one point in history, it is true for all time, including today. Truths about God's character and attributes are "timeless truths"- they form a bridge across to today.

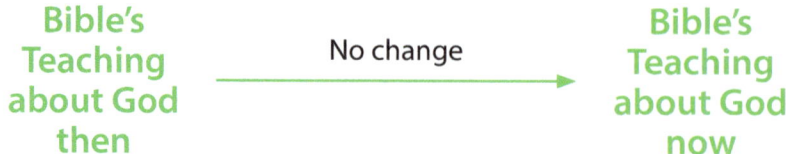

Bible's Teaching about God then — No change → Bible's Teaching about God now

"What does this passage teach about God?" is therefore a wonderful question to ask of any Bible passage, and a great place to return if ever we are struggling to understand a text.

Having said that, it still remains important to "Trace the theme forwards" for this will check our understanding of God. Are there other passages which teach what we have learned about God? Or is there a passage which contradicts it?

"What does this passage teach about God?" is always relevant, for God never changes.

### The theme of "People"

Connecting the second great theme of the Bible, that of "People", to Today's World is also relatively straightforward.

With "People" there are two things that don't change over time - human dignity given by God and sinful human nature. We can trace them backwards or forwards, but human dignity and sinful human nature remain the same. There are two exceptions for sinful human nature. Right at the beginning of time in the Garden of Eden (before sin) and right at the end in the new heavens and new earth (after sin) things are different. Otherwise sinful human nature is exactly the same today as it was then, when the Bible was written.

Using these two unchanging timeless truths we can build bridges:

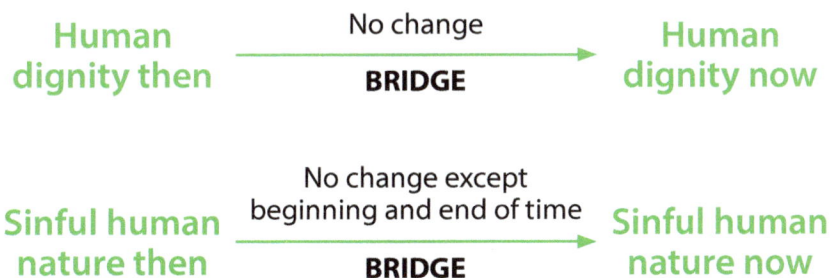

### Example: Human Dignity

**In Revelation 4:11 we read:**

"You are worthy, our Lord and our God, to receive glory and honour and power, for you created all things, and by your will they were created and have their being."

From this verse we could look at the theme of "God". The text teaches about God as creator. Equally, we could look at the verse thinking about the theme of "People".

All people according to this verse were created, and God wills their creation - God values all people.

That dignity was true when the verse was written and is timelessly true today. God doesn't make mistakes. So you and I, and all other people living today, are not just created, but are valued by God. In dealing with difficult people, or if ever we feel unvalued by others, this is a great timeless truth to remember.

### Example: Sinful Human Nature

**In Mark 12:38-40 we read:**

"[38]As he taught, Jesus said, 'Watch out for the teachers of the law. They like to walk around in flowing robes and be greeted with respect in the market-places, [39]and have the most important seats in the synagogues and the places of honour at banquets. [40]They devour widows' houses and for a show make lengthy prayers. These men will be punished most severely.'"

These words of Jesus, spoken to a large crowd, contain a strong specific teaching point for the people of his day - they are to watch out for the teachers of the law. To explain why they are to watch out, Jesus points to various aspects of their behaviour. Jesus teaches with reasoning, but his teaching is specific to the people of his day.

Nowadays, very few places have teachers of Old Testament law walking around in long flowing robes. But that doesn't make Jesus' teaching irrelevant today. To understand its relevance, we need to find a bridge. We need to "Consider the changes" (none with regard to sinful human nature) and then "Find a timeless truth". Once that is done and we have checked our timeless truth by "Tracing the theme forwards", we can cross over to Today's World - we can pick up the specific teaching in Bible Land and discover its teaching for us.

---

**EXERCISE**

Take a look at those verses again. Try to come up with a "timeless truth", an underlying principle (a statement that was true then and which is also true now) behind what Jesus teaches the crowd, and so link his teaching to us today.

HELP: Make sure the timeless truth takes into account all the details of what we are told about the teachers of the law. (There is one which at first may not appear to fit.)

---

In these verses Jesus lists a number of characteristics which describe the teachers of the law. Behind them, and common to these characteristics, is their love of being seen, respected and honoured by people. This underlying truth (concerning their sinful nature) unites what we are told about them.

But did you notice the odd one out? The comment that "they devour widows' houses" isn't connected with them loving to be seen and respected.

Rather than ignoring this, we need to think further. Who were widows? They were amongst the most vulnerable in society. The Old Testament Law commanded that they were to be provided for (Deuteronomy 24:17-21), but according to Jesus, these teachers of the law were doing the exact opposite - taking advantage of them for their personal gain.

Combining this with their love to be seen and honoured, there is an underlying principle or truth. These people may have been leaders, but they used their position for personal gain, they lived for themselves and not for God. Having identified this, we can put together a "timeless truth" which covers everything we are told about them, such as: "Jesus warns against leaders who use their position for personal gain." This, and the promise of severe punishment for such people, is the text's teaching then and (because it is a timeless truth) also its teaching for us today.

Finally, we need to check that this teaching fits with the rest of the New Testament by tracing the theme forwards. In doing this we find passages confirming the teaching (2 Corinthians 2:17, 11:9-13) and in contrast, see servant leadership as our model to follow, supremely demonstrated in Jesus himself (Mark 10:42-45).

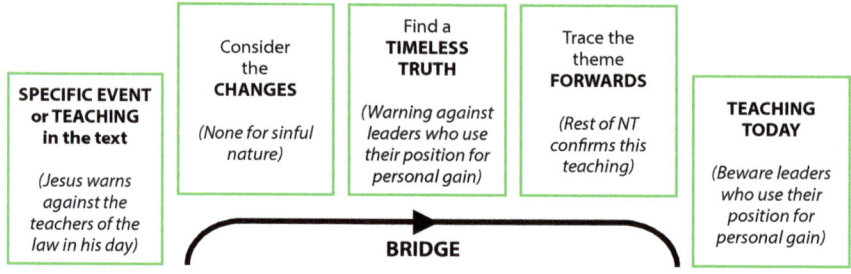

### The theme of "Relationships"

When considering the third great theme of the Bible, that of relationships, finding a bridge to Today's World is more complicated. This is because often there are changes that need to be taken into account. Despite this, the process remains the same:

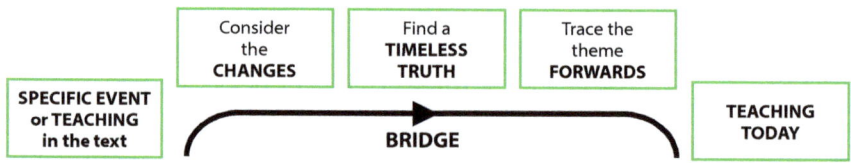

In particular, there are three types of change that need to be considered. For each we will consider a worked example, taking us from the text to its teaching today.

### Covenant Changes (The relationship between God and People)

In the Garden of Eden the relationship between God and people was unaffected by sin. Then Adam and Eve ate the forbidden fruit, sin entered the world and the relationship changed. Since then, there have been further changes in the relationship between God and people, each defined by what are known as "covenants". A covenant is a serious binding agreement describing the arrangement by which one party will relate to another. Marriage is a covenant relationship. A man makes certain promises to his wife and, in return, his wife makes promises to him. These promises then determine their relationship, so that either the covenant is kept or broken, depending on their faithfulness to their promises.

In the Bible, the covenants between God and people are different in that they don't describe a relationship of equals. God initiates the relationship and as sovereign makes promises. To live under his covenant, God's people are then required to accept the terms of the covenant relationship.

In moving from a specific event or teaching point in a text through to what it teaches today about relationships, we must take any covenant changes into account.

God's relationship with people then — Covenant changes / BRIDGE → God's relationship with people now

### Example – Deuteronomy 14:8

By way of example, think of the command in Deuteronomy 14:8 for the Israelites not to eat pork: "The pig is also unclean; although it has a divided hoof, it does not chew the cud. You are not to eat their meat or touch their carcasses."

This was a requirement for God's people then, as it was part of their covenant relationship with God. But to apply that command directly to Christians today would be a mistake, for there have been covenant changes. Christians now live under a different covenant, called the "New Covenant" under which the food laws no longer apply (Mark 7:19).

**Bible Land**                                                              **Today's World**

| Don't Eat Pork | → | Consider Covenant Changes | → | Allowed to eat Pork |

But this doesn't mean that the command to avoid eating pork is completely irrelevant today. Its relevance can be determined by moving to the next step in crossing the bridge - "Find a timeless truth". We need to find a principle behind the command not to eat pork.

So why was the command given?

The answer comes by reading the context. In Deuteronomy 14:1-2 we see that the food laws were given because God's people were to be holy, that is, they were to be different or distinct in their commitment to God. Back then, under that covenant, not eating pork showed that holiness.

Today, under the new covenant, although the food laws have gone, there is still the command for God's people to be holy (1 Peter 1:15-16). As such a timeless truth - "God's people are to be holy" - has been found connecting the teaching in the passage to Today's World.

## Be specific

But having found a timeless truth, we need to be careful not to be too general, for our timeless truth needs to be specific to the teaching of the text. "God's people are to be holy in their eating" is therefore better, but "God's people are to be holy in what they don't eat", is better still.

## The Teaching Today

Finally, to move from the timeless truth to what the passage teaches today, we need to "trace the theme forwards". To do this we must ask what else the Bible says on the identified theme (particularly to those under the new covenant) and we need to ask how the theme is fulfilled in Jesus. What does it mean to be holy in what we don't eat?

When Jesus came to earth as a man, he denied himself the joys of heaven for the sake of others. In doing so he gave up much more than just food. On the cross he emptied himself completely of all that was legitimately his - he laid down his life for you and me (John 10:11; Philippians 2:6-8). In this way Jesus fulfils the theme of holiness in giving up what is legitimately ours for the sake of others. Being holy in what we don't eat is just a small part of a much greater holiness.

Furthermore, the theme of being holy in what we don't eat is specifically taken up in the New Testament and applied to Christians. Some key texts are:

"If your brother or sister is distressed by what you eat, you are no longer acting in love. Do not by your eating destroy someone for whom Christ died." (Romans 14:15)

"All food is clean, but it is wrong for a person to eat anything that causes someone else to stumble. It is better not to eat meat or drink wine or to do anything else that will cause your brother to stumble." (Romans 14:20-21)

"So whatever you eat or drink or whatever you do, do it all for the glory of God. Do not cause anyone to stumble, whether Jews, Greeks or the church of God." (1 Corinthians 10:31-32)

These passages provide further understanding of what it means to be holy in what we don't eat. Our distinctiveness is to be people who reflect the supreme love of Jesus in his denial of self for others, to bring glory to God; and a small part of that is to not cause distress by what we eat. What exactly that means in our particular situation will then need further thought. If we sit down to eat with a friend who is very allergic to fish, it will mean avoiding that on the menu; if they are vegetarian, it will mean a willingness to avoid meat; if they are from a Muslim or Jewish background, it may still mean avoiding pork!

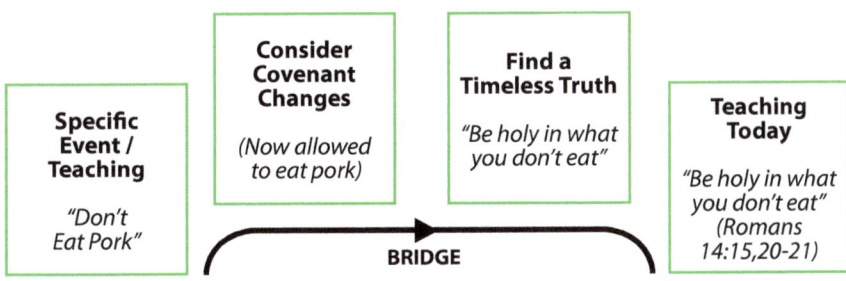

> **ADDITIONAL TIP**
>
> The Bible contains a number of covenants between God and people, made at various times in history. Although not the primary focus of this book, a good understanding of these covenants is extremely helpful. For additional reading Appendix 6 summarises the most important of these covenants, how they relate to one another and their relevance for today.

## Cultural Changes

A second area of change that is relevant to the broad theme of relationships is that of culture. Unlike covenant changes, which do not apply for most of the New Testament (for God's people after Pentecost were under the same covenant as we are today), cultural changes often apply and need to be identified. As before, once these changes have been determined, the key is to find a timeless truth by which we can cross the bridge to the teaching today.

Cultural changes

**Culture then** - - - - - - - - - - - - -▶ **Culture today**

**BRIDGE**

## Example

In four of his New Testament letters, Paul concludes with the instruction to: "Greet one another with a holy kiss." Peter does the same in 1 Peter 5:14, so this practice was clearly normal in 1st-century Israel.

Today kissing someone as a greeting may be perfectly acceptable in some cultures such as those in the Middle East, but where that is not the case, cultural changes need to be considered if we are to move from the teaching of the text to its teaching today.

Just as before, we need to find a timeless truth. What truth or principle is given in Paul's instruction that would equally apply today?

Reading through the letters where Paul brings this instruction reveals divisions within the churches. Although it is not exactly clear what Paul meant by a "holy kiss", it is apparent this was a sign of genuine affection.

Paul was not therefore just seeking a formal ceasefire between the parties he was writing to, but wanting genuine peace and love between them. Paul was instructing a greeting of genuine affection.

With the timeless truth behind Paul's command identified, we can translate his instruction into our own culture. How do we express an attitude of genuine peace and affection?

Each of us will need to work out what it means for our particular culture, but the important thing is Paul's instruction. We are to greet all believers with a sign of genuine affection, even those with whom we have a disagreement. Is there a fellow Christian you are not prepared to greet in this way?

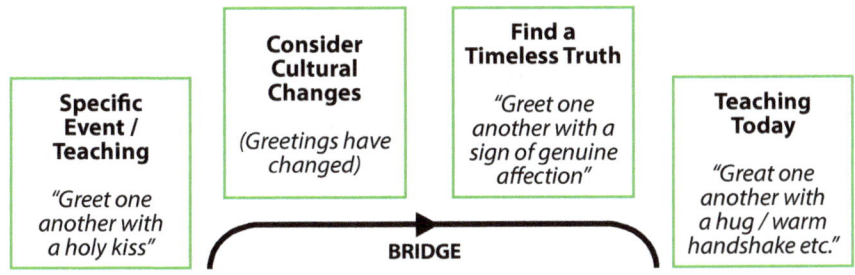

| Specific Event / Teaching | Consider Cultural Changes | Find a Timeless Truth | Teaching Today |
|---|---|---|---|
| "Greet one another with a holy kiss" | (Greetings have changed) | "Greet one another with a sign of genuine affection" | "Great one another with a hug / warm handshake etc." |

BRIDGE

### Enemy Changes

The final change to note when considering the theme of relationships is that between God's people and their enemies.

In the Old Testament the enemies of Israel were the Egyptians, Philistines, Amalekites, Amorites, Moabites etc. But for the Christian, our understanding has been transformed. Consider these two verses:

"Dear friends, I urge you, as foreigners and exiles, to abstain from sinful desires, which war against your soul." (1 Peter 2:11)

"For our struggle is not against flesh and blood, but against the rulers, against the authorities, against the powers of this dark world and against the spiritual forces of evil in the heavenly realms." (Ephesians 6:12)

The principal enemies of God's people now are sin and Satan. That has actually always been the case, but these enemies were illustrated by foreign nations in the Old Testament. The physical nations opposing Israel teach us today about our enemies of sin and Satan. As such, rather than just ignoring certain Old Testament passages as irrelevant for us, or worse still using them to justify war on other people as has sadly been done in the past, we can learn from them. These passages teach us about spiritual warfare.

| Old Testament | | New Testament |
|---|---|---|
| **Enemies of God then** | Enemy changes<br>**BRIDGE** | **Enemies of God now** |
| *(Physical nations)* | | *(Sin / Spiritual forces of evil)* |

### Example

In chapter 2 whilst looking at the first step of "Observe" we considered the armour and weapons of the terrifying Philistine champion Goliath (1 Samuel 17:4-11). We saw how the author spent time to provide us with a detailed description to make Goliath memorable. But what relevance does Goliath have for us today?

By recognising that the enemies of God then, illustrate the enemies of God now, the relevance of Goliath becomes clear. Rather than being a long dead historical figure, Goliath is a picture of Satan - the terrifying leader of the enemies of God, a man too powerful for an ordinary person to defeat.

It's a lesson we need to learn - it's a timeless truth. On our own we can't defeat Satan, for he is too powerful. Yet David, a foreshadow of Jesus our champion, crushes his head (1 Samuel 17:49-51 fulfilling Genesis 3:15), so bringing victory to God's people.

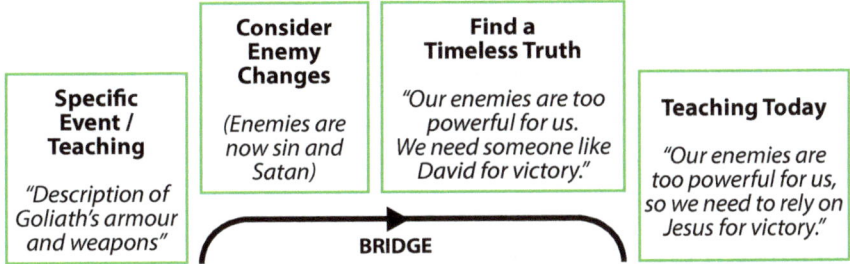

## Remember Jesus

Mrs Wise's face sparkled with excitement.

"Remember, every Bible passage points to Jesus," she remarked.

Joe and Rachel nodded in agreement.

"And we need to be wary of any teaching that you might equally find in a Jewish synagogue," she added. "The Old Testament is as much about Jesus, as the New."

"So easy to get distracted though," Rachel sighed. "But I see now, once you understand how it links with Jesus, all sorts of other things begin to make sense."

"Promises, Patterns and Bible Themes," continued Joe, "They all point to Jesus - I need to remember that!"

> **ADDITIONAL TIP**
>
> Promises, patterns and themes all point to Jesus, the centre of the Bible's teaching. But along with pointing to Jesus, promises, patterns and themes are also used to paint the canvas - the background onto which things related to Jesus are portrayed.
>
> So, there are promises in the Prophets for our future according to our relationship with Jesus. There are patterns such as Babylon for the world in opposition to Jesus, in contrast to Jerusalem which patterns the heavenly city of God. And there are themes, where Proverbs is a good example as it takes up the theme of wise living for those who follow Jesus, wisdom himself. (Appendix 4 lists some of the more important patterns used in this way.)

## Bringing it all together

At this point, having worked through every step of "MRS WISE Carefully Studies Jesus" we will hopefully have gained all sorts of insights into the text we are studying. In particular, we should now appreciate how the passage connects with Jesus. Next, we need to pause.

As we have seen, our key task has been to listen carefully to the author. We have worked through "Observe" and then "Understand" so as to grasp *their* main points and emphasis. Now as we bring our insights together, we need to focus, not on smaller topics in the text which may serve our particular interest, but on humbly accepting all of what God is saying. If we don't do this, we neglect God, for he is the supreme author.

### A summary sentence

To keep God's teaching and emphasis central (rather than picking up on particular things we want to hear) a very useful exercise is to summarise the main teaching of the text in one (ideally short) sentence.

Often this is not easy. But regardless of how successful we are (or are not) in producing a good summary sentence, it is the process of putting one together which is most helpful.

Usually, the best way to start is to list the main teaching points in the text. Typically, these will be timeless truths that can be applied today. Once the list is complete, the question of what holds the points together can be asked. This may be a common theme or a flow of logical thought.

From there we can produce the first draft of our summary sentence.

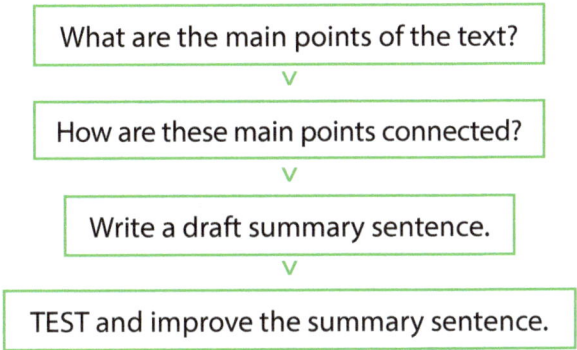

### Key questions to ask

With the first draft completed, the following questions can be used to test and improve our summary sentence. These can be remembered using the word "TEST":

### 1. Is the sentence faithful to the *Teaching* in the text?

Ideally, we need to have understood every verse in the text so that it is covered by our summary sentence.

Re-reading through the passage may identify an area where further insight is needed. Perhaps part of a verse still doesn't make sense or doesn't fit into the flow of the passage. If so, we need to persevere with our prayer and efforts to understand. Often these last puzzles unlock rich treasures.

A great help available to us in such circumstances is our friends. By discussing our insights, thoughts and struggles, greater clarity often comes to our understanding. Another help is that of commentaries. Now is the right time to read these useful books written by people who have spent time studying the Bible. Never forget however, that although commentaries (like good friends) can stimulate thought and challenge us, they may not always be correct. Commentaries are not the final authority - that is always the Bible. The treasure is in the text.

With better understanding we can revise our summary sentence and continue to revise it until our sentence reflects the teaching in the Bible passage as faithfully as possible. The summary sentence needs to reflect the teaching of the text.

## 2. Is the sentence faithful to the *Emphasis* in the text?

Along with being careful to reflect the teaching of the text, our summary sentence also needs to reflect the author's emphasis. Biblical truth needs to go hand in hand with Biblical balance.

If a passage has a great deal to say about God's judgement and then only a concluding remark about his salvation, this should be reflected in our sentence. It may not be so pleasant, but by writing this way, our author wants us to spend time thinking through God's judgement. It is meant to sink in - to affect us. Only then do they break the good news of salvation. If we pass over God's judgement too quickly in order to focus on the good news, we are not being faithful to the author's emphasis.

## 3. Is the sentence faithful to the *Structure* of the text?

Although this is not essential, it's usually very helpful, particularly when teaching a Bible passage, to follow the structure of the text. In his sovereignty God has arranged order in the Scriptures, structuring them as he has chosen. If we change that order, there will be more of us in what is heard and less of God. So where possible, follow the structure provided, particularly where the text develops a logical argument.

## 4. Is the sentence faithful to the *Tone* in the text?

As every parent will know, there are a great number of ways for a child to say "sorry" or, for a parent to instruct a child who has done wrong. The words are one thing; the tone in which they are said is another.

Discerning an author's tone is never easy. Is the author being encouraging, patient, forceful or despairing? It's not easy as we only have written words on a page, but as we have seen authors leave clues. A good summary sentence should reflect the author's tone.

---

**ADDITIONAL TIP**

For Bible teachers the importance of writing a good summary sentence reflecting the teaching, emphasis, structure and tone of the text cannot be overstated. Such a sentence can then be used to ensure that Bible study questions are most helpful or that a sermon reflects the teaching, emphasis, structure and tone of the text. Time spent here for a Bible teacher will produce the fruit of clarity and simplicity, but above all faithfulness to God and his Word.

---

### END OF CHAPTER EXERCISES

If you are only able to do one exercise, please spend your time in 2 Kings 2:19-24 as this is taken up further in the next chapter.

Suggested thoughts on each exercise can be found on pages 283-286.

### 2 Kings 2:19-24

At the end of chapter 7, in the exercises, we began to consider this passage. We saw how understanding the situation throws light on the text. Jericho was a place known for its curse, yet it received God's blessing. Bethel in contrast, known for its blessing, received God's curse.

Now we need to move forward in time and cross the bridge that we might grasp its teaching for us today.

### Read 2 Kings 2:19-24 - How does this text point to Jesus?

Remember to look for patterns and themes:
- Who patterns Jesus is this passage? And why?
- Which themes picked up in this passage find their climax in Jesus?
  (See Galatians 3:10-14; Ephesians 1:3; John 3:36; Matthew 25:34,41)

### What timeless truths connect the passage to Today's World?
### Write a summary sentence for the main teaching of the passage today.

**The Theme of God's Curse**

In chapter 6 we traced the theme of God's curse from Genesis to Deuteronomy ending with some terrible descriptions of the curses promised to the Israelites if they disobeyed God's commands (Deuteronomy 28:15-68).

Let's now cross the bridge from Bible Land to Today's World so that we might understand the relevance of this passage in Deuteronomy for us today.

**Read Deuteronomy 28:15-68**

**Consider the changes** - What has not changed? What has changed? (Consider God, People and Relationships)
HELP: How is the theme of God's curse fulfilled in Jesus?
(Galatians 3:13-14)
HELP: How is the theme of God's curse fulfilled at the end of time?
(Matthew 25:41-46; Revelation 22:3)

**Find a timeless truth** - (There are a number of these)

**Trace the theme forwards** - Check that your timeless truths are supported by the rest of the Bible (e.g. Daniel 9:11; Malachi 2:2; John 3:36; Romans 5:1, 8:1-4; 2 Peter 2:14)

Summarise the relevance of the teaching in Deuteronomy 28:15-68 for today.

# STAGE 3: APPLY

"The Bible was not given for our information
but for our transformation."
**Dwight L. Moody**

# CHAPTER 11

## APPLICATION (KEY PRINCIPLES)

---

*"Do not merely listen to the word,*
*and so deceive yourselves. Do what it says."*
**James 1:22**

"The Bible will always be full of things you cannot understand, as
long as you will not live according to those you can understand."
**Billy Sunday**

---

Rachel and Joe sat down on the garden bench, soaked in sunshine.

"How did you two get on looking at that short passage in 2 Kings?"
enquired Mrs Wise.

"It was a bit strange," replied Joe.

"At first, it didn't seem to have any relevance," added Rachel. "Elisha
throwing salt into bad water to make it good and…"

Joe interrupted: "…bears coming out of a wood to deal with some
rude boys." There was a brief pause before Joe quietly added, "I wouldn't
mind that for some of the boys I teach at school!"

"We made some real progress, thanks to your help," Rachel added
quickly with a smile. She knew Joe's real reputation. He was one of the
kindest teachers at St. Luke's.

Rachel and Joe went on to explain their understanding of the passage, much to the delight of Mrs Wise.

"I think," replied Joe, "Elisha is the one who brings God's Word, so perhaps he foreshadows Jesus?"

"That's what I reasoned," added Rachel, "Elisha is a pattern of Jesus."

"So how do you think it applies?" Mrs Wise asked. "What relevance does it have for us today? Can we call on God to bring out bears from the woods?"

"Ur... I'm not sure about that," replied Joe.

"I think, the passage teaches that we need to pay attention to God's Word," added Rachel, "then, like the people in the passage, we will be blessed."

A clear smile appeared on Mrs Wise's face. "And I was hoping you might have some good practical tips for how to do that."

A few moments passed before Mrs Wise replied. "Yes, but you need to be careful," she said. "Application is not the same as activity. It is much more, and practical things rarely come first in application."

"But that's what I look for!" replied Joe. "Little things I can do to change the way I live."

"Those are important," replied Mrs Wise, "but they come much later; our focus as we start, must be elsewhere."

## Key principles

When considering "Understand" we examined some key principles that we need to keep at the forefront of our minds. We saw how the Bible doesn't speak directly to us, but speaks first to the original hearers and then to us. We were reminded of the importance of seeing in a text only what is actually there, as opposed to what we might want to see, and how we must rely on God for our every insight.

Now as we consider how to apply the text, there are further principles to keep at the forefront of our minds.

## Be God centred

Just as with "Understand", the main danger for "Apply" comes from within our sinful hearts. Jeremiah 17:9 tells us:

"The heart is deceitful above all things".

A good question to ask of ourselves, therefore, is whether there is anything in us that will act as an obstacle to faithful application of the passage. But even with that question we need to be careful, for first and foremost, the deception of sin is to focus on ourselves rather than on God. We must never forget this. It is quite possible to come up with all sorts of good applications and yet, at the same time, move the focus from God to us. When that happens, however "good" the application, the deceit of our sinful hearts will have won the day.

The counter is to start our application with the question: "What is God saying about God in this passage?" The Bible is, above all, God speaking about God.

Before concentrating on ourselves, or even asking whether there is something in us which opposes faithful application, our aim should be to have our hearts filled with a sense of God. Then, with an awareness of his sovereignty, grace, holiness and wisdom, once we have seen and marvelled at the glory of God, with hearts transformed by that vision of him, we will want to sit at his feet and ask what he wants of us.

### God's priority in application

Another tendency can be to focus on activity, like Rachel and Joe. We naturally look for things to do, little practical things to change in our lives, in response to what we have learned.

That's not wrong, but it is rarely the Bible's key application and usually comes last. Furthermore, it can be dangerous, for if the spotlight is primarily on what we do, our sinful nature may twist our activity into feeling good about ourselves or despairing of ourselves. Either way we push Jesus aside.

So what is God's priority for us in application?

To answer this important question, consider Paul's well-known passage in his letter to the Romans:

"28And we know that in all things God works for the good of those who love him, who have been called according to his purpose. 29For those God foreknew he also predestined to be conformed to the image of his Son, that he might be the firstborn among many brothers and sisters." (Romans 8:28-29)

Spend a moment looking at those verses: What are we taught about God's will for our lives?

God's will, we are told, in all things is to work for our good. Our "good" is then explained as being "conformed to the image of his Son". That's incredible! It means that God's application for us, from every Bible passage, is that we might become more like Jesus.

To become more like Jesus involves what we do, but it signifies much more. We are to think like Jesus, be motivated like Jesus, trust like Jesus, feel like Jesus, love like Jesus, and many other things. Consequently, God's application for us is much bigger than little practical tasks. God wants to change our very selves - our hearts, minds and attitude - indeed everything about us. By way of example consider Acts 3:1-10:

"1One day Peter and John were going up to the temple at the time of prayer - at three in the afternoon. 2Now a man who was lame from birth was being carried to the temple gate called Beautiful, where he was put every day to beg from those going into the temple courts. 3When he saw Peter and John about to enter, he asked them for money. [4]Peter looked straight at him, as did John. Then Peter said, 'Look at us!' [5]So the man gave them his attention, expecting to get something from them.

[6]Then Peter said, 'Silver and gold I do not have, but what I do have I give you. In the name of Jesus Christ of Nazareth, walk.' [7]Taking him by the right hand, he helped him up, and instantly the man's feet and ankles became strong. [8]He jumped to his feet and began to walk. Then he went with them into the temple courts, walking and jumping, and praising God. [9]When all the people saw him walking and praising God, [10]they recognised him as the same man who used to sit begging at the temple gate called Beautiful, and they were filled with wonder and amazement at what had happened to him."

There is a great deal of teaching in this passage. This is the first specific episode that Luke records after Pentecost and Peter's sermon. It shows us clearly that Jesus is continuing his work through the church. There is a lesson for how much better the good news is than material riches, we see the ongoing fulfilment of prophecy (Isaiah 35:6) and there are clear eye-witness details to testify to the truth of what happened.

But the emphasis is different. Note the name of the place where this miracle happens - it's an additional detail repeated twice: at the gate "Beautiful," because what happens is beautiful. A man, lame from birth, a beggar who has so little, a beggar who doesn't even ask for healing is instantly healed and walks and jumps and praises God.

This passage, first and foremost, speaks to our hearts. The crowd "were filled with wonder and amazement at what had happened" and we too are meant to feel the same. This was beautiful. We have a gracious, loving, powerful and kind God. To be like Jesus we need to love God with all our hearts, so this passage speaks to our hearts - engaging them, for a greater appreciation of God. The passage contains virtually nothing by way of application that is very practical, but there is something else, far more important.

So, if God's chief application is for us to become more like Jesus, how does that happen?

2 Corinthians 3:18 is instructive: "And we all, who with unveiled faces contemplate the Lord's glory, are being transformed into his image with ever increasing glory, which comes from the Lord, who is the Spirit."

This verse reminds us that the work of transforming believers into the image of Jesus is the work of the Holy Spirit. But it also informs us of how he does his work - it is as we "contemplate the Lord's glory," that is, as we see Jesus.

Earlier we listened to Jesus' own words about the Bible: "These are the very Scriptures that testify about me" (John 5:39). Put these things together and what do you have? The Holy Spirit works to transform us into the likeness of Jesus as we see Jesus' glory through the words of the Bible.

### Be specific: What is the application of this particular text?

If the key to "Observe" is to "Read, read and read again" and to "Understand" is "Ask questions, again and again", the key to application is: "Be specific to the text".

Each Bible passage is unique. This doesn't mean that every part of the Bible teaches something completely different. Many texts may teach the same truth, but each Bible passage will communicate that truth in its own special way and so apply its message differently.

Failure to listen carefully to what is unique in a passage will inevitably lead to a blunting of the message that is heard and applied. The sharpness of the double-edged sword is lost and its power to change lives is weakened.

So how do we ensure our application is specific to the passage being studied?

### Consider the application to the original hearers

Just as when considering "Understand", we need to start the step of "Apply" in Bible Land rather than in Today's World. To do this we need to ask how the passage would have applied to the original hearers. Working out the author's intention for them will unlock the divine author's specific intention for us.

Often working out the application for the original hearers is easy, for it is given in the text. Addressing his hearers, James says: "My dear brothers and sisters, take note of this: everyone should be quick to listen, slow to speak and slow to become angry" (James 1:19). This is clearly telling them what they should do.

Alternatively, there may be an application in the text given by a character in the story. Joshua addressing the people of Israel says: "Now fear the LORD and serve him with all faithfulness. Throw away the gods your ancestors worshipped beyond the River Euphrates and in Egypt, and serve the LORD." (Joshua 24:14). Here the author of the book speaks (through Joshua), to encourage his original hearers to do the same.

For many passages of Scripture however, there is no specific application given in the text. For these passages, such as the story of when Elisha visits Jericho to heal its waters and then visits Bethel only to bring bears out of the woods, we need to think harder. The key is once again to put ourselves into the shoes of the original hearers.

So how would that passage apply to them? In our study we saw how an original reader would pick up on the significance of the places mentioned. Jericho was a place previously cursed by God, but it was blessed; whereas Bethel, a place previously blessed by God, was cursed. This understanding of how the original hearer would respond leads to the application for them - comfort for those who felt they were under God's curse and a warning to those complacent about God's blessing.

## Crossing the Bridge for Application to Today's World

Once the application to the original hearers is identified, we are well placed to find an application which forms a bridge into Today's World.

Again though, just as with the step of "Understand", we need to be careful. Making an application straight from the text to ourselves is likely to lead to error - we need to avoid the "crocodiles". We need a safe bridge to cross from application then, to application now.

To find a safe application bridge there are two essential tasks. First, we need to "Connect the characters" and then we need to "Connect the application".

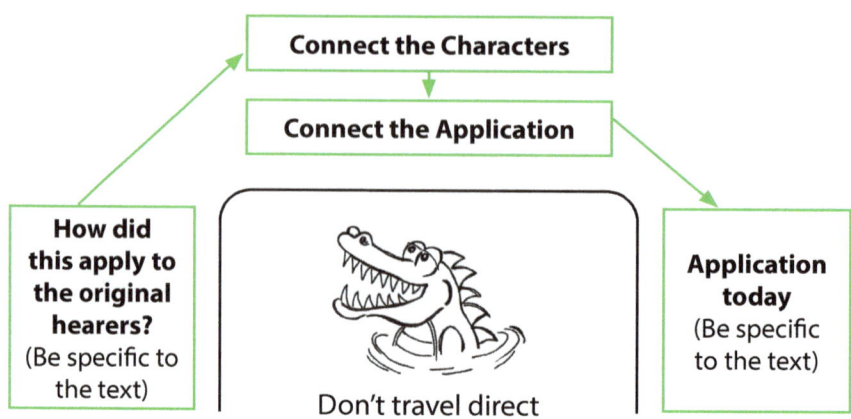

## Connect the Characters

Our first task is to think through who today, is the equivalent of those characters in the Bible text. The table below gives examples of possible equivalents to consider.

| BIBLE LAND | | TODAY'S WORLD | EXAMPLE TEXT |
|---|---|---|---|
| Old Testament | New Testament | | |
| God | | God | Exodus 34:6-7 |
| Foreshadow of Jesus | Jesus | Jesus (Exalted in glory) | See Appendix 3 Matthew 11:29 |
| O.T. Prophets | N.T. Apostles | No equivalent (The Bible) | Mark 6:8 John 16:13 |
| Leaders of God's People | | Church Leaders | 2 Timothy 4:1-2 |
| False Prophets | False Teachers | False Teachers | 2 Peter 2:1 |
| Political Leaders | | Political Leaders | Psalm 2:10-12 |
| People of God (Israelites) | People of God (Christians) | People of God (Professing Christians) | Isaiah 1:16-20 Romans 12:1-2 |
| Enemies of God* | | Those opposed to Jesus | Luke 11:39-52 |
| All people | | All people | Mark 8:34-38 |

*See Chapter 10. These may foreshadow sin / Satan. They may also illustrate people living as enemies of God.

This process of thinking through the equivalent characters is extremely important if we are to avoid "crocodiles". Take Jesus' words in John 16:13:

"But when he, the Spirit of Truth, comes, he will guide you into all truth. He will not speak on his own; he will speak only what he hears, and he will tell you what is yet to come."

How does this verse apply today?

Rather than immediately hearing the "you" in this verse as applying directly to us, we need to remember to "Connect the characters". These words were spoken to the original disciples, the apostles of Jesus, not to ordinary believers. As such there is no direct link to believers today, for we are not apostles as they were. Our words are not those of "all truth" as theirs were. To claim that authority for us is wrong. To apply the words like that, directly to ourselves, is to be eaten by "crocodiles".

But that doesn't mean this verse has no application for us. First, it confirms the reliability of the New Testament as "all truth". The New Testament was written by these very apostles (or those very closely associated with them), so we have Jesus' promise of its reliability. Secondly, this passage applies to us, because it teaches us something about the Holy Spirit - he is the Spirit of Truth.

The Holy Spirit now lives in believers (1 Corinthians 6:19) and, being God, his nature does not change. This doesn't mean the Holy Spirit will lead Christians today into all truth with the same level of understanding that the apostles were promised. But if we are struggling to make sense of a text, it does mean we can approach God in prayer with confidence, for the Holy Spirit's very nature is to reveal truth.

"Connecting the characters" is important, but sometimes it is far from straightforward. One reason is because some people in the Bible connect at a number of different levels. King David in the Old Testament is a good example. As we have seen, King David often acts as a shadow of Jesus. Just as David was a saviour, so Jesus is the saviour; just as David was a great king, Jesus is the King of kings.

On the other hand, David sometimes connects to people today

by virtue of his role as a leader of God's people, or just as an ordinary person. For every passage we need to think hard as to which way of connecting is appropriate.

One of the most tragic stories in the Bible is in 2 Samuel 11 where David sees the beautiful Bathsheba bathing as he walks on the roof top of his palace. Soon he has not only committed adultery with her, but has arranged for Uriah her husband, to be brutally murdered.

Who in this episode does King David connect to in Today's World? Take a moment to think that through.

As a human being, he connects with all of us, for we all face sexual temptation and, once we have sinned, the temptation to cover up what we have done. As a leader he also connects with political and church leaders today. The power that comes with such a position can easily be misused, so the story contains a particular warning to those in leadership. Finally, as we saw in chapter 8, David connects with Jesus - not because he foreshadows Jesus in these terrible events, but because he is the exact opposite - he reveals the need for a very different king, one who doesn't sin. As we apply the passage, we need to think carefully to "Connect the characters".

Let's now return to the passage with Elisha in 2 Kings 2:19-25 that Rachel, Joe and Mrs Wise were discussing. How do we "Connect the characters" here?

As we have seen, Elisha is a shadow of Jesus, for he brings the Word of God. The people in Jericho are believers - they welcome Elisha and ask for his help. On the other hand, the youths who reject Elisha and mock him connect with those who reject Jesus and mock him today.

This is a good start, but we must remember that, when making an application, the key is to "Be specific to the text". We need to connect as accurately as we can, so as not to lose the uniqueness of the passage and the sharpness of the Word of God.

These youths are not just those who mock Elisha, but those who come out of Bethel - a place known for being blessed by God. Their equivalent today is not people who have no knowledge of God, but those who do, those who know about his blessing. Their specific equivalent today is therefore "church-going" people, people who should know better, who yet reject and mock the Word of God.

## Connect the Application

Once we have "Connected the characters", our next task is to "Connect the application". To be effective, our bridge must not just find the equivalent people today, but also take us from the application then (in Bible Land), to our application today.

To do this, we can take the same approach as when looking at Bible themes. Then we saw how helpful it is to find a "timeless truth", a connecting principle to take us over the bridge. For application the process is identical - if we can find a timeless truth, we can then cross the bridge and "Connect the application".

In the passage with Elisha, there are two timeless truths: "receive the Word of God and you will be blessed" and "reject the Word of God and you will be cursed". These both apply at all times. As such, we can safely cross over from the application then, to the application today.

Again, however, we need to "Be specific to the text". The uniqueness of this passage is that blessing comes to a place associated with a curse, and a curse comes to a place associated with blessing. Now the application has more impact - no matter how much hardship we have experienced in the past, or how much we may feel under the curse of God, receiving Jesus and his words will bring blessing. On the other hand, no matter how much blessing we may have received in the past, if we reject Jesus and pay no attention to his Word, we invite his curse.

> **ADDITIONAL TIP – Examples to Follow and Warnings to Avoid**
> Bible passages often teach us by providing inspiring examples of behaviour to follow (Romans 15:4) or the exact opposite - warnings of behaviour to avoid (1 Corinthians 10:6,11).
>
> As we consider application, we may see a possible example to follow or a warning to avoid in the passage. But we need to remember that passages that describe a one-off event, in history,

are doing just that. They may provide an example for us to follow or a warning to avoid, but equally, they may not.

To decide between these two possibilities and avoid the danger of jumping to conclusions, we need to ask whether the Bible repeats the example or warning elsewhere or, contradicts it elsewhere. Better still, we need to ask whether there is a timeless truth behind the example or warning.

In 2 Kings 2 blessing is brought to Jericho. On its own, that doesn't mean blessing will be brought to us. But because there is a timeless truth behind what happens, namely "receiving the Word of God brings God's blessing," that serves as a bridge to "Connect the application" to today. This timeless truth is illustrated, indeed taught elsewhere (Mark 4:20; James 1:25) and never contradicted, so the people of Jericho become an example for us to follow.

| Some instances of "Examples to Follow" and "Warnings to Avoid" | |
|---|---|
| **Examples to Follow** | |
| **God** | 1 Peter 1:15-16 |
| **Jesus - The Son of God** | John 13:15; 1 Peter 2:21 |
| **Abraham** (Genesis 22) | James 2:20-24 |
| **Elijah** (1 Kings 17-19) | Romans 11:1-5; James 5:16-18 |
| **The people of faith of the OT** | Hebrews 11, 12:1 |
| **Job** | James 5:10-11 |
| **Paul** | 1 Corinthians 4:16, 10:32-11:1 Philippians 3:17,4:9; 2 Thess 3:6-9 |
| **Timothy and Epaphroditus** | Philippians 2:19-29 |
| **Warnings to Avoid** | |
| **Cain** (Genesis 4) | 1 John 3:12 |
| **Balaam** (Numbers 22-23) | 2 Peter 2:15 |
| **People of Sodom & Gomorrah** (Genesis 19) | Jude 7; 2 Peter 2:6 |
| **Israel in the Desert** | 1 Corinthians 10:6-11; Hebrews 4:11 |

**EXERCISE**

**Read Mark 6:7-13**

Connect the characters: Who are today's equivalent to the characters in this passage?

Connect the application: What is the application to the people in the passage? How can we apply this to ourselves today?

For suggested thoughts in response to these questions please see pages 286-288.

## Translate the Application

Once we have found a "timeless truth", we are ready to cross the application bridge to Today's World. Often however, on arrival, we will need to do some "translation" for our application today.

In Joshua 24:14 (mentioned earlier) Joshua addresses the people of Israel:

"Now fear the LORD and serve him with all faithfulness. Throw away the gods your ancestors worshipped beyond the River Euphrates and in Egypt, and serve the LORD."

How does this apply today?

First, we need to "Connect the characters". Here the application is to the Israelites, so the equivalent is God's people today, Christians. Next, we need to "Connect the application" using a timeless truth. In this verse a timeless truth is given to us - we are to "fear the LORD and serve him with all faithfulness." That is something that is often repeated in the Bible and never contradicted. It applies to all times and so also to us.

However, the specific application needs translation. The Israelites were to "throw away the gods your ancestors worshipped beyond the River Euphrates and in Egypt." Today we no longer worship those gods. So how does that translate into an application for today?

As always in the step of "Apply", we need to be specific. It's not wrong to list off all the general "gods" that people cling onto today, such as the gods of money, power, popularity and personal enjoyment. To throw away those is to "fear the LORD and serve him with all faithfulness." But it is better to think through the equivalent of the specific gods mentioned in the text. Why was it so difficult to throw away these gods? The answer in the passage is that these were gods their ancestors worshipped. These were not new fashionable gods that came and went with the times, but gods deeply rooted in their culture - their culture as God's people.

Which false gods that people worship are deeply rooted in your church culture today? The answer is the specific application of this passage, and these false gods need to be thrown away. For the step of "Apply" - be specific.

In the next chapter we will look further at how to be specific in our application. Meanwhile please enjoy the end of chapter exercise.

## END OF CHAPTER EXERCISE

After reading the text, aim to spend a few minutes thinking through your answer. Once you have drawn your conclusions, compare them with the suggested thoughts on pages 288-290.

**Read Deuteronomy 7:1-6**

Understanding the application for the original hearers is easy enough in this passage. But to apply it as directly speaking to us, would be very wrong. So how does it apply today?

**Connect the characters:** Who are the equivalent two sets of people in this passage today? (HELP: See the table on page 226.)

**Connect the application:** Look for timeless truths in the passage. (HELP: See 1 Peter 1:15 and 1 Peter 2:9)

**Translate the application:** How do we apply "you must destroy them totally" and "make no treaty with them" and "do not intermarry with them"? Remember to be specific.

# APPLICATION (CHRIST)

---

*"...whoever looks into the perfect law that gives freedom*
*and continues in it - not forgetting what they have heard*
*but doing it - they will be blessed in what they do."*
**James 1:25**

"Apply yourself wholly to the text;
apply the text wholly to yourself."
**Johann Albrecht Bengel**

---

"Connect the characters and connect the application. I think I am getting this." declared Rachel.

"And don't be eaten by crocodiles!" added Joe.

"Exactly!" replied Mrs Wise. "Always find a good bridge from Bible Land to the here and now."

"And be specific," she added after a pause. "We must listen carefully to the author, not impose ourselves on the text. To leave the author's purpose behind is to become a car without an engine - no power."

"Oh yes, I remember that" added Joe, "the text stops speaking in the same way. 1 Thessalonians, wasn't it? No longer will God's Word come with power, with the Holy Spirit and deep conviction."

### One truth - many applications

Throughout this book we've seen the great importance of the author's purpose. But from the one main purpose or teaching point there may be many different applications.

Think of sunlight (white light) shining into a shower of rain. Just as the light is divided into all the colours of the rainbow, so one main teaching point from an author can produce many applications of different colours.

To help think through these various colours of application, all coming from the white light of the main purpose of the text, we need to remember the word **CHRIST**. This completes our memory aid for Bible study: **MRS WISE** Carefully **S**tudies **Jesus CHRIST.**

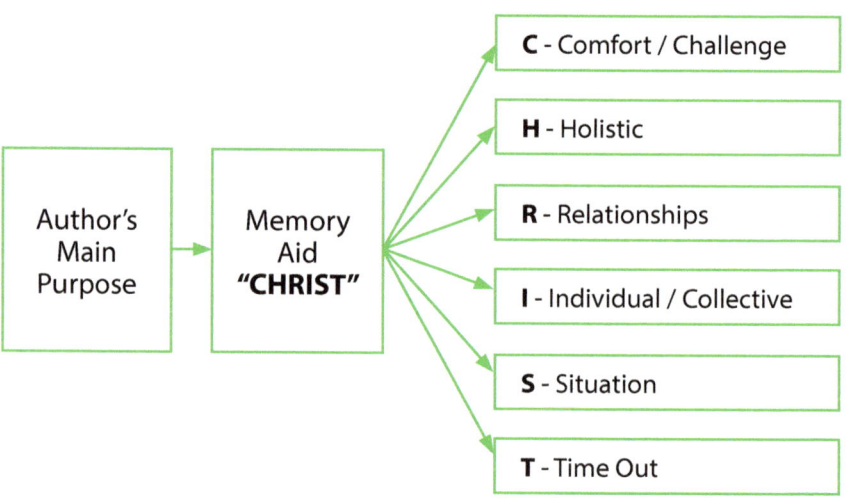

## C in "CHRIST" is for Comfort and Challenge

The first simple way in which application from a passage can be divided is to think about comfort and challenge. In his wisdom, God has ensured that in virtually every Bible passage there is both comfort and challenge. Listen to 2 Timothy 3:15:

"All Scripture is God-breathed and is useful for teaching, rebuking, correcting and training in righteousness so that the servant of God may be thoroughly equipped for every good work."

In this verse there are two positives (two comforts) - teaching and training, and there are two negatives (two challenges) - rebuking and correcting.

Teaching is to inform of the truth and motivate a positive response to the truth - it is to comfort. And to train in righteousness is to empower someone to keep going in the right direction. Like a parent holding a child's hand and encouraging them to continue on the right path, it is comforting. When we suffer and struggle, there is comfort in the Bible - teaching and training to keep going.

But on the other hand, when we are complacent, proud and self-confident, there is challenge. The Bible rebukes wrong thinking, beliefs and behaviour and corrects us - it calls us to change. The picture here is of a child travelling in the wrong direction being taken by the hand and lovingly being turned around.

For every passage we should ask:

- How does this passage bring comfort? (How does it teach and train?)
- How does this passage bring challenge? (How does it rebuke and correct?)

---

**ADDITIONAL TIP**

When considering comfort and challenge it is important to ask: "How does *this passage* bring comfort and challenge?" Each Bible passage is unique, so we need to think carefully about what is specific to the passage concerned. For comfort, the Word of God should taste like nourishing food (Matthew 4:4; Psalm 34:8), for challenge, we should feel the sharpness of the double-edged sword (Hebrews 4:12). Anything else falls short of the application intended.

---

### H in "CHRIST" is for Holistic

Good application is holistic - that is, it involves the whole person. Jesus himself teaches this in Luke 10:27 when referring to the greatest commandment: "Love the Lord your God with all your heart and with all your soul and with all your strength and with all your mind."

Jesus' emphasis here is on the repeated "all". He is not just saying that every part of us is to love God, but *all* of every part of us should love God - good application is holistic.

In describing the heart, soul, strength and mind, Jesus describes four aspects of who we are as people. The four overlap considerably in biblical thought, but there is enough difference to consider each separately for the purposes of good application.

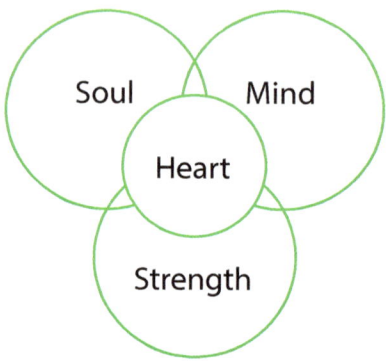

## 1. Our Heart

The heart in biblical thought is the centre of who we are. The heart is our headquarters - it drives us and defines us. Consequently, the heart determines what we value and trust. It directs our attitudes and is the place where we worship. The heart is in fact the most important part of us.

Application to the heart is therefore crucial. If the Word of God is not applied to our hearts, it's not really applied to us at all.

And because we can hide our heart, we can deceive others. We can look good on the outside, appearing to apply the Bible; yet be very different at the centre of our being, in our hearts.

Furthermore, sin in the heart is so deceitful we can even deceive ourselves. Outward visible change may persuade us that we are good enough, whilst our hearts remain just as sinful as before. In application it is always good therefore, to reflect and ask whether there has been any change in the heart - in what we trust in and value and worship. If there has been no impact here, we may been living with deceit. Application must be to the heart, the very centre of our being.

**Questions for application to the heart include:**

How does this passage reveal God as the one to be supremely valued, praised and worshipped?

What does this passage teach us to value and put our trust in? What would it mean for us to value and trust these things?

What false gods (delights / things of value) does this passage tell us to avoid? Are our hearts avoiding them?

## 2. Our Soul

As mentioned above, there is a great deal of overlap with these four aspects of who we are. The emphasis when considering the soul is to see it as the place of our emotions and desires. The soul determines what we love and what we hate, what makes us angry and what makes us happy - the soul is the place of our feelings.

**Questions for application to the soul include:**

What emotional impact is the text meant to have on its hearers?

What is there here that makes me stop? Stop in fear and so repent, or stop in wonder and so praise?

How does this passage comfort and how does this passage challenge at the level of what I feel?

**ADDITIONAL TIP**

To aid application to the heart and soul, it can be helpful to use "heart words" in the questions we ask. Such words help us to focus on our desires, values and emotions, rather than on external actions.

Examples might include:

Is there anything that I react to as unfair, sad, challenging or frustrating? Why is that? What does that reveal about me?

What is there here that is appealing, meaningful, invigorating or makes me happy? Why is that? What does that reveal about me?

### 3. Our Strength

By "strength" Jesus means the strength of our will - the power to do what we should do, as opposed to what we sinfully want to do. Application to our "strength" therefore concerns behaviour - our actions and what we say.

**Questions for application to the strength include:**
What behaviour does this text insist is avoided?
What actions does this text encourage or command?
How does this text address the content of what I say?

### 4. Our Mind

The mind is the place where we think. It's also where we dream, where we imagine and where we understand.

To apply to the mind, means making the good thinking of the text our thinking. It is to improve our understanding and imagination.

**Questions for application to the mind include:**
What does this passage teach as true, or teach as a lie?
What does this passage instruct that we should, or should not, think about?
What would be helpful to remember from this text?

### R in "CHRIST" is for Relationships

After teaching his disciples the greatest commandment, Jesus said: "and the second is like it: 'Love your neighbour as yourself'" (Matthew 22:39).

The word "neighbour" literally means someone who is near. That might be family, friends, work colleagues, strangers, people in authority and as Jesus taught, even enemies (Luke 10:25-37). A neighbour is anyone who is near.

Because of this, the white light of one Bible truth or one purpose in a Bible passage, can be considered by thinking through the many neighbours in our lives. Take for example the application to "value others above yourselves" (Philippians 2:3). This will look different for each of these various neighbours and running through them in our thinking may highlight the need for change, in one of our relationships.

### I in "CHRIST" is for Individual (versus Collective)

Another important consideration for application is to think through how a text applies to the individual, and then how it applies collectively.

In many parts of the world, such as the UK where I live, our tendency is to think of ourselves just as individuals. But if we are to reflect the image of our creator (in Trinity) as God intends (Colossians 3:10), then we must think and act as individuals in community. As Christians we are each members of the body of Christ, the church. Consequently, we should apply the Bible at both the individual and at the collective level if we are to be faithful to its teaching.

---

**EXERCISE**

Read through **Matthew 5:3-12.**

These verses were spoken to Jesus' disciples as a group.

What would it mean for a local church (as a whole), to demonstrate each of the beatitudes?

---

### S in "CHRIST" is for Situation

"I'm home," announced Joe. "And exhausted. Sorry I am so late - it's been quite a day at school!"

"Only just got back myself," replied Rachel, "absolute chaos all day!"

Rachel and Joe looked at each other. It was clear neither had much energy to think about dinner.

Just then the doorbell rang. "Oh no!" Rachel exclaimed, "who can that be?"

Slowly Joe opened the door. "Pizza for two," announced a young man standing at the entrance, handing Joe a colourful box and some drinks.

"From the old lady next door," explained the man. "She's also written you a note."

Joe and Rachel wasted no time in opening the box. The pizza was superb. "To help you think through application." Mrs Wise had written. "Each slice represents a different aspect to 'The Feast' of life. Enjoy your meal."

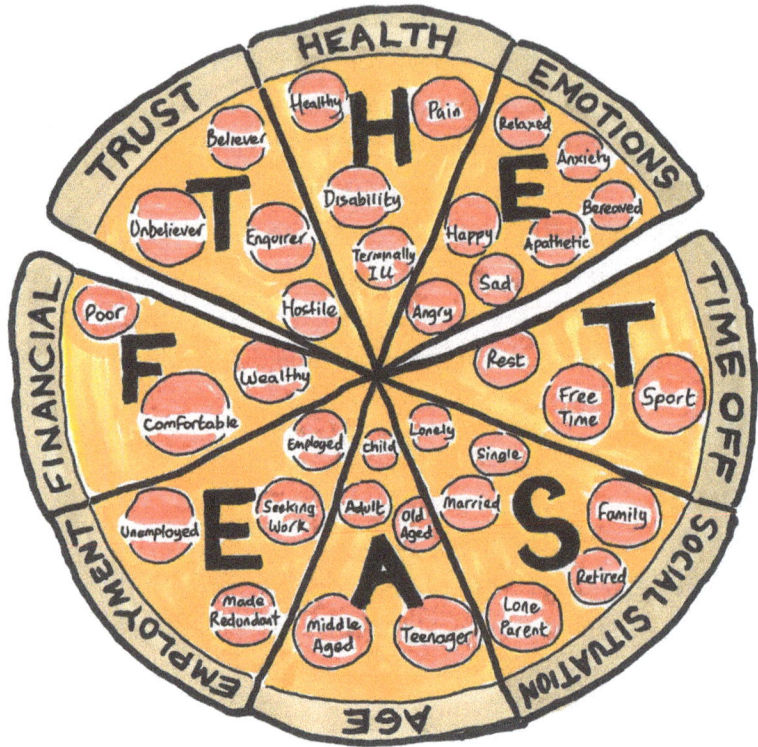

In chapter 7 we saw how considering the situation has great importance for our understanding of how the original hearers would have responded. Now as we come to our own application, situation is no less important.

If you are a Bible teacher, the full range of situations people may be experiencing in Today's World needs to be considered. Even if an application doesn't appear particularly relevant to us now, it is good to think through in preparation for what life might bring in the future.

Each slice of the pizza - "THE FEAST" - helps us to think through situation. Each letter stands for a different aspect of life.

For "Trust" for example, people may be in many different situations. They may be strong believers in Jesus, doubting believers, enquirers, unbelievers or hostile. For "Social Situation" people may be lonely, single, married, with young children, single parents, retired etc. Thinking through how the text specifically applies to people in each of these situations (each slice of the pizza), helps our application to be specific and relevant.

### T in "CHRIST" is for Time out (for reflection)

We have come now to the final step in the method described in this book. Having put in so much effort to work through all the steps of MRS WISE Carefully Studies Jesus CHRIS, this last step "T" is easily avoided. But it is perhaps the most important step of all. We must take time out for reflection.

Almighty God has spoken to us in his Word. Our creator - our all-wise, all-knowing and perfectly loving heavenly Father has spoken. Now we need time to reflect.

How has God particularly spoken to us? What as a result, do we need to enjoy, change, remember or do? As James tells us, we must not be like those who look in a mirror and immediately forget what we look like. We need to be those who don't forget what we have heard and put it into practice (James 1:22-25).

### Practical Tips for Reflection

So how do we not forget what we have heard? Above all, as James instructs, we need to "Do what it says" (James 1:21). To help, here are a few practical tips:

• **Pray**

Prayer is a wonderful way to reflect on God's Word. To pray is to bring ourselves to God and to focus on God. In prayer we can bring before him everything brought to light by a text - every truth, every encouragement, every challenge and need. From there we can thank God, praise him, repent and ask for his help, confident of his provision (John 14:13-14).

- **Memorise Texts**

  Another help is to commit the passage, or part of the passage, to memory. Perhaps there is a key verse in the text. This can be written down, placed in a pocket and read as we have opportunity during the day. Alternatively, a key verse might be pinned to a wall. A summary sentence from a text also works well.

- **Look for biblical motivations**

  Along with teaching points, Bible texts often provide motivations for obedience. There may be reasons in the text to obey, illustrations or the example of Bible characters. A focus on these strengthens our resolve.

- **Look for human examples**

  Similarly, Christians down the ages who persevered in their faith (Hebrews 12:1) inspire obedience. Christian biographies retelling the wonderful ways in which God has worked through others, can stir our hearts to faithfulness. But it need not be a biography - simply the memory of a friend or family member we witnessed putting their faith into practice is likewise inspiring.

- **Develop Associations**

  The teaching of a text can also be brought to mind by connecting the content of a passage to an object or activity in our everyday lives. This way of aiding memory is used in the Bible, not just with illustrations, but in specific episodes. Why, in 2 Kings 2:20, did Elisha ask for a new bowl and for salt to be put into it, before throwing the salt into the bad water of Jericho? Could he not have healed the water without this?

  At one level the answer is symbolism: the new bowl represented a new start for Jericho and salt was known for its cleaning effects, but there is something else going on too. The new bowl and the salt were being associated with the blessing - the truth that God gives new starts. From that day on in Jericho, anyone using a new bowl or salt would likely remember the miracle and what it taught. The objects became linked to the truth.

  All of God's creation speaks of him, and everything in the

experience of our lives in some way points to, or reflects, the truths of the Bible. The sun is like the glory of God, the rain the water of life, the clouds like sin blocking blessing from God etc. - the list goes on and on. The same is true for man-made objects - a strong front door reminds us of the security God provides, the internet that God is all-knowing, and so forth.

Such associations can work as opposites too - an impatient boss at work contrasts with the patience of God, a dishonest work colleague with the truthfulness of God or an unfaithful friend with our need to be faithful. With a bit of thought, any object or experience can be linked to a truth in the Bible. By linking what we have learned to an object or an activity, we are helped to remember it.

- **Ask what opposes us making the application**
Rather than being won over with the need to apply the Bible, our sinful nature and Satan himself will work tirelessly against our faithful obedience. Excuses, counterarguments, distractions and a focus on the world's solutions (applications) are just some of the ways in which they will resist what God wants. But by anticipating this opposition, by asking "Where am I most vulnerable?" and resolving not to listen, we will be better prepared for when the conflict comes.

- **The help of others**
Finally, just as other people can be helpful for learning, so others are a great source of strength for application. "Two are better than one… if either of them falls down, one can help the other up." (Ecclesiastes 4:9-10). Application with a friend enables mutual encouragement and honesty about our struggles.

Which of these tips for your own application will you work on this week?

## END OF CHAPTER EXERCISE

The object of this exercise is to think through how a single truth, or in this case instruction, can be divided into many different specific applications.

**Read Romans 12:9-13.**

Choose two or three of the commands in these verses. Using the steps of **CHRIST,** think through how each applies today.

Once you have spent some time thinking through these commands there are additional questions to help you think further on page 290.

# CONCLUSION

On 11th February 1554 a lady called Jane Dudley (née Lady Jane Grey) took up her pen to write. She had been made Queen of England, but her reign had lasted just nine days. Now, she awaited her execution. But a sincere offer had been made - all she had to do was abandon her faith in Jesus and she would have her freedom.

As she lifted her pen, her thoughts were of Katherine her younger sister. Her subject was the living Word of God:

"…which shall lead you to the path of eternal joy; and, if you with a good mind read it, and with an earnest mind do purpose to follow it, it shall bring you an immortal and everlasting life. It shall teach you to live, and learn you to die."

The following morning, without any apparent fear, she proved the truth of her own words. Jane Dudley was just 16 years old.

# CONCLUSION

---

*"…one thing I do: forgetting what is behind and straining towards what is ahead, I press on towards the goal to win the prize for which God has called me heavenwards in Christ Jesus."*
**Philippians 3:13b-14**

"The enjoyment of God is the only happiness with which our souls can be satisfied. To go to heaven, fully to enjoy God, is infinitely better than the most pleasant accommodations here…
[These] are but shadows; but God is the substance.
These are but scattered beams; but God is the sun.
These are but streams; but God is the ocean."
**Jonathan Edwards**

---

"Sometime in the new year I must have you back," announced Mrs Wise. "There is more I want to share with you on the various styles of Bible writing.[1] But for now, I have one last thing to show you, one last very important thing."

"It's in my bedroom," she continued. "I put it there, as a reminder for me every day when I get up."

Intrigued, Rachel and Joe followed as Mrs Wise led the way. The bedroom was small, but colourful and well organised. Next to her bed was a comfortable looking chair with a little table beside it.

---

1. A detailed look at the various styles of Bible writing (biblical "genres") with tips for understanding each of them will be covered in a sequel to "Life from the Living Word".

Rachel noticed a Bible on the table, but Joe's eyes were drawn to the framed photograph alongside it. Rather than being a picture of people, as might be expected, it was a river scene in the countryside. A few small sailing boats were pointing up the river. Behind the boats, downstream, there were rocks and the water appeared dangerous, but ahead, the river looked wonderful in the sunshine.

"It's a picture a friend took of me years ago," remarked Mrs Wise. "I'm there - that tiny figure in the blue boat." There was a moment, as the three of them took in the picture. Rachel and Joe wondered why it was so significant.

Mrs Wise broke the silence. "I want you to remember that picture," she said with a serious tone to her voice, "that picture is very important for Bible reading."

"Now this is eternal life: that they may know you, the only true God, and Jesus Christ, who you have sent." (John 17:4)

Knowing God, life from the living Word, has been the subject of this book. We have seen how Jesus is revealed in all the Bible and that to be in relationship with Jesus Christ is eternal life.

But remembering the photograph is important.

Each of us, like Mrs Wise in the photograph, is alone in our small sailing boat. There are others nearby in their boats. They will encourage us, but as individuals, we each need to have a relationship with Jesus.

Against us is the flow of the river. It pushes us backwards towards the dangerous waters and rocks. Hebrews 2:1 warns us: "We must pay the most careful attention therefore, to what we have heard, so that we do not drift away." Neglecting our Bible is to neglect Jesus, it is to drift downstream and for some, even leads to "shipwreck of their faith" (1 Timothy 1:19).

## The need for the wind

To move upstream, to experience the pleasant waters of a deeper relationship with Jesus, is not straightforward. The boat has no engine, there isn't a paddle and there are no oars. In fact, there is no way at all for us to move the boat forwards with our own efforts.

But realising our total inability is God's starting point for our progress. For we are not in boats with any power of their own: we are in sailing boats that rely on the wind.

"The wind" says Jesus, "blows wherever it pleases…So it is with everyone born of the Spirit" (John 3:8). To move forwards, to move upstream, we must rely completely on the Holy Spirit. Sometimes he will blow so strongly that the boat will be pushed along without any sail, but usually he is a gentle wind and sometimes virtually no wind at all. To "keep in step with the Spirit" (Galatians 5:25) and so move forwards, we will need to raise the sail.

## The need for effort

To raise the sail requires effort, hard work and struggle on our part. Bible reading, observation, understanding and application are all part of that struggle. It's my prayer that the steps of "MRS WISE Carefully Studies Jesus CHRIST" are all helpful in raising the sail for you, but, on their own, they are as useless as raising a sail on a day with no wind. No amount of effort on our part, no amount of expertise or experience will be of any help if there is no wind.

Equally however, without the sail, the boat will rarely move forwards and may drift back in the current. We must therefore make every effort to raise the sail.

Before moving on, I need to address a possible objection. Perhaps you are troubled and asking: Are we not saved by grace alone? Is it not all God's work and not ours?

Absolutely yes! But the knowledge that there is nothing we can do to save ourselves mustn't lead to the false understanding that there is then nothing for us to do.

Paul tells us to put off the old person and put on the new (Colossians 3:5-14), Peter tells us to make every effort to develop Christ-likeness (2 Peter 1:5), but these commands are never divorced from the work of the Spirit. The wind blows, but we have to raise the sail.

Does our raising the sail make the wind blow? Of course not! Can we pay the wind to blow? Equally no: "the wind blows wherever it pleases" (John 3:8).

The wind and the sail work together. Paul puts it like this for his own life: "I worked harder than all of them - yet not I, but the grace of God that was in me" (1 Corinthians 15:10) and "I labour, struggling with all his energy which so powerfully works in me." (Colossians 1:29 - NIV 1974).

And it is the same for us. We are to "keep in step with the Spirit" (Galatians 5:25). We are to "work out your salvation...for it is God who works in you" (Philippians 2:12). We are to raise the sail. "Grace is not opposed to effort, it is opposed to earning."[2] We show our dependence on the wind, not by doing nothing, but by putting up the sail.[3]

## Travelling up the river

Faced with the knowledge that travelling up the river will require regular effort and struggle, we need to ask an important question. Do

---

2. Dallas Willard - Article in Christian Herald 14th April 2001 "Live Life to the Full"
3. This is what Paul calls the "obedience of faith" (Romans 1:5 ESV). As Christians we are not called to obedience as one usually thinks of obedience - that is, God issues a command, and we then act on that command. Such thinking implies we respond either "I can do this" followed by obedience, or "I can't do this" followed by no action. Either way the emphasis is on us. Instead, we are called to "the obedience of faith". This says, "Of course I can't do this, but HE can do this in me - so I will do it!"

I really wish to make this journey?

Do I want to travel upstream and know Jesus better? Do I, with Paul, really "want to know Christ"? (Philippians 3:10)

Perhaps, what we actually want is something different? We may profess Jesus as Lord, but are we willing to go wherever he takes us?

Are we instead accepting him only on our terms? We want Jesus to serve us - our true god is not the God of the Bible: our true god is still ourselves.

Perhaps instead, we are satisfied with what we already have? If so, we will rarely raise the sail and will drift backwards towards the rocks.

Maybe we want an easy journey; we want a power boat to take us upstream without any effort. But no such boat exists. Jesus has not saved us for an easy life, but for an eternal life.

We need to face the question: Is the greatest desire of my heart to know Jesus better, or is it something else? If it is something else, the effort and struggle to raise the sail will always become a duty, a chore. Keeping in step with the Spirit will become just one more thing for us to do, another thing to add to an already long list.

But if, we do want to know Jesus, if going upstream is the greatest desire of our hearts, then raising the sail will become a joy. It will still be hard work. Sometimes it will be very hard work and at times frustrating when there is little wind, but it will always be a joy. For when we raise the sail we can expect to feel the wind blowing - that is hear God's voice and so know that the boat is making progress. The key is to keep on looking up the river. We must fix our eyes on Jesus the author and perfecter of our faith and knowing him better (Hebrews 12:2).

### Opening the sail

As we have seen, for a sail to effective in the wind it first needs to be raised. The method described in this book can be likened to lifting up the sail. There are other vital aspects to this process such as dependent prayer, but when we spend time struggling to observe, understand and then working out how to apply a Bible text, we are lifting the sail.

Stopping there however, would be virtually pointless. The sail needs to be opened if the wind is to move the boat forwards.

"Do not merely listen to the word and so deceive yourselves," says James, "Do what it says." (James 1:22).

We need to open the sail. We need to work with the Spirit so that the wind provides power to the boat. To open the sail is to obey the wind.

Jesus said, "Whoever has my commands and keeps them is the one who loves me. The one who loves me will be loved by my Father, and I too will love them and show myself to them." (John 14:21). When we open the sail, when we keep the commands of Jesus, there is this promise - the wind will drive us further up the river.

But opening the sail is not the end. Any sailor will tell you that, once open, the sail needs to be held open. Left alone, it will blow straight and the wind will no longer be as effective. So it is with Bible application. We need constantly to be holding the sail open and working with the wind, continuously reflecting, praying and putting the teaching of God's Word into practice.

### Remove the barnacles

On the underside of boats small animals called barnacles will collect, often unseen to those in the boat.

These animals hang onto the hull and increase drag - that is, they slow down the progress of the boat, for they work with the current in pushing the boat back down the river.

If we are to move up the river to a richer joy and deeper relationship with God, we need to pay attention to anything causing drag on the boat.

The letter to the Hebrews puts it this way when describing a race: "…let us throw off everything that hinders and the sin that so easily entangles." (Hebrews 12:1).

We, like the Hebrews, need to throw off the sin that so easily entangles. We need to remove the barnacles and keep on removing them, for they will keep on collecting. Without repenting of our sin, we should expect little progress.

"So will you do that?" asked Mrs Wise. "Will you make it your daily practice? Will you lift the sail and open the sail, and then hold it open throughout the day and scrape off the barnacles as you find them?"

"That's the priority. That is why this little photograph is so important."

She paused. And looking upwards she smiled. "Above all though, depend on the wind, and keep your eyes upstream - he is glorious!"

## END OF CHAPTER EXERCISE

In Appendix 7 (page 317) you will find a summary of the main principles and the method described in this book. (A single double-sided page version of this method summary, designed to be cut out and placed in the back of your Bible, can be printed out free of charge at www.livingwordliterature.com).

**Have a read through Appendix 7. What one or two things have been most helpful to you?**

**Pray that God would provide all that you need to daily lift the sail, open the sail, hold it to the wind and remove the barnacles.**

May the Holy Spirit blow with power so that you might know Jesus better, that is have life to the full - life from the living Word.

# APPENDICES

# APPENDIX 1

# Suggested Thoughts for Chapter Exercises

## Chapter 2: Memorable, Repeated and Surprising

**M is for Memorable – 1 Samuel 17:4-11**

At the start of this famous Bible story our author gives a full eight verses to introduce Goliath. Every detail fixes into our memories how fearsome an enemy he was. He is a "champion" about three metres tall, with heavy and complete armour. He is equipped with mighty weapons - just the tip of his spear weighed almost 7kg! His voice is loud and defiant. Everything about this man instils fear into Saul and all the Israelites. As readers, our author wants us to realise and then feel something of that awe and terror which Goliath created.

So how do we apply such a passage to ourselves today? There will be much more on this in later chapters so don't worry too much about how to draw out the application just yet. But, as we will see, Goliath is a picture of the supreme enemy of the people of God. As Christians our supreme enemies are sin and Satan. They, like Goliath, are mighty foes, and we should recognise their strength and power. Like the Israelites, we cannot fight them and win, but wonderfully we too have a saviour. Just as Goliath is a picture of our enemy, so David is a picture of the Lord Jesus, who (like David) gains the victory.

Have you fully understood the power of our great enemies with a sense of fear and dread? Without that, we will never appreciate our saviour, the Lord Jesus the way we should.

**R is for Repeated – Mark 10:35-52**

The passage describes two separate episodes, first the request of James and John and second Jesus healing blind Bartimaeus. Connecting the two together is the question Jesus asks them both: "What do you want me to do for you?" It's a repeated question that receives two very different answers. Noticing the repetition leads us to compare the accounts and particularly those answers.

Whereas James and John want glory for themselves, which Jesus rejects, Bartimaeus simply wants to see and is healed.

Earlier in Mark's gospel (8:22-26) another blind man is healed, and his seeing is immediately linked with Peter's "seeing" that Jesus is the Messiah (8:29).

So here the repetition of a blind man being cured carries with it the idea of understanding. Bartimaeus (whose name means "son of uncleanness") understands his need, so asks Jesus for mercy to see. James and John on the other hand, though physically seeing, don't see their need. Instead they have a perceived strength (10:39) so they ask Jesus for glory.

The question "What do you want me to do for you?" therefore is a challenge for us all. Are we like James and John wanting Jesus to serve us and give us riches, pleasure and glory, or are we like blind Bartimaeus, knowing our need and simply wanting to see Jesus - that is have Jesus revealed to us in all *his* glory?

In truth, which of these do you really want Jesus to do for you?

**S is for Surprising – John 11:1-16**

There is surprise enough in v4 with Jesus' remarkable confidence about the future for Lazarus. An experienced doctor alongside their patient might be able to provide such reassurance, but Jesus is nowhere near him. The real shock, however, is that John then says, "Now Jesus loved Martha and her sister and Lazarus. So when he heard that Lazarus was ill, he stayed where he was two more days." This is outrageous. Surely if Jesus loved Lazarus, he wouldn't delay but depart immediately to go to him.

Then there is some surprise in the fact that Jesus takes no account of the danger of travelling to Bethany to see Lazarus (v8-10). There is further surprise when the disciples think Jesus is talking about Lazarus sleeping (v13) and surprise that Thomas is willing to follow even to his own death. But in v15 we get another enormous shock. Jesus says, "Lazarus is dead, and for your sake I am glad I was not there, so that you may believe. But let us go to him."

So what is John (following Jesus) drawing our attention to with these surprises?

Not just Jesus' remarkable authority, but his remarkable love. Jesus' primary concern is the glory of God (v4) and the faith of his followers (v14), not our physical health! This is a tough truth to learn, but in a reality where death is not the end because Jesus has authority over death - God's glory and our faith really are more important than our ill-health or even our death. Jesus genuinely loved Martha, her sister and Lazarus and he truly loves us today when he delays or allows things to seemingly get worse. Why? Because, despite our lack of understanding, he is always working for our good (Romans 8:28).

## Matthew 4:18-22

**Memorable:** In this passage the scene itself is memorable. The author vividly describes Jesus walking alongside the lake, seeing fishermen casting / repairing their nets and calling to them before they leave to follow him. Particularly memorable is Matthew's deliberate insertion of Jesus' wonderful phrase "I will send you out to fish for people." The idea of "fishing for people" sticks in our minds.

**Repeated:** There are many repetitions in these verses. There are two lots of two brothers, two pairs of fishermen, two callings by Jesus and, in both episodes, the brothers leave to follow him.

**Surprising:** To leave one's livelihood to follow someone is surprising enough, but Matthew adds the detail "at once / immediately" (same repeated word in the original Greek) to add to the shock.

**Conclusions:** A comparison of the two episodes is also revealing. In the first episode we are uniquely given Jesus' memorable comment "I will send you out to fish for people" and in the second we are uniquely told that they leave their boat "and their father".

Putting all this together, our author is drawing our attention again and again to the remarkable authority of Jesus. This is a man who simply has to speak and people will follow him. They don't hesitate, but obey immediately, leaving their livelihoods and their family to become fishers of people. His authority is then repeated in the next four verses where Jesus' power is demonstrated over every sickness.

Do we see Jesus in this clear light, with the authority to call people as he does here? If so, what difference would it make to us?

### 1 Samuel 16:1-13

**Memorable:** This whole passage is an unforgettable account of how David, being the very last to be considered, is then chosen by the LORD. In v7 the LORD's rebuke of Samuel's thinking is particularly memorable, not only because of the surprise of the prophet being rebuked, but because it addresses us all with a challenging truth: "People look at the outward appearance, but the LORD looks at the heart."

**Repeated:** The repetition in this passage is that of an action, the consideration of each son in turn, accompanied by the repeated phrase "The LORD has rejected / not chosen…" (vv8,9,10). This highlights the LORD's rejection of Jesse's sons (despite their outward appearance) until the choosing of David.

In most English versions there is also a repetition of the words "look at" in v7, though the repetition in the original Hebrew is more pronounced.[1]

---

1. Using STEP, in the original Hebrew the same word root is repeated seven times in these verses. As a verb it is rā'āh meaning "provide" (v1) or "see, look at" (vv6,7-three times) and as nouns meaning "appearance" (vv7,12). Observing this repeated Hebrew word, further confirms our understanding of the author's main point that how God sees, rather than how people see, is what matters. However, because of the author's skill in using a variety of means to communicate their central point, even though our English translations lose a little of this repetition, their main point remains very clear.

**Surprising:** As the youngest and seemingly least important, it's surprising that David is chosen. This is highlighted by the fact he is not invited to the sacrifice and not even named until v13. There is perhaps a surprise in the fact that we are told that David "had a fine appearance and handsome features," for this may appear to go against the teaching in v7. But this corrects a misunderstanding. The point is not that the LORD rejects a fine appearance: it is just that outward appearance neither qualifies, nor disqualifies. In choosing his leader, outward appearance is just not something that matters to the LORD.

There is also a surprise in v2 and v4 in that both Samuel and the elders of Bethlehem are fearful of each other. We are not told why, but perhaps this is because Bethlehem is seen as on the side of Saul, so Samuel is both fearful of them and they of him. Regardless, in v2 the LORD provides Samuel with a cover for his true reasons to go to Bethlehem - another possible surprise which generates ethical questions.[2]

**Conclusions:** The repeated emphasis in the passage is summed up in v7. Whereas people reject and select leaders[3] based on how impressive they appear, God selects according to what he sees in the heart. Nowhere is this more wonderfully seen than in the selection and rejection of Jesus. He is supremely "the living stone - rejected by humans but chosen by God and precious to him" (1 Peter 2:6). By way of application, we must be wary of choosing outwardly impressive leaders, the movers and shakers, the entertainers, the "big" people. We should rather look for leaders like Jesus with humility, prayerfulness, courage in evangelism, faithfulness in preaching and a heart that weeps over sin.

---

2. On the ethics of the concealment of v2 see Walter Kaiser, Jr. "Toward Old Testament Ethics" (Grand Rapids: Zondervan, 1983), p224-227.
3. This passage is not addressing the issue of how God chooses people to salvation, but rather to office, not election to eternal life but election to a particular function within God's kingdom.

## Chapter 3: Words and Images

**Words - 1 Corinthians 15:58**

**Q - Quoted Words**

There are no quoted words in this verse.

**U - Unfamiliar Words**

Perhaps the word "vain" is unfamiliar to you. A quick Google search provides the answer: To do something "in vain" means to do something "without success, achievement or result."

**A - Added Words**

There are a number of "added" words in this verse. These include "dear", "firm", "always" and "fully". The phrases "of the Lord" and "in the Lord" are also added. (The core of the verse is "Therefore, my brothers and sisters, stand. Let nothing move you. Give yourselves to the work, because you know that your labour is not in vain.")

**C - Connecting Words**

"Therefore" is a connecting word. It links the verse back to Paul's argument from 1 Corinthians 15:1 onwards (or arguably concludes his argument for the whole book). "Because" is also a connecting word linking the last two parts of the verse together.

**K - Key Words**

The two key words / phrases in this verse are "stand firm" and "work in the Lord". (Because "work" is so strongly connected to "in the Lord" the whole phrase "work in the Lord" should be regarded as key.)

Later in chapter 6 we will look in more detail at how to investigate and so understand key words and key phrases. At this stage we should note the key words and any questions we may have about the words. Such questions now will produce useful fruit later.

"Stand firm" is not just a key phrase, but is repeated in the idea of "let nothing move you," so this is being emphasised. The questions "Stand firm in what?" and "How do we stand firm?" and "What might move me?" would be good to note.

The idea of "work of the Lord" is also repeated in the phrase "labour in the Lord". Again this raises questions such as "What is the work of the Lord?"

But careful thought also helps provides some insight. This is work *"of the Lord,"* it is his work, with him in control. This therefore is not working for ourselves or for others, but for Jesus. Do we *always, give ourselves, fully,* to the work of *the Lord*? Each word brings challenge.

Finally, we must never forget every word matters. Careful observation will notice two differences between "work of the Lord" and "labour in the Lord". It is not just "work" and "labour" that are different, but *"of* the Lord" and *"in* the Lord" that are not the same. Paul could easily have said "labour of the Lord" to repeat his point, but he doesn't, and we do well to ask why?

Paul's point is not just that our work is God's work and is therefore "not in vain", but that our work is *in* the Lord - we work in union with Jesus - and so we work in the strength that he provides. That too makes it "not in vain".

**Galatians 5:13-15**

In these verses Paul writes to persuade his readers not to abuse their call to freedom by indulging their self-centred sinful desires, but rather to serve one another in love.

**Quoted Words:** Paul draws emphasis to the importance of love by quoting Leviticus 19:18, "Love your neighbour as yourself."

**Unfamiliar Words:** The word "flesh" may be unfamiliar. This is translated "sinful nature" in other versions (e.g. NIV 1984). A dictionary or internet search will give a definition. The flesh is that part of a person's inner self which is constantly opposed to God.

**Added Words:** "my brothers and sisters" is added to show affection. "Humbly in love" is added to qualify what it means to "serve one another". It is the "entire" law which is "fulfilled" in keeping the "one" command.

**Connecting Words:** "But" and "rather" in v13 and "For" in v14 are connecting words. This sets up the structure as:

Main idea (you were called to be free) …but…don't use that freedom to indulge the flesh…rather…serve one another…For…this is the summary of the law.

A warning using an image (of biting and devouring) is then used to conclude with impact.

**Key Words:** "called to be free", "indulge the flesh" and "serve" are key words /phrases which need to be understood well for good comprehension.

**Image:** In v15 the passage concludes with an image to create impact. In sharp contrast to "serve one another humbly in love" we are told that to indulge the flesh is to "bite and devour each other," as a savage animal might treat its prey. The end-result is devastating, "you will be destroyed by each other."

Is that how we think of indulging our sinful desires? Like a savage animal biting and devouring others leading to destruction?

### Isaiah 11:6-9

At one level, these verses teach two straightforward things. First, in the new earth there will be perfect safety and peace; and second, this will come about because there will be complete knowledge of God, that is perfect relationship with him.

But rather than just stating those truths as simple facts, our author wants us to experience something of just how wonderful that will be.

As such, images are used. These are memorable (the picture of animals which would normally be hostile, living, lying down and eating together), repeated (wolf with lamb, leopard with goat, calf with lion etc.) and surprising (the child's hand in a viper's nest, but no harm).

To this, added words bring home the perfection of the safety. It is a "little" child who leads them, and their "young" will lie down together.

Finally, the key words add to the picture of safety and peace. These are "live", "lie down", "eat" and "play" - all summed up in v9: "They will neither harm, nor destroy on all my holy mountain." (Note the repetition and the added words "all" and "holy".)

In the second image (to describe the earth's knowledge of the LORD), the picture is of the waters covering the sea. Again, this communicates completeness and perfection, an emphasis aided by the added word "filled" in v9. Life in the world to come will be that of perfect safety, perfect peace, perfect knowledge of God and perfect relationships. Incredible!

## Chapter 4: Structure and Emphasis

### Judges 3:12-30

### What is the structure of these verses?

The text is most easily split according to scenes, as if watching a film:

**v12:** An Introduction (this is not part of the film)

**v13-14:** Defeat in battle - Israel subject to Moab.

**Connecting word "Again"**

**v15-17:** God raises up Ehud in response to a cry from Israelites. Presents tribute.

**Connecting word "After"**

**v18-19**: Servants leave. Ehud and Eglon alone by stone images - secret message.

**Connecting word "then" and change of location**

**v20-23:** Ehud and Eglon alone in upper room - message from God - Eglon killed.

**Connecting word "After" and change of location**

**v24-26:** Servants embarrassed. Find Eglon dead.

**Change of location**

**v27-28a:** Passes stone images. Blows trumpet and calls out for followers.

**Connecting word "So"**

**v28b-30:** Victory in battle - Moab subject to Israel.

Reviewing these scenes, the overall structure is both linear and mirror line. There is a linear movement from Israel doing evil and being subject to Moab, to Moab being subject to Israel.

The key stages in that linear progression are:

Israelites do evil
v
Defeat in battle - Israel subject to Moab
v
Repentance of Israel
v
The LORD raises up a deliverer
v
The deliverer defeats the enemy king
v
The deliverer raises an army
v
Victory in battle - Moab subject to Israel

In addition, the structure is mirror line:

**v12 Introduction:** Israelites do evil and so the LORD gives them over to Eglon king of Moab

**v13-14:**   Defeat in battle - Israelites subject to Moab for 18 years

**v15-17:**   A cry - to the LORD and the LORD provides a deliverer
Ehud goes to the king of Moab with tribute
(leading the submission)

**v18-19:**   Ehud at stone images
A secret message - king is about to die
King's servants leave him

**v20-23:**   Ehud enters upper room
Message from God

**- MIRROR LINE**

King Eglon killed
Ehud leaves upper room

**v24-26:**   King's servants come to him
A secret - king is dead
Ehud passes stone images

**v27-28a:**   Ehud returns from the king of Moab with a trumpet
(leading the rebellion)
A cry - "Follow me - LORD has given Moab into your hands"

**v28b-30:** Victory in battle - Moab subject to Israel for 80 years

The mirror line brings emphasis to the central event, the message from God and defeat of king Eglon.

## What unifies these verses?

These verses are held together by the theme of "Ehud and what the LORD did through him." This is what makes them an individual unit.

## What is the emphasis in the passage?

**Memorable:** The killing of Eglon with its graphic details is certainly memorable as is the secret of the sword and the embarrassment of the king's servants whilst Ehud gets away.

**Repeated:** The theme of secrets - secret sword, secret message, secret of king's death. The "message" is repeated - it is both "secret" (v19) and "from God" (v20). The idea that God is behind what happens is also repeated (vv12,20,28).

**Surprises:** The sword was certainly a surprise to Eglon! Perhaps the fact that Ehud's left-handedness[4] was enough to get him past the guards is a surprise. He may have been left-handed because his right hand was crippled. If so, he appears weak and so not a threat. Either way he is an unexpected deliverer.

**Words:** There are a large number of added words (detail) particularly associated with Ehud being left-handed, the secret of the sword, the killing of king Eglon and the embarrassment of the king's servants.

**Images and Structure:** The story is deliberately slowed down with details to paint a graphic image for us in v21-22 of Eglon being killed. The story also slows down around the central event in v18-19 and v24-26.

Combining these observations, the emphasis of the text is on the humiliating defeat of Eglon by the LORD's unexpected deliverer who had a secret message from God.

---

4. Ehud is from the tribe of Benjamin (v15), which literally means "son of my right hand". This too draws attention to his unexpected left handedness.

## A reassuring note

How did you get on? Having worked through this passage and my suggested thoughts, it may be that you were able to see the linear structure, but missed the mirror line. Perhaps you had slightly different scenes in your film?

Please be reassured. It is not that you got it wrong. Seeing a mirror line structure is helpful (and wonderful to appreciate the beautiful construction of God's Word), but it is not essential. God has so written his Word that the mirror line structure is just one of the many ways in which he brings out his emphasis. Did you see that the emphasis has something to do with secrets, the unexpected deliverer and the defeat of king Eglon? Did you see the progression from the Israelites living under king Eglon to victory and peace? If so, you are absolutely on track.

Finally, perhaps after looking at the passage you are asking: "How does this passage apply to me today?" That's a good question to ask and we will get there, but not just yet. The next step before "Apply" is to "Understand".

## Matthew 7:7-12

### What is the structure in these verses?

**Change in content:** The largest changes are between v7-8 (encouragement to pray) and v9-11 (further encouragement to pray) and between v11 and v12.

**Connecting words:** In this passage these are "For" in v8, "Or" in v9, "Or" in v10, "then" in v11, "how much more" in v11, "So" in v12 and "for" in v12. (Note some English versions don't translate the "or" in v9 (e.g. NIV) but others are truer to the Greek (e.g. ESV). This illustrates why it is helpful, if they are available, to study with two different English translations to hand.)

Using the connecting words and thinking about the changes in content, I suggest that the overall structure is linear, though to start with it repeats:

Three instructions to pray, each with encouragement (ask/seek/knock) (v7)

→For… three-fold promise of answering (receives/finds/door opened) (v8) Or (to put it another way - a repetition):

Two examples of asking and receiving good (not bad) gifts (This subsection uses contrast as its structure) (v9-10)

→Then… if you are evil and give good gifts when asked, how much more will your heavenly Father do this (v11)

→So (concluding point) v12

**What is odd about v12?**

V12 is different in that it introduces a new, seemingly unrelated topic to the passage - namely, "doing to others what you would have them do to you, for this sums up the Law and the Prophets." This doesn't appear to fit, even though it is clearly joined to the passage by the connecting word "so".

At this stage an odd verse like this, which appears simply to stand on its own, needs to be noted. We will return to it and its significance in the next chapter.

**What unifies these verses?** Teaching on prayer.

**What is the emphasis in the passage?**

We can be confident prayer will be answered.

# Chapter 5: Context (Part 1) – Immediate and Book Context

**Genesis 12:10-20**

Considering "MRS WISE" the following are suggested observations:

**Memorable:** The whole story, particularly with its deception, is memorable.

**Repetition:** "Famine" is repeated twice in v10, with the added word "severe" for further emphasis. The idea of "seeing" that Sarai is "beautiful" is repeated three times (vv12,14,15) with the added word "very" in v14 further emphasising her beauty. Pharaoh's repeated question (three times) in v18 draws our attention, as does Pharaoh's repetition of his order for Abram and Sarah to go (vv19,20). Finally, Abram's plan is repeated in v13 and v19.

**Surprises:** Abram's deception is a surprise, as is Pharaoh's letting Abram go with Sarai rather than simply killing Abram for his deception.

**Words:** There are no quoted or particularly unfamiliar words. "And when Pharaoh's officials saw her they praised her to Pharaoh" (v15) are "added" words. They are not needed for the plot of the story, but their presence adds further repetition to the emphasis on Sarah's beauty, as noted above. There are no obvious key words on which the meaning depends, but the repeated words will need further thought (which we will cover in the next chapter) as these have been highlighted by the author.

**Images:** The whole story is an image that sticks in our minds for it is portrayed vividly by the author. There are, however, no specific images in the passage.

**Structure:** There are five scenes arranged in a mirror pattern:

**A** - v10: Abram and Sarah travelling to Egypt in poverty.
  **B** - v11-13: Just about to enter Egypt - Abram's plan of deception to keep himself safe.
    **C** - v14-16: In Egypt. Abram's plan appears to work. Abram is blessed, not harmed.
                                                    **- Mirror Line**
    **C'**- v17: In Egypt. The LORD's intervention. Serious diseases on Pharaoh and household.
  **B'**- v18-19: Just about to leave Egypt - Pharaoh's judgement of Abram's plan.
**A'**- v20: Abram and Sarah travelling from Egypt with wealth.

This structure highlights the centre. Although Abram's plan appears to be successful, it is not in accordance with God's will; and - despite Abram's failings - the LORD still intervenes.

**Emphasis:** From just observing the passage, the author's emphasis is unclear. Certain themes are highlighted, the famine, the deception of Abram, seeing the beauty of Sarai, the LORD's intervention, the judgement of Pharaoh on Abram's plan and his command to leave. We are left needing to understand more. Context is the key.

### Considering the Immediate Context

### Before the passage: Genesis 12:1-9.

The verses before Genesis 12:10-20 start a new main section in the book of Genesis with God's call to Abram whilst he was at Haran. In them God makes some great promises:

v2: To make Abram into a great nation (so making his name great)

v2: To bless Abram

v3: To bless those who bless Abram

v3: To curse those who curse Abram

v3: To bless all peoples on earth through Abram

v7: To provide a land for Abram's offspring

In 12:10-20 there is a notable contrast with this preceding passage of promises. Instead of staying in the land of promise, Abram and Sarai move to Egypt. Instead of trusting in God's promise for a great nation of offspring, Abram fears for his own life and lies about his wife, saying Sarai is his sister, leading to her being taken into Pharaoh's palace. It now appears that God's promises of land and a great nation will not happen.

But despite Abram and Sarai's failings to trust God, so making the promises seem unlikely to come true, God is at work. Abram continues to be blessed (v16), and the LORD works by "inflicting serious diseases on Pharaoh and his household" (v17) so that Sarai is returned to him as his wife and Pharaoh allows him to leave to return to the land of promise.

The immediate context therefore encourages us that, despite the great failings of those who receive his promises, God will work to ensure that his promises are fulfilled. How good is that!

**After the passage: Genesis 13:1-18**

A comparison of Genesis 13:1-4 with 12:8-10 reveals a contrast in Abram's wealth. When he entered Egypt "the famine was severe", but he left "very wealthy". Further comparison notices a repetition of place names and action, but in reverse. The movement earlier was from a place between Bethel and Ai (where he pitched his tent, built an altar and called on God's name), to the Negev (the name given to the dry lands before coming to Egypt) and then Egypt itself. Now the sequence is repeated, but in reverse. The movement is from Egypt to the Negev and on to the place between Bethel and Ai where Abram pitched his tent. It ends as Abram again "called on the name of the LORD."

This repetition in reverse, adds an outer layer to the mirror structure given on page 266, but most importantly draws our attention to God's complete reversal of what has happened.

So, by 13:5 Abram and Sarai are back in the promised land, but there is a problem in that Lot and Abram can't stay together (v6-7).

Abram's response is to offer Lot the choice of land before them. Lot looks around and sees that the land to the east is "well watered" and "like the land of Egypt." This immediately should raise concern, for Lot wants to be in a place like Egypt just as Abram had in 12:10. In case we missed it, the author adds a further note to indicate that this is not good, by mentioning Sodom and Gomorrah. The resulting separation (v11) highlights the difference between Lot (who "lived among the cities of the plain and pitched his tent near Sodom" where the people were "wicked" and were "sinning greatly against the LORD") and Abram. Rather than trusting in what looked good to him, a land which looked like Egypt, Abram now trusts God's promise and "lived in the land of Canaan".

The passage ends, back where 12:1-7 started, with a repetition of God's great promises. Careful observation reveals that the promises are now also expanded. Now the promise is not just "this land" but "all the land that you see" and it is a land "for you" as well as "your offspring" and it is "for ever". Now the offspring are as uncountable as the "dust of the earth". As Abram again pitches his tent and builds an altar in 13:18, God's promises stand firm and we have learned the importance of faith in his promises, rather than what looks attractive to our natural judgement.

Do you trust in what God promises or in what seems best in your thinking?

## Matthew 6:22-23
To understand the images Jesus uses in these verses the context is vital.

## Immediate Context
The immediate context is Matthew 6:19-21 beforehand and 6:24 afterwards. These two passages are linked by the theme of what we desire. We should desire to store up treasure in heaven, but not desire treasure on earth. We should desire and so be devoted to God, but not Money.

With this theme of desire in the immediate context, the "eyes" of v22-23 represent our desires. This makes sense from our experience. Our eyes focus on what we desire, an association made by Jesus in Matthew 5:28-29.[5]

In v21-22 we are told that "the eye is the lamp of the body" and that our eyes can either be "healthy" or "unhealthy". If our eyes are healthy, that is, if our desires are healthy, the result is "your whole body will be full of light", but if unhealthy "your whole body will be full of darkness."

So what is this "light" and what is this "darkness" that come depending on the health of our desires and what they are focused on? To answer that question the wider "Book Context" is helpful.

## Wider Book Context
As identified on pages 112-113, these verses fall into a section marked out by two bookends (Matthew 5:17 and 7:12). The bookends inform us that the verses in between are held together by Jesus' teaching on fulfilling the Law and the Prophets, or as he puts it in 5:19, "practising these commands" or 5:20 practising "righteousness".

Reading through the section, the warnings of 6:1,2,5 and 16 (all

---

5. The O.T. also associates eyes with desire. See Psalm 119:36-37.

relating to acts of righteousness and their rewards) are followed by another warning in 6:19. Storing up treasure for yourself on earth (with its rewards) is therefore in parallel with practising "acts of righteousness" (giving, prayer and fasting) so as to "be honoured by others" and "having your reward in "full". This contrasts with the healthy desire of a reward from God (6:1,4,6,18) - labelled "treasure in heaven" in 6:19.

Looking ahead to the verses which follow (6:25-34), the connecting word "therefore" carries forward the theme of desire with its close sister worry. To worry is to have an unhealthy desire for security on earth, or to put it another way, to have little faith in God. That is to be like pagan unbelievers. In contrast a healthy desire (eyes) is given in v32-33. We should seek "God's kingdom and his righteousness," with the promise that it will be given.

Putting these things together, the light that comes when our desires are healthy is God's kingdom. God's kingdom is his rule, where we follow his commands (5:19), do good deeds (5:16) and a righteousness, which exceeds that of the Pharisees (5:20). These are God's reward for those who seek righteousness and are pure in heart (5:6,8).

Darkness (6:23), on the other hand, is the absence of such righteousness. The outward appearance of righteousness, such as the Pharisees have, may appear to be light to them, but it is actually great darkness, for it prevents them from receiving God's true righteousness.

So how do we have healthy desires and so be filled with light? Jesus will go on to give further instruction about this, but he provides two important teaching points in these verses.

First v21, "where your treasure is there your heart will be also." In other words, the heart follows the treasure. If by faith we focus on and value treasure in heaven, our hearts with their desires will follow.

Secondly in v24, "you cannot serve both God and Money." If we are to have healthy eyes (desires) we must no longer serve (desire) Money[6]. It is one or the other, we cannot have both. The two are not compatible.

---

6. The Greek word translated "Money" is wealth represented as a person. This "person" stands in opposition to God, so represents not just wealth but anything people serve that is not God.

**Is your body full of light?**

To ask this question is to ask the wrong question. The Pharisees thought they were full of light, but they were full of darkness (6:23). The correct test is to ask instead: Are our eyes healthy? - that is: What do we desire? If we desire God, his rule and his righteousness then we can be confident that our whole body will be full of light, with righteousness from God (6:22). But to focus on our works, our acts of righteousness and so conclude they are acceptable is to be like the Pharisees. This is why Jesus repeatedly instructs us not to focus on ourselves and on our acts of righteousness (6:1,2,3,5-6,16), but on God and his righteousness (6:20, 32-33). If we are downhearted and mourn and hunger because we long for more of God's righteousness in us, we can be greatly comforted (5:3-6).

## Chapter 6: Context (Part 2) – Whole Bible Context

**The Pattern associated with 40 days**

In his sovereignty God allowed it to rain for 40 days on Noah and spent 40 days with Moses on Mount Sinai, and he made sure that the Israelite spies completed 40 days searching out the promised land.

So, what do they have in common? Each 40-day period was followed by an episode revealing that God's people fail to be faithful to God. Noah became drunk, the Israelites built a golden calf and instead of trusting and entering the promised land, the people in the desert rebelled against God.

From this pattern of association (using 40 days to connect the episodes) we are being told something about the theme of people. Repeatedly people fail the test of faithfulness and so we need a saviour. (We will return to this pattern of association with 40 days in chapter 9.)

**Romans 12:20 – "heap up burning coals on his head"**

The context of Romans 12:17-21 is one of "peace with everyone" (v18). Rather than "repay anyone evil for evil" (v17) we are to "overcome evil with good" (v21).

With such a context, the understanding that "heap burning coals on his head" implies a worsening of the day of judgement for your enemy can be excluded. This is supported by the last line of Proverbs 25:22 (the line omitted by Paul in his quotation), for it says that by giving our enemies food to eat and water to drink, "the LORD will reward you." There is no personal reward in seeing an enemy suffer at the final judgement. God himself does not delight in the death of anyone (Ezekiel 18:32).

That excludes a wrong understanding, but what is the correct way to take this phrase?

Looking at other uses of the Greek word for "heap" (*sōreuō*) takes us to 2 Timothy 3:6 where it is variously translated "burdened", "loaded down", or "overwhelmed" when referring to a person's sins.

This suggests[7] that to "heap burning coals on his head" is to bring about a burden or a loading down of an inward, unpleasant burning in the head because of sin. This "conviction" of sin comes when we are practical in our love towards our enemy, for then our good actions contrast with their sin. Such a burden may lead our enemy to repentance. If so, evil is overcome with good (v21), and in that there is a reward for us (Proverbs 25:22).

## Genesis 12:10-20

### Word-Threads

By repeating the idea that Sarai's beauty was *seen* three times, our author is deliberately drawing our attention to what has happened earlier. In Genesis 3:6 and 6:2 we note the same pattern of "seeing", then desiring what is seen, then "taking" (sin) and finally the consequences of the action. Noting the pattern, we should ask how this new episode increases our understanding. Here, in contrast to the sins of 3:6 and 6:2, Pharaoh is unaware of what he is doing in taking Sarai, but the consequences are just the same, for God's anger is provoked (12:17).

---

7. With only one other use of the word translated "heap" in the Bible, it is important to be humble in our understanding. Some things are known only to God (Deuteronomy 29:29). If others disagree where the Bible is not very clear, rather than asserting our understanding, we do well to "live at peace with everyone" (Romans 12:18).

Ignorance doesn't prevent an action from being sinful. God's anger at such sin remains.

The repetition of Pharaoh's question summed up as "What have you done?" also picks up an earlier phrase used in Genesis 3:13 and 4:10. The question ties what Abram has done in lying about Sarai to the sin of Adam and Eve in the garden and to the murder of Abel by Cain.[8] Lying to protect yourself is not a small thing to God. It is serious.

### Themes

The passage brings up a number of important Bible themes:

**God:** God's promises cannot be invalidated - even by the failings of those to whom he makes his promises. God rescues his people from the consequences of their unfaithfulness. God is angered by sin even if it is committed in ignorance. Having only one sexual partner within marriage is important to God.

**People:** Rather than trusting God in hard times, people trust in their own clever solutions - solutions that may even work to some extent (12:16).

**Relationships:** When we are prosperous and succeed in our plans, it doesn't mean that we have God's approval. (Abram's plan is successful and he leaves Egypt rich, but he has not been faithful to God.) Lying has negative consequences for relationships between people.

Which of the above truths do you find most challenging?
Praise God that whatever our failure, his promises never fail!

### The theme of God's curse

The theme of God's curse begins in the Garden of Eden. It is God's righteous response to the snake, who is cursed first. Although punished, Adam and Eve are not specifically cursed, but the ground is cursed because of their sin - which has consequences for them. In

---

8. Later the same phrase "What have you done?" is used in Genesis 20:9 and 26:10. As such our author connects these two later episodes to this passage. They too involve lying about wives to protect the husband concerned. Neither Abram, nor his son Isaac, learned from Abram's earlier error. We are being taught sin persists despite the negative experience of correction.

contrast to Adam and Eve, Cain is specifically cursed by God after his murder of Abel (Genesis 4:11).

In Genesis 5:29 we are introduced to Noah, who will "comfort us in the painful toil of our hands caused by the ground the LORD has cursed." Here is a person who will bring comfort despite the curse. By Genesis 8:21, in response to Noah's sacrifice, the LORD says in his heart: "Never again will I curse the ground because of humans, even though every inclination of the human heart is evil from childhood."

A new idea is being introduced - that of a man who will bring comfort from the curse of God, a man whose sacrifice changes the way God views sinful mankind and the curses that follow.

In Genesis 12:1-3 God brings his great promises to Abram. These promises contain the line: "I will bless those who bless you and whoever curses you I will curse." The theme of who is blessed or cursed by God is being developed. Here we learn that whether it is God's blessing or his curse that is received by someone, depends on their response to a particular person. Initially this person is Abram, but that is also developed, for it is clear the promise also applies to his offspring (Genesis 27:29).

In Deuteronomy 27 the theme of who is cursed returns, this time strongly associating God's curse with sin - the breaking of God's law. This brings the devastating conclusion of Deuteronomy 27:26: "Cursed is anyone who does not uphold the words of this law by carrying them out." The contents of the curses are then graphically and repeatedly described in all their horror in Deuteronomy 28. The author makes us face their impact. This is what it is to be under the curse of God.

By the end of Deuteronomy, the Bible's progressive revelation has taught us that everyone who sins is under a curse, with terrible consequences to follow. The thread leaves us close to despair, but there has also been a hint of hope. One man, Noah, was able to bring comfort despite God's curse. Furthermore, God has made a promise to bless or curse, not dependent on obedience to rules, but dependent on a relationship to a particular person and their offspring. To understand fully, we will need to trace the thread forwards - the subject of chapter 10.

## Chapter 7: Situation

**2 Kings 2:19-24**

Paying attention to where events occur in the Bible is often helpful for our understanding.

2 Kings 2:19-22 occurs at Jericho (see v18). Jericho was a place of God's destruction and curse (Joshua 6:20-21,26; 1 Kings 16:34) which lived on as "the water is bad and the land unproductive," things associated with God's curse (Genesis 3:18-19; Deuteronomy 29:23-27).

But through Elisha, the LORD heals the water and the land, just as he had in Exodus 15:22-26. A place under God's curse can still receive God's blessing.

In contrast, Bethel (1 Kings 12:23-24) was a place associated with God's blessing. It was here that Jacob met God and declared, "This is none other than the house of God; this is the gate of heaven." (Genesis 28:10-22).

More recently, however, it had become a centre for idol worship (1 Kings 12:25-33). The place of blessing had become a place of false religious activity. As Elisha approaches, some youths come out of the town and call him "baldy" (a term of insult) and tell him to "Get out of here," showing he is not welcome. In consequence, Bethel becomes a place under God's curse (v24). These are no ordinary bears, they are bears sent by God, for in response to turning away from him, God had promised "I will send wild animals against you and they will rob you of your children" (Leviticus 26:22).

A place previously under God's blessing can still receive God's curse. In chapter 10 we will consider this further and how it teaches us today.

**Matthew 8:1-3**

Leprosy was not just a terrible disease, but - according to the Law of God - made the sufferer "unclean" (Leviticus 13:45). This meant that the affected person would have to live alone, outside the camp (Leviticus 13:46). Leprosy itself was seen as a punishment from God for sin (Numbers 12:9-12; 2 Kings 5:27) and its healing was something that only God could do (2 Kings 5:7).

In the chapters before this passage (Matthew 5-7) Jesus' teaching has highlighted the poverty and weakness of everyone because of sin. We are all naturally like lepers - separated from God. Then, quite deliberately, Matthew tells us of this man with leprosy - a man who is subsequently healed.

Rather than becoming unclean himself by touching this man as everyone else would have been (Leviticus 15:7), Jesus' touch makes him clean. Jesus has the will and power to make even the most unclean person right with God.

However "unclean" we may feel; indeed however "unclean" we are or impossible our healing may appear to be, Jesus can, and is, willing to make us clean! The richness of this truth only comes through an understanding of the situational context.

## Chapter 8: Jesus (Part 1) – Promises

**Genesis 3:15**

This verse, spoken by God shortly after Adam and Eve ate the forbidden fruit, contains promises concerning the snake and its offspring, and the woman (Eve) and her offspring.

First there is the promise of enmity or hostility between the two. At its simplest level, human beings and snakes will live with that relationship. But because the snake represents Satan (Revelation 12:9,17), this verse teaches the ongoing spiritual hostility between Satan and his offspring[9] and the woman and her offspring.

The second part of the verse then develops this theme. Ultimately, the head of the snake will be crushed - the snake will lose.

Careful observation notes that "offspring" in the first part of the verse, is in parallel with the singular words "he", "you", "head" and "heel" in the second part of the verse.[10] Genesis 3:15 promises a future

---

9. By the "offspring" of Satan, the reference is probably both to demons and to people who oppose God, for both Jesus and John refer to "children of the devil" (Matthew 13:38; John 8:44; 1 John 3:10). By this they mean all people not born again as children of God, not a special category of unbelievers.
10. For a detailed defence of this point see: "A Syntactical note (Genesis 3:15): Is the Woman's Seed Singular or Plural?" Jack Collins. Tyndale Bulletin 48.1 (1997) p139-148.

singular offspring of the woman who will defeat Satan.

Being born of a virgin, Jesus is literally the offspring of a woman (Matthew 1:25; Galatians 4:4). He came to "destroy the devil's work" (1 John 3:8) and "break the power of him who holds the power of death - that is the devil" (Hebrews 2:14). Jesus' victory, however, is only promised at the expense of his suffering (or death, for poisonous snakes kill) for Satan is told "you will strike his heel."

As for all promises, this idea of a singular offspring of the woman crushing the head of Satan, can be traced through the Bible. The promise is taken up by Balaam in his prophesy (Numbers 24:17) and it is no co-incidence that Jael crushes Sisera's head with a tent peg (Judges 4:21) or that David lands a stone from his sling onto Goliath's head (1 Samuel 17:49). Such shadows pick up the promise of Genesis 3:15.

So how is this promise fulfilled?

In his life, Jesus begins the fulfilment as he drives out demons. At the cross he "disarmed the powers and authorities" (Colossians 2:15), so landing the crucial blow to guarantee victory. But Satan's activity continues. In Revelation 12 we are told that the hostility between the woman (the church) and the snake will continue until the end.  But the end will come. Then the devil will be "tormented day and night forever and ever" (Revelation 20:10) and the victory will be complete.

Meanwhile we need to wait, but with encouragement for, as Paul puts it, "The God of peace will soon crush Satan under your feet." (Romans 16:20).

## Psalm 2:7-9

As I am sure you will have seen, Psalm 2:7-9 contains several glorious promises all fulfilled in Jesus.

In v7, we are given the promise of a son. This is another description of God's king (Psalm 2:6) and is fulfilled in Jesus (Matthew 17:5; Hebrews 1:5). In v8, we are told this son will receive an inheritance, that of the nations - also fulfilled in Jesus. Then in v9 we are promised the son will be appointed as ruler of the nations with a rod of iron. This develops a promise made earlier (Genesis 49:10) and is completely fulfilled at the return of Jesus (Revelation 12:5, 19:15). But did you notice the timing of all this promise fulfilment?

According to Acts 13:32-34 the "Today" in Psalm 2:7 occurred at the resurrection of Jesus. This was when Jesus received his inheritance (Psalm 2:8 with Acts 13:34), the day Jesus became the ruler of the nations. As a result, after his resurrection, Jesus declared: "All authority in heaven and on earth has been given to me." (Matthew 28:18).

Furthermore, in Romans 1:4 we are told that it was at the resurrection of Jesus that he was "appointed the Son of God in power". Jesus is eternally the Son of God, but his resurrection was a unique day when this was revealed in power, a day fulfilling Psalm 2:7.

But then, did you also see the surprise in Revelation 2:26-27?

These verses clearly state that the promise of authority to rule rests with Jesus for the speaker (Jesus) says "just as I received authority from my Father." But at the same time, Jesus also states that this same authority, "over the nations" and "to rule with an iron sceptre" will be given to "the one who is victorious and does my will to the end." This is truly amazing. The Christian who perseveres in doing the will of Jesus will rule with Jesus!

For now, the promises of Psalm 2:7-9 are fulfilled in Jesus. Christians are also now sons of God (Romans 8:15-16). One day however, those followers who persevere to the end will also be declared in power to be sons of God at their resurrection. And on that day, they will inherit the nations (Daniel 7:27; Matthew 5:5; Romans 8:17) and rule with Jesus (1 Corinthians 6:2-3; 2 Timothy 2:12; Revelation 5:10). How wonderful will that day be!

## Chapter 9: Jesus (Part 2) – Patterns

**Judges 3:12-30**

In chapter 4, where we considered "Structure" and "Emphasis", we saw how this text draws our attention to the humiliating defeat of King Eglon by an unexpected deliverer with a hidden sword - a secret message from God.

In context, Ehud is just one of many deliverers in the book of Judges all of whom fall into a repeated sequence structure, first laid out in Judges 2:7-11.

All are patterns of Jesus as the deliverer of God's people. Like Jesus, all are sent by God and defeat their enemies to bring peace to Israel.

But each deliverer is also unique, with their own particular emphasis pointing forward to Jesus in their own specific way. For Ehud, the humiliation of the enemy king is particularly strong, as is the secret means of victory. Just as the Moabites didn't see the hidden sword, so the "rulers of this age" in Jesus' time didn't see the secret wisdom of God (1 Corinthians 2:7), the wisdom of the cross, the wisdom of Christ crucified.

The story of Ehud encourages us to rejoice, for not only has our God rescued us from our enemies, but he has humiliated them (Colossians 2:15). Ehud encourages us to laugh, just as God himself laughs (Psalm 2:4). God's enemies are not just defeated, but completely outwitted. For God is sovereign - indeed: "the foolishness of God is wiser than man's wisdom and the weakness of God is stronger than human strength." (1 Corinthians 1:25). Do you laugh at the defeat of evil as well as rejoice in your rescue from evil? Ehud teaches us to do so.

## Numbers 21:4-9

At first sight, this account of what happened to the Israelites in the wilderness may seem far from pointing to Jesus. But by taking Jesus at his word - that all the Scriptures point to him, we will look for how this passage does that.

First, Moses foreshadows Jesus. As the leader, God's people come to him and repent (v7). Moses then prays for the people's deliverance (v7) and he obeys God to provide salvation. All this foreshadows Jesus.

But second, there is a shadow of an object as the bronze snake is raised up on a pole. Any Israelite who is bitten and facing death can look up at the raised bronze snake and live, ideas repeated twice in v8-9 so drawing attention to their importance. This is a shadow of Jesus raised up on the cross, as Jesus himself confirms (John 3:15). Anyone who looks to him will be saved.

As with all shadows, the bronze snake doesn't just point to Jesus, it also helps us to understand Jesus better. In John 3:15 Jesus says: "Just as Moses lifted up the snake in the wilderness, so the Son of Man must be lifted up, that  everyone who believes may have eternal life."

There is a clear parallel between "look at" the snake and "believes". We are being taught about what it means to "believe", an important theme in John's gospel (John 20:31).

First, there is no requirement for achievement. Indeed, the Israelites did the exact opposite of anything to please God.  After a longer than expected journey, they became impatient and spoke against God and Moses. They even complained about their salvation (being brought out of Egypt) and against their ongoing salvation (the manna in the desert) (Numbers 21:5). There is no doubt they deserved judgement. But even those who have rejected God's salvation are not beyond God's saving grace. After repentance, looking to the means of salvation that God provided gave them life. It is the same for us, for our God remains the same. Whenever we feel the bite of our sin, we too simply need to look - nothing else, but look - to Jesus, lifted up on the cross, and our promise is eternal life.

Why though, does God use a bronze snake raised on a pole to represent Jesus lifted up on a cross? Snakes were after all, unclean (Leviticus 11:41-42) and associated with evil (Genesis 3). The answer is not specifically given, but two reflections may help. To be raised on a cross was to be considered cursed and despised, it was a hated thing, just like snakes - it was a "stumbling block to Jews and foolishness to Gentiles" (1 Corinthians 1:23). Others may despise Jesus on the cross, yet this is the saviour to whom we must look. There is no room for shame of our saviour on the cross.

Secondly, God is sovereign. Satan has no realm of authority, not even over snakes. If God wants to use a snake as a symbol of salvation for his purposes, he will. Satan can do nothing to stop him!

**1 Samuel 16:1-13**

Despite his impressive outward appearance (1 Samuel 10:23-34) Saul had proven unfaithful to God (1 Samuel 15). The LORD's verdict opens this passage: "I have rejected him as king". In contrast, God tells Samuel that he has chosen one of Jesse's sons to be king, but the identity of the exact son is kept hidden from Samuel. Eliab the eldest, is the obvious choice. He looks like Saul, but is rejected - as are all the other sons of Jesse who are present.

"Are these all the sons you have?" asks Samuel. "There is still the youngest," Jesse answered. "He is tending the sheep."

And so David is introduced. The youngest, considered so unimportant that he hadn't even been invited to the sacrifice. David had, in effect, been rejected.[11] He is a lowly shepherd, just one who looks after the sheep.

But David is the one chosen by God, for v7: "People look at the outward appearance, but the LORD looks at the heart." It is upon David that the Spirit of the LORD comes.  Although unrecognised as king, David then helps those affected by evil spirits (v14-23) and, though he looks so unimpressive, rescues the people from the oppression of their enemy (1 Samuel 17:1-58).

The original hearer would have seen very little of how this all patterns the great shepherd king to come. But as Christians, with our eyes opened to the glory of Jesus, we can see his shadow - his identity kept from the Old Testament prophets (1 Peter 1:10-11), his rejection by his people (Isaiah 53:3; John 1:11), his coming from Bethlehem as the shepherd king (2 Samuel 5:2; Matthew 2:6; John 10:11), his anointing by the Spirit (Matthew 3:16) leading to healing of those with evil spirits (Mark 1:32) and the rescue of his people from their oppressive enemy (Colossians 2:13-15).

How does this shadow teach us more than we can learn from just the New Testament? The answer lies in the emphasis this passage would have on an original hearer - the LORD looks, not at the outward

---

11. In 1 Samuel 17:20 we are told that David was able to leave the sheep in the hands of another shepherd to deliver food for his brothers facing the Philistines. Samuel's visit and sacrifice was a big event. Why could David have not come with a similar arrangement, unless he was rejected? Further evidence of his rejection comes in 1 Samuel 17:28-30.

appearance, but at the heart. It's instructive for us to look at the heart of our leaders, but (above all) the heart of our saviour king. This theme, the heart of the king, continues throughout 1 Samuel as the heart of David is followed. Remarkably, only in one place in the New Testament does Jesus tell us about his own heart - some of the most wonderful words ever spoken: "I am gentle and lowly in heart" (Matthew 11:29), but in 1 and 2 Samuel, from the shadow, we can learn much more of what this means.

## Psalm 1:1-3

In chapter 4 we considered the structure of this opening psalm and saw that v1-3 serve as a sub-section, for they describe the godly person in contrast to the wicked of v4-5, before a conclusion in v6.

Examining an alternative Bible translation is helpful to connect this passage with Jesus. The ESV more accurately has (emphasis mine): "Blessed is the *man* who…" (v1) and "*his* delight is…" (v2) and "*He* is like…" (v3) and "in all that *he* does, *he* prospers" (v3). For these verses describe one person, a man - Jesus.

Only Jesus fits v1-3, for he alone is without sin (2 Corinthians 5:21). Jesus perfectly delights in the law of the LORD and is supremely like the fruitful tree of v3.

Further evidence of Jesus being the subject of these verses comes from the end of Psalm 2 which concludes: "Blessed are all those who take refuge in him." This ending acts as a bookend with Psalm 1:1 and is a verse which clearly refers to Jesus. The "him" is the "son" of 2:12 and 2:7, verses which are directly applied to Jesus in the New Testament (Acts 13:33; Hebrews 1:5, 5:5).

How then should Psalm 1 be applied to us? The first thing to recognise is that, apart from Jesus, we are the wicked of v4! We will not stand in the judgement for we are sinners (v5), so our future without Jesus is destruction (v6).

But in v5 there is an "assembly of the righteous" and in v6: "the LORD watches over the way of the righteous." So who are the righteous? Not those who meet the standards of v1-3, for those verses describe a single, unique man - Jesus. The righteous, are those whose righteousness was bought by the one righteous man, and then, because they are bought, increasingly reflect his righteousness in their lives. We must never forget that first and foremost all the Scriptures point to Jesus.

## Chapter 10: Jesus (Part 3) - Bible Themes

### 2 Kings 2:19-24 - How does this text point to Jesus?

### Patterns

Being a true prophet of God, Elisha brings God's Word. As such he patterns the Lord Jesus as the ultimate prophet of God (Acts 3:20-22).

A further study of 1 and 2 Kings strengthens this pattern of Elisha pointing to Jesus, because Elisha is preceded by another prophet, Elijah who patterns John the Baptist.

Elijah, like John, wears camel hair clothing with a leather belt (2 Kings 1:8; Matthew 3:4). Both Elijah and John are dismayed by the sin of Israel (1 Kings 19:10; Luke 3:7-9) and are told that their successor will bring judgement (1 Kings 19:16; Luke 3:17). Furthermore, both prophets are persecuted by the wife of the king (Jezebel in 1 Kings 19:1-2; Herodias in Mark 6:17-25). Finally, just as Elijah passes on his ministry to Elisha at the waters of the Jordan, so John baptises Jesus to begin his ministry at the Jordan (2 Kings 2:1-14; Mark 1:9-11).

The ministry of Elisha and Jesus is also very similar. Though both are appointed as judge (2 Kings 19:16; Acts 17:31), both instead begin their ministry with salvation, indeed Elisha means "God saves" just as Jesus means "Yahweh saves". 2 Kings 2:19-24 therefore, right at the start of Elisha's ministry introduces us to what will follow - first salvation, but later judgement.

### Themes

As we saw in Chapter 7, this passage picks up the important themes of God's blessing and God's curse.

The text in 2 Kings 2:19-24 is teaching us about who receives God's blessing and who receives God's curse. But because these themes involve the relationship between God and his people it is important to consider covenant changes when applying to us today. Now under the new covenant, Jesus has "…redeemed us from the curse of the law by becoming a curse for us, for it is written; 'Cursed is everyone hung on a pole.'" (Galatians 3:10-14). Instead, now, "every spiritual blessing in Christ" belongs to his people (Ephesians 1:3).

In addition, the New Testament teaches us that "whoever rejects the Son will not see life, for God's wrath remains on them." (John 3:36). The responses to Elisha in 2 Kings 2:19-24 therefore point forward to our response to Jesus, for at the final judgement it will be that which determines whether we are blessed or cursed (Matthew 25:34,41).

**What timeless truths connect the passage to Today's World?**
When thinking through timeless truths, it is important to ensure that we are specific to the passage being considered. "Accepting God's Word brings blessing" is good, but "accepting God's Word brings blessing, even to those under curse" is better.

By identifying Elisha as a pattern (foreshadow) of Jesus, we can then clarify the timeless truths illustrated by this passage:

"God's Word (Jesus himself) brings blessing even to those under curse" and "God's Word (Jesus himself) brings curse (judgement) even to those previously blessed."

These timeless truths find support elsewhere in the Bible (e.g. Matthew 7:24-27; John 3:36, 5:24) and are not contradicted.

**Write a summary sentence for the main teaching of the passage today.**
My suggestion (yours may be better) is: "Regardless of past blessings or curses from God, the way we relate to Jesus (God's Word) determines whether we are under his blessing or curse today."

### The Theme of God's Curse (Deuteronomy 28:15-68)

### Consider the changes
Deuteronomy 28:15-68 contains specific teaching for the Israelites living under the Covenant of the Law (the Mosaic Covenant). It describes the

terrible curses that will come upon them for disobedience to God's commands, curses that are repeated in the Prophets (Daniel 9:11; Malachi 2:2).

Since then, God has not changed and neither has human sinful nature. But there have been important covenant changes for Jesus has fulfilled the requirements of the Law. As Galatians 3:13 declares: "Christ redeemed us from the curse of the law by becoming a curse for us, for it is written: 'Cursed is everyone who is hung on a pole.' [the cross]"

With Jesus taking the curse upon himself, the result for Christian believers is "peace with God through our Lord Jesus Christ" (Romans 5:1) and "no condemnation for those who are in Christ Jesus" (Romans 8:1). Because of Jesus the Christian can never experience the curse of God. Revelation 22:3 wonderfully declares: "No longer will there be any curse."

But for those who reject Jesus "God's wrath remains on them." (John 3:36). They are "accursed" (2 Peter 2:14) and on the day of judgement Jesus will say: "Depart from me, you who are cursed, into the eternal fire prepared for the devil and his angels." (Matthew 25:41).

### Find a timeless truth

Thinking about God's unchanging nature, the passage in Deuteronomy teaches us of God's hatred of sin and his demand for justice. God's character remains the same. Each and every sin, even today, evokes God's righteous and dreadful anger.

Reading the text carefully also reveals that despite the suffering for sin the people continue in their sin and so suffer more (Deuteronomy 28:64). This is a timeless truth of sinful human nature. Punishment will often make no difference to our ongoing sin (Leviticus 26:14-39; Isaiah 1:5-6) for the law cannot save us (Romans 8:3).

The emphasis of the passage, however, lies with a different timeless truth - how truly terrible it is to experience the curse of God. Repetition after repetition brings home the horror with graphic images. It's drawn-out again and again so that we feel its impact. It is a dreadful thing to fall into the hands of the living God (Hebrews 10:31).

This terror was experienced by Jesus on the cross. For the Christian,

Jesus willingly became "a curse for us" (Galatians 3:13) so that we no longer have to face God's curse. Every verse of horror is met by his grace. What can we do but praise and thank him.

But that terror still awaits those who reject Jesus. Every sin provokes his anger yet further. The text of Deuteronomy pleads with those not trusting in Jesus to repent and it calls upon Christian believers to pray for them and to speak to them of the saviour.

# Chapter 11 – Application (Key Principles)

**Mark 6:7-13**

**Connect the characters**

In this passage Jesus addresses his original twelve disciples (v7) giving them specific commands and authority (v7-11) with wonderful results (v12).

Connecting the characters, Jesus is still the same (Hebrews 13:8). This passage therefore teaches us about Jesus' authority. But what about the authority he gives to his twelve original disciples to heal and drive out demons? Does he promise to give that authority to each of us today?

To conclude that would be a mistake, for Jesus' promise of authority was specific to his twelve original disciples (called apostles) and we are not those people. Therefore, when we preach, we should not assume that we can drive out demons or heal many people. By God's grace that may occur, but it would require something beyond the ordinary: a special enabling by God for that particular situation.

But that doesn't mean the passage contains no application for us. In so far as these twelve people were entrusted with "preaching that people should repent" (v12) they are like us and so can, in that way, be connected to ourselves.

**Connect the application**

Having identified how to connect the characters, our next task is to find a timeless truth behind Jesus' specific command to them.

Jesus said to them: "Take nothing for the journey except a staff - no bread, no bag, no money in your belts. Wear sandals but not an extra shirt. Whenever you enter a house, stay there until you leave that town. And if any place will not welcome you or listen to you, leave that place and shake the dust off your feet as a testimony against them." (v8-11)

What timeless truth lies behind these specific instructions to the twelve apostles?

At first, it may appear there is a timeless truth for Christians to rely only on God for the provision of what we need as we preach the good news. But that doesn't cover everything in these verses, for there is also the command to stay in a house that is welcoming and leave a house that is unwelcoming, with a visible sign of rejection.

Reflecting further, there is a connection between these commands, for they all concern how to relate to those to whom we preach.

Having no spare money or provisions meant that the twelve disciples would relate to those around them in a certain way. They would be dependent on those they met. They would need to be accommodated by others and be fed by others. Furthermore, they wouldn't be offering the false gospel of "if you believe you will receive riches".

So, by obeying these commands, the twelve disciples needed those people to whom they spoke.

Today it is still very easy for a wealth gap to become a barrier to healthy relationships. It can foster pride and it brings power. Dependence on others, on the other hand, develops humility, thankfulness and a sense of control for others. It also doesn't advertise a gospel of material riches.

Behind Jesus' commands, therefore, lies an important timeless truth. This is not just that we should rely on God for all that we need, but that our relationship with unbelievers to whom we speak the gospel, should in no way exercise power over them. We are taught by Jesus elsewhere to serve others in their need. Here he teaches us the importance of letting others serve us in our need.[12]

---

12. Tracing the theme forwards Paul's words in 1 Corinthians 10:32 pick up this principle: "Do not cause anyone to stumble" and in 1 Corinthians 9:19-23: "To the weak I became weak, to win the weak. I have become all things to all people so that by all possible means I might save some."

## Translate into the language of Today's World

Finally, we need to bring the application home to ourselves, remembering to "Be specific". We need to ask: Does my relationship with those who don't yet know Jesus demonstrate this kind of equality? If not, how could it do so? What role do possessions and money have in my relationship with unbelievers? Are these stumbling blocks? Perhaps I need to become less independent, less powerful, less controlling and instead show vulnerability and some reliance on my unbelieving friends?

## Deuteronomy 7:1-6

Passages such as this one in the Old Testament are often neglected. Their commands to the original hearers to "destroy them totally", "make no treaty with them" and "do not intermarry with them" are shocking and seemingly against the teaching of loving our enemies in the New Testament. But to neglect passages like these is to neglect rich teaching and application for Christians today.

## Connect the Characters

The Israelites as the people of God connect to Christians today, the present people of God. The enemy nations (Hittites, Amorites, Canaanites etc.) correspond to the enemies of Christians today - namely sin (in all its various forms) and Satan.

## Connect the application

The passage contains a number of timeless truths.

First with regard to God - that he will bring his people into his promised land (7:1) and deliver his people from their enemies (7:2); the deliverance of the Israelites foreshadowing his great deliverance through Jesus at the cross.

Secondly with regard to people, there are timeless truths in that God's people are described as "holy to the LORD your God" (7:6) and as "chosen" (7:7). These descriptions are supremely true of Jesus (Luke 9:35; Revelation 3:7) and because of him for all Christians (Colossians

3:12; 1 Peter 2:9). In their status, the people of God (both then and now) are holy (separate and devoted to God) and chosen (out of the nations) to be his people.

Consequently, just as then, God's people today must live in accordance with this status before God as holy and chosen (1 Peter 1:15). But what does this mean practically?

### Translate the application

The practical application for the Israelites in Deuteronomy 7 was to make no treaty with their enemies, form no marriage relationship with their enemies and destroy them totally. How then do we translate that application to Christians today?

As Christians our enemies are different. The foreign nations in Deuteronomy are not our enemies, but instead, foreshadow sin and Satan.

So, to make no treaty with our enemies is to make no deals with the longings of sin and Satan. It is to accept no compromise. To not marry means to have no close relationship. Rather than listening to sin and Satan or entertaining evil thoughts, we are instead to reject the teaching of Satan (1 Timothy 4:1) and put sin to death (Romans 8:13). That is, we are to destroy them totally.

Realising this, the passage challenges us to stop and ask: Is that how I relate to sin and the thinking of the devil? God's command is for total destruction, no toleration, no relationship. Do I take this seriously?

We'd do well to examine ourselves for compromise. Are we making deals in our minds and so allowing some aspects of sin to remain? Do we show mercy to our enemies in any way, or will we destroy them totally? Do we recognise the truth of v4?

Finally, in this passage we should note that God doesn't command that some enemies are to be destroyed, but that all enemies are to be destroyed. The application today is therefore to all sin and to all thinking of Satan. And as we have seen, with application it is wise to "Be specific". We need to ask ourselves: To which particular sin am I most likely to show some mercy? Which individual sin am I not totally destroying? And what specifically would it mean for me to destroy that sin and leave no trace of it in my life? (v5) That, we must then do in the power which God provides.

## Chapter 12 – Application (CHRIST)

**Romans 12:9-13**

I hope this exercise was useful and helped you to think through some good applications. By way of further thought, here are some additional questions to ask of your answers:

1. Is your application God-centred? Does it start with God?
2. Is your application consistent with God's overall purpose - "being conformed to the likeness of his son" (Romans 8:28-29)?
3. Could your application be made more specific to the text?

# APPENDIX 2

## The Story of Israel

The diagram on the next page shows how the content of the Old Testament books fits into the overall Bible storyline.

Some key characters in the storyline are also included.

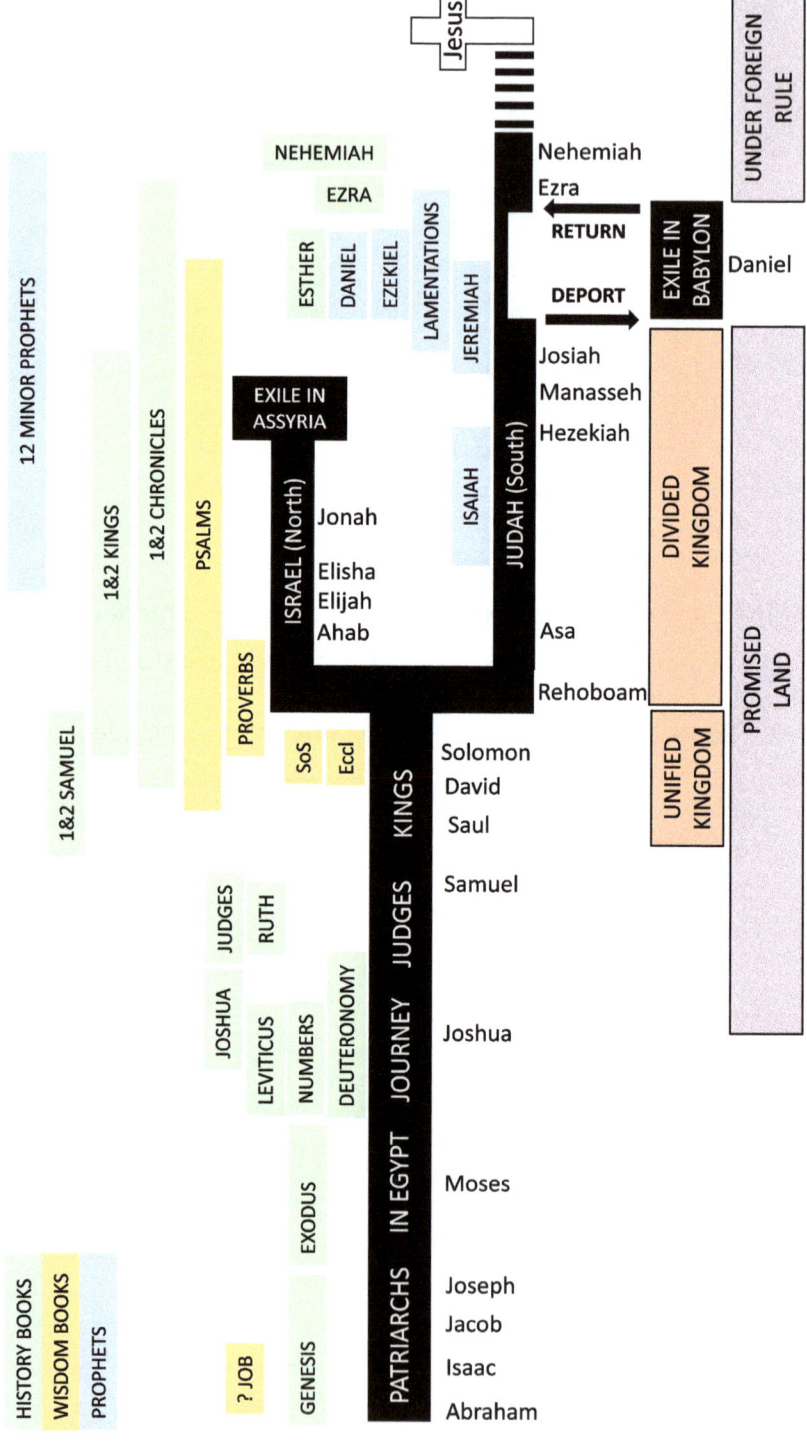

# APPENDIX 3

## Foreshadows of Jesus

| | OT Shadow (with examples) | OT Reference | NT Fulfilment |
|---|---|---|---|
| ROLE | **Head of humanity** **(Adam)** | Gen 2-3 | Rom 5:14 1 Cor 15:45-47 |
| | **Holder of keys** (Eliakim) | Is 22:20-22 | Rev 3:7 |
| | **Husband** | Ezek 16; Hosea 2:16 | Eph 5:32 |
| | **King** (David) (All Kings) | Ps 2 2 Sam 7 Eze 34:23-24; 37:24 | Matt 1:1,6; Luke 1:69; Matt 9:27 Heb 1:1-5; Acts 4:23-31;13:30-39; 13:34-39; Luke 1:32 |
| | **Kinsman-Redeemer** (Boaz) | Lev 25:48; Ruth 4:4-8 | 1 Peter 1:18 |
| | **Mediator** (Abraham) (Moses) (Samuel) (Job) | Gen 19; 20:7 Ex 32:31-32; Num 21:7 1 Sam 7:9; 12:19 Job 42:8 | 1 Tim 2:5; Heb 7:25 |
| | **Merciful Judge** (Esau) | Gen 33:10 | Heb 8:12; Rev 22:4 |
| | **Person of Faith** (Abraham) (Esther) (Moses) (Noah) (Rahab) (Ruth) (Many others - See Heb 11) | Gen 12:1-9; 22:1-18 Esther 4:15-16 Gen 6:9-8:22 Josh 2:8-13 Ruth 1:16-17 | Heb 12:2 Heb 11:8-10 James 2:21:24 Heb 11 Matt 2:13-15; Heb 3:2 Heb 11:24-28, 11:7 James 2:25 |
| | **Priest** (Aaron) (Melchizedek) (Samuel) (Ezra) | Lev 21 Ex 28:1-4 Gen 14; Ps 110:4 1 Sam 7:2-14 | Heb 9:11, 10:11-13 Heb 5:4-5 Heb 5-7 |
| | **Prophet** (All prophets) | Deut 18:15 | Acts 3:20-26 |
| | **Lord** (Jacob) (Joseph) | Dan 7:14 Gen27:29; Gen 43:28 | Phil 2:10 |
| | **Son** (Isaac) (Israel) | Gen 3:15; Ps 2:7; Hos 11:1 Ex 4:22; Deut 8:5 | Mark 1:11, 9:7 Matt 2:15 |
| | **Saviour / Rescuer** (David) (Gideon) (Samson) (Samuel and all Judges) | 1 Sam 17 Judges 7 Judges 16:30 1 Sam 7:2-14 | Luke 2:11; Col 2:15; 1 Jn 4:14 Acts 13:23 |
| | **Serpent's head crusher** | Gen 3:15 Judges 4:22; 1 Sam 17:51 | Rom16:20 Heb 2:14 |
| | **Shepherd/Leader/ Ruler** (All leaders) | 2 Sam 5:2; Ezek 34 Num 27:17-18 1 Chron 11:2, 29:22 | John 10:11; Rev 1:5 Luke 22:26-29 Acts 5:31 |
| | **Suffering Servant** (Job) (Joseph) | Is 53 Gen 37-46 | Acts 8:32-33 James 5:11 Acts 7 |
| | **Teacher** | Eccl 1:1-2, 12:9 | John 13:13 |

| OT Shadow (with examples) | OT Reference | NT Fulfilment |
|---|---|---|
| **Branch** (Descendant from whom comes blessing) | Is 4:2, 11:1-2 Jer 23:5, 33:15 Zech 3:8, 6:12 | Matt 1:6; Rom 1:3 |
| **Bronze Serpent** (Look to this and you will be saved) | Num 21:4-9 | John 3:14-16 |
| **Cities of Refuge** (Flee to this place and you will be safe) | Num 35 | Matt 11:28; Rom 8:33-39 Heb 6:18-19 |
| **Great Fish (Jonah)** (Picture of death and new life) | Jonah 1:17 | Matt 12:40 |
| **Ladder (Jacob's)** (Access point to God) | Gen 28:12 | John 1:51 |
| **Living Stone** (Something to build your life on or something that will crush you) | Is 8:14; Dan 2:34,44 Ps 118:22 | Luke 20:17-19; Acts 4:11 Eph 2:20; 1 Peter 2:4-8 |
| **Manna in the desert** (Necessary food for life) | Ex 16 | John 6:32-33 |
| **Noah's Ark** (Means of salvation through judgement) | Gen 6-9 | 2 Peter 2:5-9; Matt 24:37-38 Luke 17:26-27; Heb 11:7 1 Peter 3:20 |
| **Rock in the Wilderness** (Drink from this and you will live) | Ex 17:5-7 Num 20:2-11 | 1 Cor 10:4 |
| **Sacrifices** (Abel) (Isaac) (Heifer) (Lamb) (All OT sacrifices) | Lev 17:11 Gen 4:8-10 Gen 22:2 Num 19:2-5 Ex 12:1-13; Is 53:7 | Heb 9:11-15 25-28; 10:1-12 Heb 12:24<br><br>Heb 9:13-14 John 1:29; Rev 5:6-13 Acts 8:32; 1 Cor 5:7 1 Peter 1:17-21 |
| **Scape Goat** (Removal of sins) | Lev 16:20-22 Is 53:6,12 | Heb 10:4,10 1 John 3:5 |
| **Tabernacle/Temple (Zion)** (Place of God's presence / sacrifice / place to meet with God) | 1 Kings 8:10-11; Ps 132:13 Is 56:7 | John 1:14, John 2:19-21 1 Cor 6:19 Heb 8:5 1 Peter 2:4-5 |
| **Vine and its branches** (Life in the kingdom of God) | Is 5:1-7; Ps 80:8-9 | John 15:5 |

OBJECT

# APPENDIX 4

## Other Bible Patterns

| Other Bible Patterns | | |
|---|---|---|
| **OT Shadow** | **OT Reference** | **NT Fulfilment** |
| **Exile** (A repeated pattern of God's judgement) | Many references including Gen 3:23-24, 4:14 Deut 28:62-68 2 Kings 17:6, 25:8-21 2 Chron 36:20-21 Jer 39:9-10 | Matt 25:41 Col 1:21 2 Thess 1:9 |
| **Life for God's people in Exile** | Jer 29:1-23 | Christians (citizens of heaven - Phil 3:20) as exiles: Heb 11:13 James 1:1 1 Peter 1:1,17, 2:11 |
| **The Exodus** (A pattern of God's salvation) | Many references - particularly in Exodus, Numbers and Deuteronomy | 1 Cor 5:7, 10:4 1 Peter 1:15-19 |
| **Dry bones coming to life** | Ezek 37:1-14 | Matt 27:52-53 |
| **Passing through the Red Sea** | Ex 14 | 1 Cor 10:1-2 |
| **The Veil of the Tabernacle and Temple** | Ex 26:37; Lev 16 | Matt 27:51 Mark 15:38 Heb 9:3, 10:19-20 |
| **Jonah** (Asleep in a storm, with terrified sailors, which is miraculously calmed leading to the fear of God) | Jonah 1:4-16 | Mark 4:35-41 |
| **The Passover** | Ex 12-13 | 1 Cor 5:7 |
| **Unleavened Bread** | Ex 12:17 | John 5; 1 Cor 5:6-8 |
| **First Fruits** | Ex 23:9-14; Jer 2:3 | 1 Cor 15:20-23 |
| **Day of Atonement** | Lev 16 | Heb 13:11-13 |
| **Israel** (God's people) | Many references | Christians - many references |
| **Enemies of God and his people** | Amalekites Amorites Egyptians Philistines Moabites Many others | **Satan / Spiritual forces** Eph 6:11-12; 1 Peter 5:8; Rev 14:7 **Sin**: Rom 8:13; 1 Peter 2:11 **World**: Matt 13:38, 18:7; John 15:18-19, 16:33; Phil 1:19-30 Col 2:8; James 4:4; 1 John 2:16 |
| **Queen of Sheba** (Gentiles coming to Jerusalem to honour the king) | 1 Kings 10 2 Chron 9:1-12 Is 2:1-5 | Matt 12:42 Luke 11:31 |

The left margin labels read vertically: **EVENTS** (spanning the first eight rows), **FESTIVALS** (spanning The Passover through Day of Atonement), **PEOPLE** (spanning Israel through Queen of Sheba).

| Other Bible Patterns | | |
|---|---|---|
| OT Shadow | OT Reference | NT Fulfilment |
| **Jerusalem**<br>(The dwelling place of God and the church in glory) | Many references | Gal 4:26<br>Heb 12:22-23<br>Rev 21 |
| **Babylon**<br>(The world in opposition to God and his people) | Many references including:<br>Gen 10:10; 11:1-9<br>2 Kings 17-25<br>2 Chron 32-36<br>Is 47 | 1 Peter 5:13<br>Rev 14:8, 17:3-7, 18:1-24 |
| **Sodom & Gomorrah** | Gen 19 | Matt 11:23-24<br>Luke 10:12; 17:28-29,32<br>Jude 7<br>2 Peter 2:6-7 |
| **Temple**<br>(Shadows heavenly temple)<br>(Place from which comes life) | Ezek 47:1-12 | Heb 8:5, 9:1,24<br>Rev 21 |
| **The Promised Land**<br>(Place of rest) | Many references - particularly in Exodus, Numbers, Deuteronomy and Joshua | Heb 3:7-4:11<br>Rev 14:13 |
| **Wilderness**<br>(Place between rescue from Egypt and the promised land - corresponds to life on earth now for the Christian) | Many references - particularly in Exodus, Numbers and Deuteronomy | Mark 6:32<br>Luke 4:1<br>Rev 12:6, 14 |

PLACE

# APPENDIX 5

# New Testament References to the Old Testament

The following list of references should not be taken as a comprehensive list. My hope is that they prove useful in the study of the Old Testament, revealing as they do the unity of the Scriptures. The verses in italics are allusions rather than direct references.

## GENESIS

**Chap 1** - *Heb 11:3*; **1:3** - 2Cor 4:6
**1:27** - Matt 19:4; Mark 10:6
**2:2** - Heb 4:4,10; **2:7** - 1Cor 15:45
**2:20-23** - 1Cor 11:8-9
**2:24** - Matt 19:5; Mark 10:7-8
1Cor 6:16; Eph 5:31
**Chap 3** - 1Tim 2:13-14; **3:15** -
*Matt 1:25; Rom 16:20; Col 2:15*
*Heb 2:14; 1 John 3:8; Rev 12:17*
**3:22** - *Rev 22:2*
**Chap 4** - Heb 11:4; 1John 3:12
Jude 11; **4:8-12** - Luke 11:51
**5:18-24** - Heb 11:5; Jude 14-15
**Chap 6** - Matt 24:37-39
Luke 17:26-27; **6:9-8:22** -
1Peter 3:20-21; 2Peter 2:4-5, 3:6
**6:8-9:29** - Heb 11:7
**12:1** - Acts 7:3; **12:1-9** -
Luke 1:72-73; Heb 11:8-10
**12:3** - Gal 3:8; **12:7** - Gal 3:16
**13:15** - Gal 3:16
**14:17-24** - Heb 7:1-10

**15:5** - Rom 4:18; **15:6** - Rom 4:3,
4:19-25; Gal 3:6; James 2:23
**15:13-14** - Acts 7:6-7
**Chap 16** - Gal 4:21-31
**Chap 17** - Rom 4:11-12
**17:5** - Rom 4:17; **17:7** - Gal 3:16
**18:10,14** - Rom 9:9
**18:18** - Gal 3:8
**Chap 19** - Matt 11:23-24
Luke 17:28-29; **19:1-25** -
Luke 10:12; **19:1-29** - Jude 7
**19:23-29** - 2 Peter 2:6-7
**19:26** - Luke 17:32, *Luke 9:63*
**21:1-3** - Heb 11:11-12
**21:1-21** - Gal 4:21-31
**21:10** - Gal 4:30
**21:12 -** Rom 9:7; Heb 11:18
**Chap 22** - Heb 11:17-19
James 2:21-22; **22:2** - *Matt 3:17*
**22:17** - Heb 6:14
**22:18** - Acts 3:25; Gal 3:8
**24:7** - Gal 3:16
**25:23** - Rom 9:11-12

**25:31-34** - Heb 12:16
**26:4** - Acts 3:25
**27:27-40** - Heb 11:20
**27:34-40** - Heb 12:17
**28:12** - John 1:51
**28:14** - Acts 3:25
**47:28-48:22** - Heb 11:21
**48:22** - John 4:5
**49:9-10** - Rev 4:5; **49:10** - Rev 12:5
**50:24-25** - Heb 11:22

## EXODUS

**Chap 1** - Acts 7:17-19
**2:1-2** - Heb 11:23; **2:1-10** -
Acts 7:20-22; **2:11-15** - Acts 7:27-28
Heb 11:24-27; **2:24** - Acts 7:34
**3:6** - Matt 22:32; Mark 12:26
Luke 20:37; **3:1-10** - Acts 7:30-35
**Chap 7f** - Acts 7:36; **7:14-12:30** -
*Rev 8:6-9:11, 16:1-11*
**9:16** - Rom 9:17
**Chap 12** - Heb 11:28
**12:46** - *John 12:36, 19:36*
**13:2** - Luke 2:23; **13:12** - Luke 2:23
**Chap 14** -1Cor 10:1-2
**14:22** - Heb 11:29
**Chap 16** - John 6:32-35,49-51
1Cor 10:4; **16:4** - John 6:31
**16:18** - 2Cor 8:15
**Chap 17:1-7** - 1Cor 10:4
**Chaps 19-20** - Heb 12:18-21
**19:5** - 1Peter 2:9; *Tit 2:14*
**19:12-13** - Heb 12:20
**19:16,19** - *Rev 1:10*
**20:12** - Matt 15:4; Mark
7:10; Eph 6:2-3; **20:12-16** -
Matt 19:18-19; Mark 10:19

**EXODUS Continued**
Luke 18:20; **20:13** - Matt 5:21
**20:13-14** - James 2:11; **20:13-17** -
Rom 13:9; **20:14** - Matt 5:27
**20:17** -Rom 7:7; **20:19** - Gal 3:19
**21:17** - Matt 15:4; Mark 7:10
**21:24** - Matt 5:38
**22:28** - Acts 23:5
**23:4-5** - *Matt 5:44*
**24:28** - Heb 9:20
**25:40** - Heb 8:5
**28:17-19** - *Rev 21:19*
**Chap 32** - Acts 7:39-42
**32:6** - 1Cor 10:7
**33:19** - Rom 9:15
**34:29-53** - 2Cor 3:7-14
**40:34-35** - Rev 15:8

## LEVITICUS

**Whole book** - Heb 7:11
**11:44-45** -1Peter 1:16
**12:8** - Luke 2:24
**Chap 16** - Heb 9:7-10:15
**18:5** - Rom 10:5; Gal 3:12
**19:2** - 1Peter 1:16
**19:12** - Matt 5:33
**19:18** - Matt 5:43, 19:18-19, 22:39
Mark 12:31 Luke 10:27; Rom 13:9
Gal 5:14 James 2:8
**20:7** - 1Peter 1:16
**20:9** - Matt 15:4; Mark 7:10
**24:20** - Matt 5:38
**26:12** - 2Cor 6:16

## NUMBERS

**9:12** - John 19:36
**12:7** - Heb 3:5

**16:1-35** - Jude 11
**16:5** - 2Tim 2:19
**20:1-13** - 1Cor 10:4
**21:4-9** - John 3:14-15; 1Cor 10:9
**Chap 22-24** - 2Peter 3:15-16
Jude 11; Rev 2:14
**24:17** - Rev 22:16
**25:1-9** -1Cor 10:8

## DEUTERONOMY

**4:24** - Heb 12:29
**5:5** - Gal 3:19; **5:16** - Matt 15:4
Mark 7:10; Luke 15:20; Eph 6:2-3
**5:16-20** - Matt 19:18-19
Mark 10:19; Luke 18:20
**5:17** - Matt 5:21
**5:17-18** - James 2:11
**5:17-21** - Rom 13:9
**5:18** - Matt 5:27; **5:21** - Rom 7:7
**6:4-5** - Mark 12:29-30;
**6:5** - Matt 22:37; Luke 10:27
**6:8** - *Rev 13:16*; **6:13** - Matt 4:10
Luke 4:8; **6:16** - Matt 4:7; Luke 4:12
**8:3** - Matt 4:4; Luke 4:4
**9:19** - Heb 12:21
**13:5** -1Cor 5:13
**17:6** - Heb 10:28
**17:7** - 1Cor 5:13
**18:5** - Acts 7:37-38
**18:15,18-19** - Acts 3:22-23
**19:15** - Matt 18:16; 2Cor 13:1
**19:19** - 1Cor 5:13
**19:21** - Matt 5:38
**21:23** - Gal 3:13
**22:21** - 1Cor 5:13;
**22:24** -1Cor 5:13
**24:1** - Matt 5:31

**DEUTERONOMY Continued**
**24:1-4** - Matt 19:7-8; Mark 10:4-5
**24:7** - 1Cor 5:7
**25:4** - 1Cor 9:9; 1Tim 5:18
**27:26** - Gal 3:10
**29:4** - Rom 11:8
**30:12-14** - Rom 10:6-8
**31:6** - Heb 13:5
**32:21** - Rom 10:19
**32:35** - Rom 12:19; Heb 10:30
**32:36** - Heb 10:30
**32:43** - Rom 15:10; Heb 1:6

## JOSHUA

**Chap 2** - Heb 11:31; James 2:25
**6:1-21** - Heb 11:30
**24:32** *via Gen 33:18-19 and*
*Gen 45:22 - John 4:5,12*

## JUDGES

## RUTH

**Whole book** - Matt 1:5

## 1 SAMUEL

**21:1-9** - Mark 2:25-26; Luke 6:3-4

## 2 SAMUEL

**7:14** - 2Cor 6:18; Heb 1:5; *Rev 4:5*
**22:50** - Rom 15:9

## 1 KINGS

**8:10-11** - *Rev 15:8*
**Chap 10** - Matt 12:42; Luke 11:31
**Chaps 17-18** - James 5:17-18
**17:7-24** - Luke 4:26
**19:10-18** - Rom 11:2-4

## 2 KINGS
**Chap 5** - Luke 4:27

## 1 CHRONICLES
**17:13** - Heb 1:5
**21:5** - 1Cor 10:10

## 2 CHRONICLES
**5:13-14** - *Rev 15:8*
**Chap 9** - Matt 12:42; Luke 11:41
**24:20-21**- Luke 11:51

## EZRA

## NEHEMIAH

## ESTHER

## JOB
**Whole book** - James 5:11
**5:13** - 1Cor 3:19
**41:11** - Rom 11:35

## PSALMS
**2:1-2** - Acts 4:25-26;
**2:7** - Matt 17:5; Acts 13:33
Heb 1:5, 5:5; 2Peter 1:17
**2:9** - Rev 2:27, 12:5, 19:15
**4:4** - Eph 4:26
**5:9** - Rom 3:13
**8:2** - Matt 21:16; **8:4-6** - Heb 2:6-8
**8:6** - 1Cor 15:27; Eph 1:22
**10:7** - Rom 3:14
**14:1-3** - Rom 3:10-12
**16:8-11** - Acts 2:25-28
**16:10** - Acts 2:31, 13:35
**18:49** - Rom 15:9

**PSALMS Continued**
**19:4** - Rom 10:18
**22:1** - Matt 27:46; Mark 15:34
**22:6** - *Matt 2:23 (John 1:45-6)*
**22:7-8** - Mark 15:31
**22:9** - Matt 27:39; Mark 15:29
**22:16** - Matt 27:38; Mark 15:27
Luke 23:33; **22:18** - Mark 15:24
Luke 23:34; John 19:24
**22:22** - Heb 2:12; **22:31** - John 19:30
**24:1** - 1Cor 10:26
**31:5** - Luke 23:46
**32:1-2** - Rom 4:7-8
**34:20** - John 19:36
**34:12-16** - 1Peter 3:10-12
**35:19** - John 15:25
**36:1** - Rom 3:18
**40:6-8** - Heb 10:5-9
**41:9** - John 13:18, *John 17:12*
**44:22** - Rom 8:36
**45:6-7** - Heb 1:8-9
**46:2** - Rev 6:14; **46:4** - Rev 22:1
**51:4** - Rom 3:4
**53:1-3** - Rom 3:10-12
**62:12** - Rom 2:6
**68:18** - Eph 4:8
**69:4** - John 15:25
**69:9** - Matt 27:44; Mark 15:32
Luke 23:39; John 2:17; Rom15:3
**69:21** - Matt 27:34; Mark
15:23; Luke 23:36; John 19:29
**69:21** - John 19:29; **69:22-23** -
Rom 11:9-10; **69:25** - Acts 1:20
**78:2** - Matt 13:35
**82:6** - John 10:34
**91:11-12** – Matt 4:6; Luke 4:10-11
**94:11** - 1Cor 3:20

**95:7-8** - Heb 3:15, 4:7,10
**95:7-11** - Heb 3:7-11
**95:11** - Heb 4:5
**102:25-27** - Heb 1:10-12
**104:4** - Heb 1:7
**109:8** - *John 17:12*; Acts 1:20
**110:1** - Matt 22:44, 26:64
Mark 12:36; Luke 20:42-43
Acts 2:34-35; Heb 1:13, 10:12-13
**110:4** - Heb 5:6; Heb 7:17,21
**112:9** - 2Cor 9:9
**116:10** - 2Cor 4:13
**117:1** - Rom 15:11
**118:6-7** - Heb 13:6
**118:22** - Luke 20:17
Acts 4:11; 1Peter 2:7
**118:22-23** - Matt 21:42
Mark 12:10-11
**118:25-26** - Matt 21:9
Mark 11:9-10; John 12:13
**118:26** - Matt 21:9, 23:39
Luke 13:35, 19:38
*126:5-6 - 2Tim 2:6; James 5:7-8*
**121:6** - *Rev 7:16*
**140:3** - Rom 3:13
**145:13** - Rev 11:15
**146:6** - *Rev 14:7*

## PROVERBS

**3:11-12** - Heb 12:5-6
**3:34** - James 4:6; 1Peter 5:5
**4:26** - Heb 12:13
**11:31** - *1Peter 4:18*
**22:18** - John 19:24
**24:12** - Rom 2:6
**25:21-22** - Rom 12:20
**26:11** - 2Peter 2:22

## ECCLESIASTES

**1:2** - *Rom 8:20*
**7:20** - Rom 3:10
**12:8** - *Rom 8:20*

## SONG OF SONGS

## ISAIAH

**1:9** - Rom 9:29
**2:2-3** - Heb 12:22
**2:10,19,21** - Rev 6:15
**6:1-4** - Rev 4:6-8, *Rev 15:8*
**6:9** - Luke 8:10
**6:9-10** - Matt 13:13-16
Mark 4:12, Acts 28:26-27
**6:10** - John 12:40-41
**7:14** - Matt 1:23
**8:12-13** - 1Peter 3:14-15
**8:14** - Rom 9:33; 1Peter 2:8
**8:17-18** - Heb 2:13
**9:1-2** - Matt 4:15-16
**10:22-23** - Rom 9:27-28
**11:1** - Rev 5:5
*11:4 - Rev 19:15*
**11:10** - Rom 15:12
**13:9-13** - Rev 6:12-13
**13:10** - Matt 24:29; Mark 13:24-25
**13:13-19** - Rev 18
**21:9** - Rev 14:8
**22:13** - 1Cor 15:32; **22:22** - Rev 3:7
**25:8** - 1Cor 15:54; Rev 7:17
Rev 21:4
*26:11 - Heb 10:27*
*26:20 - Heb 10:37*
**28:11-12** - 1Cor 14:21
**28:16** - Rom 9:33; Rom 10:11
1Peter 2:6

**29:10** - Rom 11:8; **29:13** -
Matt 15:8-9; Mark 7:6-7; **29:14** -
1Cor 1:19; **29:16** - Rom 9:20
**34:4** - Matt 24:29
Mark 13:24-25; Rev 6:13-14
**34:9-10** - Rev 14:10-11
**35:5-6** - Matt 11:5; **35:6-7** -
John 7:38; **35:10** - Rev 21:4
**35:56** - Luke 7:21-23
**40:3** - Matt 3:3; Mark 1:3
John 1:23; **40:3-5** - Luke 3:4-6
**40:6-8** - 1Peter 1:24-25
**40:13** - Rom 11:34; 1Cor 2:16
**40:19** - 1Cor 2:16
**42:1-4** - Matt 12:18-21
**45:9** - Rom 9:20; **45:23** -
Rom 14:11; Phil 2:10-11
**47:7-9** - Rev 18:7-8
**48:20** - *Rev 18:4*
**49:6** - Acts 13:47; **49:8** - 2Cor 6:2
**49:10** - Rev 7:16; **49:26** - *Rev 16:6*
**50:6** - Matt 27:29-30; Mark 15:20
Luke 23:36
**52:5** - Rom 2:24; **52:7** -
Rom 10:15; **52:11** - 2Cor 6:17
**52:15** - Rom 15:21; *1Cor 2:9*
**53:1** - John 12:38; Rom 10:16
*53:3* - *Matt 2:23 (John 1:45-46)*
**53:4** - Matt 8:17; **53:4-6** -
1Peter 2:24-25; **53:7** - Matt 27:31
Mark 15:16; Luke23:26; **53:7-8** -
Acts 8:32-33; **53:9** - Matt 27:59-60
Mark 15:43-46; Luke 23:51-53
1Peter 2:22; **53:12** - Luke 22:37
**54:1** - Gal 4:27; **54:13** - John 6:45
**55:1** - Rev 21:6, 22:17
**55:3** - Acts 13:34

**ISAIAH Continued**

**56:7** - Matt 21:13; Mark 11:17
Luke 19:46
**59:7-8** - Rom 3:15-17
**59:20-21** - *Rom 11:26-27*
**60:1-3** - Rev 21:23-24
**60:11** - Rev 21:25
**60:19-20** - Rev 21:23, 22:5
**61:1-2** - Luke 4:18-21
**61:10** - *Rev 19:8*
**63:2-3** - *Rev 19:13,15*
**63:2-6** - Rev 14:20
**64:4** - 1Cor 2:9
**65:1-2** - Rom 10:20-21
**65:17** - 2Peter 3:13; Rev 21:1
**65:19** - Rev 21:4
**66:1-2** - Acts 7:49-50
**66:24** - Mark 9:48

## JEREMIAH

**7:11** - Matt 21:13; Mark 11:17
Luke 19:46
**9:24** - 1Cor 1:31; 2Cor 10:17
**18:6** - Rom 9:21
**19:1-13** - Matt 27:9
**31:15** - Matt 2:18; **31:31-34** -
Heb 8:8-12; **31:33** - Heb 10:16-17
**31:34** - *Rom 11:27;* Heb 10:17
**32:6-9** - Matt 27:9
**32:38** - 2Cor 6:16
**Chaps 50-51** - Rev 18
**50:15,29** - Rev 18:6
**51:6** - *Rev 18:4;* **51:7-8** - Rev 14:8,
18:2-3; **51:8** - Rev 18:9; **51:45** -
Rev 18:4; **51:63-64** - Rev 18:21

## LAMENTATIONS

## EZEKIEL

**Chap 1** - Rev 4
**3:3** - Rev 10:9
**Chap 27** - *Rev 18:11-20*
**36:22** - Rom 2:24
**36:26-27** - John 3:5-10
**37:27** - 2Cor 6:16
**37:27-28** - Rev 21:3
**38:1-39:16** - Rev 20:5-9
**39:17-9** - Rev 19:17-18,21
**40:17-19** - *Rev 11:1-2*
**47:1-12** - Rev 22:1-2
**48:30-34** - Rev 21:12-13

## DANIEL

**2:44** - Rev 11:15
**Chap 7** - Rev 13:1-10
**7:9** - *Rev 1:14;* **7:10** - Rev 21:12
**7:11** - Rev 13:5-6, 19:20
**7:13** - Matt 26:64; Rev 1:7,13, 14:14; **7:14** - Rev 11:15
**7:25** - Rev 11:3, 12:6 14, 13:8
**7:27** - Rev 11:18, 22:8
**8:10** - *Rev 12:4*
**9:27** - Matt 24:15; Mark 13:14
**10:4-11** - Rev 1:13-18
**11:31** - Matt 24:15; Mark 13:14
**12:11** - Matt 24:15; Mark 13:14
**12:7** - Rev 11:3, 12:6,14, 13:5
**12:9-10** - Rev 22:10-11
**12:11** - Matt 24:15; Mark 13:14

## HOSEA

**1:10** - Rom 9:26-27
**2:23** - Rom 9:25; 1Peter 2:9-10 Rev 21:3
**6:6** - Matt 9:13; Matt 12:7

## HOSEA Continued

**10:8** - Luke 23:30; Rev 6:16
**11:1** - Matt 2:15
**13:14** -1Cor 15:55

## JOEL

**Whole book** - *Rev 9:1-11*
**2:28-32** - Acts 2:17-21
**2:32** - Rom 10:13
**3:13** - Rev 14:14-20
**3:17** - Rev 21:27

## AMOS

**5:25-27** - Acts 7:42-43
**9:11-12** - Acts 15:16-18

## OBADIAH

## JONAH

**Chap 2** - Matt 12:39-40; Matt 16:4 Luke 11:29-30
**Chap 4** - Matt 12:41; Luke 11:32

## MICAH

**5:2** - Matt 2:6
**7:6** - Matt 10:35-36

## NAHUM

*1:15 - Rom 10:15*

## HABAKKUK

**1:5** - Acts 13:41
**2:3-4** - Heb 10:37-38
**2:4** - Rom 1:17; Gal 3:11

## ZEPHANIAH

**3:13** - Rev 14:8

## HAGGAI
**2:6** - Heb 12:26-27

## ZECHARIAH
**2:7** - Rev 18:4; **2:10** - Rev 21:1
**4:3,11-14** - Rev 11:4-12
**6:1-6** - Rev 6:1-8
**9:9** - Matt 21:5; John 12:15
**11:12-13** - Matt 27:9-10
**12:10** - John 19:37; *Rev 1:7*
**13:7** - Matt 26:31; Mark 14:27
**14:8** - Rev 22:1-2

## MALACHI
**1:2-3** - Rom 9:13
**3:1** - Matt 11:10; Mark 1:2
Luke 7:27
**4:5** - Matt 11:14; **4:5-6** - Luke 1:17

## WHOLE OLD TESTAMENT
Matt 5:17; Luke 24:27, 44
John 5:39; Acts 13:16-25, 28:23
Rom 15:4; 1Cor 10:11

## CHARACTERS
**Aaron** Acts 7:40; Heb Chap 7
**Abel** Matt 23:35; Luke 11:51
Heb 11:4, 12:24
**Abraham** Matt 3:9; John 8:31-41,
52-58; Acts 7:2-8,32; Rom Chap 4
Gal 3:6-9; Gal 3:14,16,18,29
Gal 4:21-31; Heb 7:1-2, 11:8-12,
17-19; James 2:21-24
**Adam** Rom 5:12-19; 1Cor 15:22
1Cor 15:45; 1Tim 2:13-14
**Balaam** 2Peter 2:15-16; Jude 11
**Barak** Heb 11:32; Rev 2:14
**Cain** Heb 11:4; 1John 3:12; Jude 11

**David** Acts 7:45-46; Heb 11:33
**Elijah** Matt 17:3; Mark 9:4-6, 9:12-13
**Enoch** Heb 11:5; Jude 14
**Esau** Rom 9:13; Heb 12:16
**Eve** 1Tim 2:13-14
**Gideon** Heb 11:32
**Hagar** Gal 4:21-31
**Isaac** Acts 7:8,32; Rom 9:7,10
Gal 4:28; Heb 11:9,20
**Jacob** John 4:5-6,12
Acts 7:8-16,42,46; Heb 11:21
**Jephthah** Heb 11:32
**Jezebel** Rev 2:20
**Job** James 5:11
**Joseph** Acts 7:9-16; Heb 11:22
**Lot** Luke 17:28-30
**Lot's wife** Luke 17:32
**Melchizedek** Heb 5:5,10, 6:20
Heb Chap 7
**Moses** Matt 17:3; Mark 9:4-6
John 5:45-46; Acts 7:20-45
Heb 3:1-6, 9:19, 11:23-28
**Naaman** Luke 4:27
**Noah** Luke 17:26-27; Heb 11:7
1Peter 3:20; 2Peter 2:4-5
**Queen of Sheba** Matt 12:42
Luke 11:31
**Rahab** Matt 1:5; Heb 11:31
James 2:25
**Samson** Heb 11:32
**Samuel** Heb 11:32
**Sarah** Rom 9:9; Gal 4:21-31
Peter 3:1-6
**Solomon** Luke 12:27; Acts7:47
**Tamar** Matt 1:3
**Zarephath** Luke 4:26
**Zechariah** Matt 23:35; Luke 11:5

# APPENDIX 6

# The Bible Covenants

This appendix aims to provide a brief overview of the most important covenants between God and people, and how the covenants relate to each other. From this, a greater understanding may be gained for how each covenant applies today.

## Covenant of Works (Adam)

The first covenant in the Bible between God and people is often referred to as the "Covenant of Works". Having created mankind in his own image (Genesis 1:27), God entered into a covenant with Adam and Eve to bless them further. Eternal life was theirs, but it depended on them being obedient to his command not to eat from the tree of the knowledge of good and evil. With disobedience would come the penalty of death (Genesis 2:16-17). Obedience to God's command (works) was therefore required to receive the blessing, so explaining the covenant's name.

Today, the Covenant of Works is still in effect in that the punishment for breaking that covenant - death - is still in operation. The disobedience of Adam and Eve brought death to them and, because they, the first of all mankind, broke the covenant, works can no longer be the means of salvation by which we, their descendants, gain eternal life.

Jesus however was born of a virgin, so was not a descendant of Adam. Unlike Adam he never sinned, he remained obedient to God and so his perfect life fulfilled the Covenant of Works. Consequently, he enjoys the blessing of eternal life and, if we are united to him, we too share in that blessing (Romans 5:18-19).

## Covenant with Noah

In contrast to the covenant with Adam, the covenant God made with Noah was unconditional. God promised Noah, his descendants, every living creature and the earth in general, that there would never again be a worldwide flood.

Because it was unconditional, God will keep this promise regardless of mankind's obedience or disobedience - and, to remind Noah and his descendants of his covenant promise, God gave us the rainbow. Today this promise is still kept by God, so every time we see a rainbow we should rejoice and remember God's faithfulness.

## Covenant of Grace (Abram, David and New Covenant)

The most important unconditional covenant in the Bible is commonly known as the "Covenant of Grace".

Like the Covenant of Works, this also starts in the Garden of Eden. God promises a descendant of the woman who will defeat Satan (Genesis 3:15). This is then expanded in the promises (covenant) to Abram (Genesis 12:1-7, 13:14-17, 15:1-21, 17:1-14) and then, as we saw in Chapter 6, it is developed further at the time of King David with more promises (Psalm 89:19-37; 2 Samuel 7; 1 Chronicles 17:11-14). Later still, the prophets announce a coming "New Covenant" (Jeremiah 31:31-33; Ezekiel 36:26-27) - a further expansion of the unconditional promises of God.

This New Covenant is then announced by Jesus himself (Luke 22:20) and begun with Christ's resurrection and ascension and the outpouring of the Holy Spirit at Pentecost. The New Covenant is the covenant under which Christians live today.

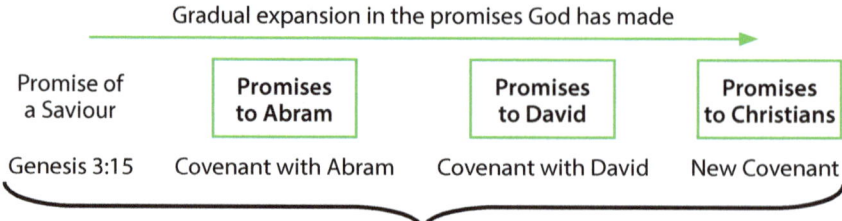

| Gradual expansion in the promises God has made | | | |
|---|---|---|---|
| Promise of a Saviour | Promises to Abram | Promises to David | Promises to Christians |
| Genesis 3:15 | Covenant with Abram | Covenant with David | New Covenant |

**Covenant of Grace**

As the one to whom all the promises point, Jesus fulfils the Covenant of Grace and so all the promised blessings come to him.

Wonderfully, through faith in Jesus, which by grace unites us to Christ by his Spirit, Christians today share in those blessings (Ephesians 1:3).

### The Mosaic Covenant (The Law of Moses)

Finally, there is the important covenant in the Bible which God made at Mount Sinai with Moses and the nation of Israel (Exodus 19-24). It is sometimes referred to as the "Law of Moses" or just simply "the Law".

Many Christians regard the Law as an expansion of the Covenant of Works for the people of Israel (Hosea 6:7). God promised his people blessings for obedience, but also punishment and curses for disobedience (Deuteronomy 28).

It is, however, important not to misunderstand this. The Mosaic Covenant was never given as a way to be saved (Deuteronomy 31:24-29; Galatians 3:21), for the promises were made to people already under the Covenant of Grace.

The Israelites after Moses were therefore under two covenants. The Mosaic Covenant did not replace the Covenant of Grace (Galatians 3:17), but the two worked alongside each other. The Covenant of Grace was their means of salvation and then later the Mosaic Covenant was added, so that through obedience their salvation might be demonstrated and that they might receive further blessing.[1] Unfortunately, many people in Israel didn't live under the Covenant of Grace - that is live by faith for their salvation (Romans 9:32; Hebrews 3:18-19). Instead, they twisted the Law into an alternative way of meriting God's favour. They saw it as the means of salvation, rather than as the right response to it.

At this point it is necessary to avoid a common mistake. We may grasp that Christians are not saved by works, for the Law cannot save us, but we still think that Christians remain under the Mosaic Covenant

---

1 Exodus 20:2 is helpful here. The commandments given in 20:3-17 (the Mosaic Covenant) follow on from the salvation described in v2. Rather than being a means to salvation, the commandments are therefore given to an already saved people as a means of response to their salvation and as a development of their blessing. (See also Exodus 19:4).

today, or something like it. In this misunderstanding, Christians are saved unconditionally under the New Covenant brought in by Jesus, but then any blessing in this life is dependent on our obedience to various rules.

Hebrews 8:13 corrects this wrong understanding:

"By calling this covenant 'new', he has made the first one obsolete; and what is obsolete and outdated will soon disappear."

Also Ephesians 2:14-15:

"For he himself is our peace, who has made the two groups one…by setting aside in his flesh the law with its commands and regulations."

For the Christian, the Mosaic Covenant is no longer binding. In Romans 7:1-3 the apostle Paul explains this by asking us to imagine two men, representing the Law and Jesus. The people of God were married to the Law (under the Mosaic Covenant), but that husband has now died. Because of this we are free to be united to Jesus, our new husband.

Paul goes on to explain that, not only has the old husband died, but when Jesus gave his life for us on the cross we also died - we "died to the law" so that we might "belong to another, to him who was raised from the dead" (Romans 7:4). Our previous husband is dead and we have died to him. As Paul puts it: "by dying to what once bound us, we have been released from the law so that we serve in the new way of the Spirit, and not in the old way of the written code" (Romans 7:6).

Shortly we will look at what Paul means by our serving "in the new way of the Spirit". Before that however, we need look at what he meant by: "the way of the written code".

### The Schoolmaster

In Galatians 3:24-25 Paul describes the Law as a "guardian" or "schoolmaster". The Greek word is *paidagogos* which describes a person responsible for the care of children in a household. They had a measure of authority tutoring the children and applying strict discipline to ensure good behaviour and safety. To be under the schoolmaster was beneficial, for the Law was a teacher and a guardian. On the other hand, it was also to be under slavery (Galatians 4:3), for the teaching was focused on rules to follow, rules that were impossible to keep and rules that required punishment when they were broken.

## The Helper

With the coming of faith in Jesus the authority of the Law ended. Rather than being under the strict slavery of the schoolmaster, faith in Jesus has brought "adoption to sonship".[2] And "because you are his sons, God sent the Spirit of his son into our hearts, the Spirit who calls out, 'Abba, Father.' So you are no longer a slave, but God's child; and since you are his child, God has made you also an heir." (Galatians 4:6-7).

Now for Christians, instead of the external and strict schoolmaster, we have been given the Spirit of Christ in our hearts - inner motivation, not external constraint.

In John's gospel the Spirit is described as a counsellor or helper (John 14:16, 26, 15:26, 16:7). The Greek word here is *parakletos,* meaning "one who is called alongside" with the purpose of helping, encouraging or acting as an advocate. And the principle means by which he fulfils this role is by speaking to us through God's Word. Importantly that includes teaching us holiness of life, from the Mosaic Law.

## The blessing of the Mosaic Covenant for Christians

As we have seen, the blessing of the Mosaic Covenant for Christians is not dependent on our obedience to it. Instead, its blessing comes through our union with Christ who fulfilled the Law and through what the Spirit teaches us by it (2 Timothy 3:16).

First, the Mosaic Covenant teaches us about God. It reveals to us what pleases God and what offends him - it reveals his holiness, beauty and perfection.

Second, the Law teaches what a sinless life looks like. As such, it describes Jesus. What is more, it describes what all Christians will be like in the new heavens and new earth by God's grace. To read the Law

---

2. The Greek word for "adoption to sonship" is a legal term, referring to the full legal standing of an adopted male heir in Roman culture. This privilege equally applies to women (Galatians 3:28).

is to open a window into the perfect life of heaven.

Third, in sharp contrast, the Law is a light which shines into the darkest parts of our lives. The Law opens our eyes to see just how far short we fall of God's perfection. As Paul puts it: "through the law we become conscious of our sin" (Romans 3:20) and "I would not have known what sin was had it not been for the law" (Romans 7:7). This light shines to keep us dependent on Jesus for our salvation, and dependent on the Spirit for transformation into the likeness of Christ.

Finally, and most importantly, the Mosaic Covenant teaches us about Jesus in that all the laws and sacrificial system in the Mosaic Covenant point to Jesus. He is the reality to which all its shadows point. He is both the one who obeys the covenant by fulfilling the law (Matthew 5:17) - so bringing the promised blessings - and who, by dying on the cross, "redeemed us from the curse of the law by becoming a curse for us" (Galatians 3:13).

In summary, the Mosaic Covenant is now fulfilled in Christ. As such it has died, and as Christians we have died to it. The Law has lost its power to punish and condemn Christians for "there is now no condemnation for those who are in Christ Jesus" (Romans 8:1). But the Law has not been abolished (Matthew 5:17), for it remains a rich source of blessing to the Christian through what it teaches.

**Serving in the new way of the Spirit**
So, if Christians are no longer under the Law, what should our response be to the Law? We have already seen how the Law teaches us about God, righteousness and sin, and how it all points to Jesus who fulfils it, but what about obeying the Law? Should Christians obey the Law?

The answer is both "no" and "yes" (with a correct understanding).

First: "no". To obey the Law out of a sense of compulsion or fear or shame that otherwise there is no salvation is wrong. In fact, it is far worse than that, it is to reject Jesus and "fall away from grace" (Galatians 5:4). If our motivation for obedience is salvation (or to earn any favour from God), we should stop obeying the Law and instead repent and return to the free grace of Christ.

But the answer is also "yes - we should obey the Law". If as Christians we are not obeying the Law, that is also wrong. So how should Christians obey the Law?

First, we need to appreciate that we are only to obey the Law as fulfilled in Jesus. Elsewhere Paul describes this as the "law of Christ" (1 Corinthians 9:21; Galatians 6:2). This can be summarised as the law of love, for "love is the fulfilment of the law" (Romans 13:10) - it is obedience to God, which is love towards him and love towards others. This is to "serve in the new way of the Spirit".

So Christians obey the Law as fulfilled in Christ. We do this because we have been saved, justified freely by his grace. But this is no mere external thing. The work of God "for us" through Christ is always recognised in our experience as the work of God "in us" by his Spirit. Christians are not just those with a set of doctrinal beliefs, but those who are united to Christ by the Spirit - the Spirit who is at work in us, to conform us to the will of God and the image of Christ.

Led by the Spirit, the Christian is empowered by him and taught by him. As our Helper he uses the Law to encourage us. The Spirit shows us the glory of God and the beauty of Christ through the Law that we might be attracted and follow out of love in our hearts. But he also shows us the ugliness of sin. He convicts and challenges that we might flee from sin and cling to Jesus, but he will never condemn or threaten or punish like the schoolmaster.

Instead as our Helper, he empowers our will to love God, for "God's love has been poured out in our hearts" (Romans 5:5 CSV) as God has promised, "I will put my Spirit in you and move you to follow my decrees and be careful to keep my laws" (Ezekiel 36:27). The Christian is increasingly changed on the inside by the Spirit, so that we hate what is evil and cling to what is good. Our obedience to the law of Christ is the "fruit of the Spirit" (Galatians 5:22) as he "works in us what is pleasing to him" (Hebrews 13:21) that we might become transformed into the image of Jesus (Romans 8:29).[3]

---

3. For an in-depth study of the Spirit's work in believers see: "Providence" by John Piper p635-658.

## Summary of the Covenants:

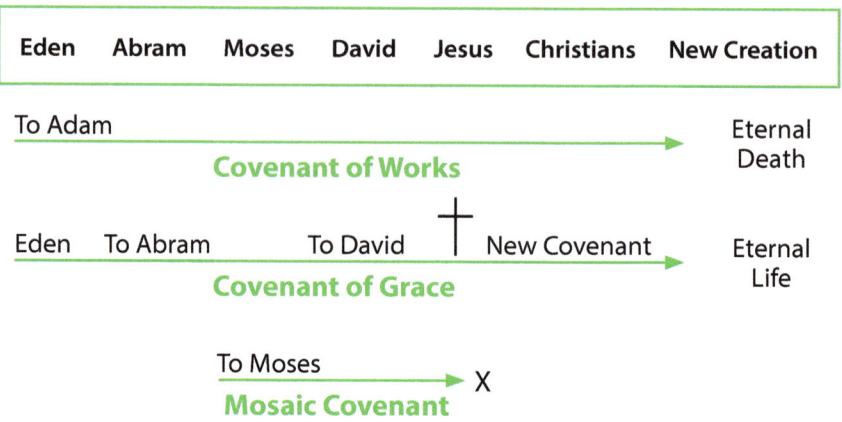

# APPENDIX 7

## Summary

There are two parts to this appendix. First, a summary of the overall journey we must make for good Bible understanding, highlighting important principles for us to remember. Secondly, there follows a detailed summary of the MRS WISE method.

A single double-sided page version of this method summary, designed to be cut out and placed in the back of your Bible, can be printed out free of charge at www.livingwordliterature.org.

### Overall Journey and Principles

**The Start**

We need to recognise:

- Every word of the Bible is God's Word and so every word of the Bible is important.
- The whole Bible is God primarily speaking about God, revealed in the person of Jesus Christ.
- We need to depend on God and be willing to obey God as we come to his Word.

**The Journey**

- We must start in Bible Land imagining ourselves as an original hearer of God's Word.
- Once we understand what it meant to them, we need to find a bridge to Today's World and so understand what it means to us. Finally, we can then apply to ourselves.

## Stages of the Journey

| Stage | Main Task | Main Question |
|---|---|---|
| Observe | Read, read and read again | What is the author's emphasis? |
| Understand (Part 1) | Ask questions again and again | What did the text mean then? |
| Understand (Part 2) | Find a safe bridge | What does the text mean now? |
| Apply | Be specific | How does the text apply now? |

## Whilst on the journey remember:

- The danger of our sinful desire to impose our understanding on the Bible rather than humbly listen to God.
- Good observation takes time.
- Context is king.
- To find a safe bridge - Never go direct from Bible Land and so be eaten by crocodiles.
- Every Bible passage points to and brings glory to Jesus.
- All Bible promises are fulfilled in Jesus, all Bible patterns point to Jesus and all Bible themes have their climax in Jesus.
- The three great themes of the Bible are God, People and Relationships.
- To conclude with a summary sentence.
- To check the summary sentence with **TEST** (Faithfulness to the **T**eaching, **E**mphasis, **S**tructure and **T**one of the text).
- To be God centred in application.
- God's priority in application is to transform us into the likeness of Jesus.
- To take time out for reflection.

# MRS WISE Carefully Studies Jesus CHRIST

## Observe – Read, read and read again

**M**emorable – What is most memorable? - Any actions / details / phrases / irony?

**R**epeated – Is anything repeated? - Words / Phrases / Ideas / Actions by a character. Why the repetition?

**S**urprising – Is anything surprising? (In the actions / teaching / the tense of a verb) (Put yourself in the shoes of an original hearer)

**W**ords – Every word matters. Look particularly for (QUACK):

| | |
|---|---|
| **Q**uoted | - Note words quoted from elsewhere e.g. O.T. |
| **U**nfamiliar | - Use a dictionary to look up these. |
| **A**dded | - Words added to the core sentence. What difference would it make if this word / phrase were not there? What alternative word / phrase could have been used, but wasn't? |
| **C**onnecting | - For structure e.g. "then", "therefore", "so", "because", "but", "for", "afterwards" etc. |
| **K**ey | - Words which form the backbone of a sentence and if changed would alter the meaning considerably. |

**I**mages – **Are there any images used to draw our attention?**

**S**tructure
### 1) Identity the component parts
- Where does the content change?
- Are there any connecting words to help divide the text?

For each subsection, try to give a title or write a summary statement.

### 2) Consider the structure of each individual unit
Three common types of structure for individual units:
1. Linear – to convey movement and bring emphasis to the end.
2. Contrast – to bring out the truth of what is being taught.
3. Mirror line – with emphasis at the mirror line.

Look out for helpful introductory and concluding statements. For each unit, try to give a title or write a summary statement.

**E**mphasis – Put all the observations together: What is the author's emphasis in the passage?

## **Understand** – Ask questions again and again.

## **Carefully (Context)**

- **Immediate Context:** How does this unit connect to the passage which comes before it / after it?

- **Book Context:** What is the purpose of the book as a whole?
  Look out for: Key verses / Repeated words, phrases or themes / Comparisons / Introductory comments / End markers
  What is the structure of each major section / the book as a whole? (Linear / Comparison / Mirror Line / Spiral / Other)

- **Whole Bible Context: (jigsaw and coloured threads)**
  **Words (Incl. Quotes/ Phrases / Images)**
  Consider: Timing / Context / Weight of influence
  How does this word / phrase / quote / image add understanding to what the author is saying?
  How does this word / phrase / quote / image affect the impact of what the author is saying?
  **Promise Fulfilment** - Are any promises being made / fulfilled?
  **Patterns** - Are there any Patterns of Association / Foreshadows?
  **Themes** - Are any themes being developed? Particularly:
  - **God**
  - **People**
  - **Relationships**

## **Studies (Situation)** –What is the situation? Consider **C to I**:

**C**ulture / **D**angers / **E**motions / **F**alse Teaching / **G**eography / **H**istory / **I**nternational Relations

To work out the situation:

> Examine the **passage** being studied
> v
> Read through the whole **book** containing the passage being studied
> v
> Consider the **rest of the Bible** for relevant content
> v
> (Clues from outside the Bible)

## Jesus – How does this text point to Jesus?

Consider:

- **Promises – Are there any promises fulfilled in Jesus?**
- **Patterns – Are there any patterns pointing to Jesus?**
  (of association or foreshadows)
- **Bible Themes – Are there any themes reaching their climax in Jesus?**

**Crossing the Bridge with a Bible Theme:**

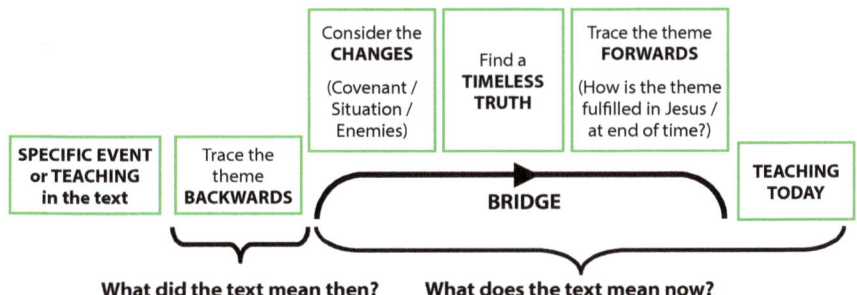

## Conclusion to Understand

**Write a one sentence summary** – Remember **TEST**

The summary should reflect the author's:

**T**ruth
**E**mphasis
**S**tructure
**T**one.

## Apply – Be specific to the text

**Be God centred and remember his priority** – to transform us into the likeness of Jesus.

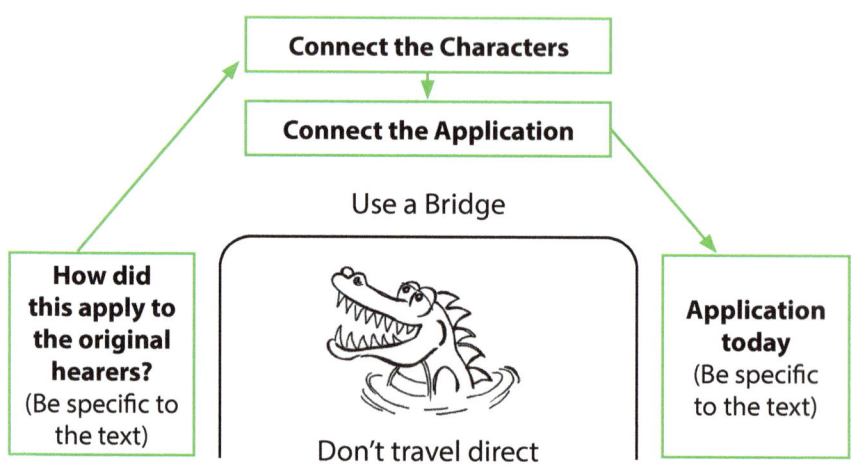

**Comforting /** - How does this passage bring comfort?
**Challenging**     (How does it teach and train?)
            - How does this passage bring challenge?
              (How does it rebuke and correct?)

**Holistic**      - How does this passage apply to the Heart / Soul /
              Mind / Actions?

**Relationships** - To God / Neighbour - Family, Friends, Work
              colleagues, Strangers, People in authority, Enemies

**Individual /**  - How does this apply to the individual and how on
**Corporate**     a corporate level, e.g. whole church?

**Situation**     - How does the passage apply to the whole range of
              situations we / others may be in: **THE FEAST**
              - **T**rust / **H**ealth / **E**motions / **F**inancial / **E**mployment
              / **A**ge / **S**ocial Situation / **T**ime off

**Time out for**  - Take Time / Pray / Memory Aids
**reflection**